FOUNDATIONS OF A FAITH

by Simon Greenberg

To Betty
Proverbs 31:29

Index by Jerome H. Kanner, Ph.D., L.H.D.

Library of Congress Catalogue Card Number: 67–31666

MANUFACTURED IN THE UNITED STATES OF AMERICA
BY AMERICAN BOOK–STRATFORD PRESS, INC.

Foreword

Professor Simon Greenberg, a singular combination of Jewish theologian and educator, offers in this book a series of guides and suggestions to a confused community, as it looks to its future. The value of this work inheres in its lucidity, its orderly approach to complex problems and its courageous facing of the issues confronting Jewry and mankind in our time.

It is the merit of Dr. Greenberg that the book reflects the wise and generous humanitarianism of the author, as the wise and generous humanitarianism of the author are practical applications of the insights in the book.

His very first essays on "The Pattern of a Faith" and "God, Man, Torah, and Israel" set the tone of the volume. Professor Greenberg adheres to the traditional faith of Israel, but with his mastery of modern thought is able to translate that faith in terms intelligible to modern man and conforming to all accepted knowledge. He avoids any effort to hedge and is never uncertain of himself. His doctrine of God is clearly rooted in his lifelong study of Maimonides. In his concept of Torah, he becomes the mystic as well as the philosopher. He declines to take sides in the age-old controversy as to whether all the commandments may be logically explained. But he insists, traditionalist that he is, that whether or not each commandment can be rationally explained, it is vital to Judaism. He bases this doctrine on the clear and unambiguous assertions of the Talmud. His concept of Israel is informed even further with a mystic reverence for the Chosen People, an idea which, however, is interpreted as that of the "Covenant People." The question, raised in the Talmud, as to whether God chose Israel, or Israel chose God, is answered in a new way—each chose the other. The miracle of the survival of Judaism—for a miracle it certainly is—testifies, according to Professor Greenberg, to two facts: the desire of God that Israel should survive as His people; and the desire of the people to survive in conformity with their covenant with God.

His essay on "God, Man, Torah, and Israel" is a remarkable effort to clarify the mature thought of a great teacher to a skeptical age. Here he propounds a thesis which may serve as a uniting statement for all those concerned with the survival of Judaism as a faith. He recognizes and deals with those problems raised by physical science and history which appear to challenge the tradition of the Jews, as all other religious traditions. But he frankly faces the opposing views and, beginning with his experience as educator and interpreter of Judaism, arrives at a formulation of Jewish doctrine which is at once ancient and modern: deeply rooted in the Jewish tradition, and yet, to one reader at least, entirely in conformity with the dominant philosophies of our day.

His essay on "Symbols and Symbolism" is outstanding in its profundity, clarity and frankness. He recognizes that many action-symbols in Judaism which at one time may have been believed to have scientific validity, can have only historical validity for our generation. But he regards such historical symbolism as no less important than the original scientific symbolism, had it proven valid, would have been. He believes it essential to have the generations tied to one another and regards religious symbolism in general, and Jewish symbolism in particular, as such a tie.

In his great essay, "Judaism and the Democratic Ideal," Professor Greenberg traces the significance attaching to the individual and to freedom across the ages, from the Prophets to the teachers of our own time. This universal interpretation of Judaism is supplemented with one entitled "The Concept of K'lal Yisrael," in which Solomon Schechter's notion of "Catholic Israel" is further interpreted and developed.

Professor Greenberg opposes all sectarianism within Judaism. The people of Israel are one. He insists that in order to have unity within Judaism, we must recognize that some individuals are less loyal to the faith than others. It is the duty of the educator to clarify to the student that while he must love his fellow-man and fellow-Jew, he must not be misled into the notion that anything done by such a fellow-man or fellow-Jew is right. Like Cyrus Adler before him, Professor Greenberg insists on the two concepts of Zechariah, "Truth" and "Peace," and is unwilling to sacrifice either for the sake of the other.

From these essays he turns naturally to a discussion of Judaism's contributions to civilization. In the essay entitled, "Some of Judaism's Eternally Relevant Contributions to Civilization," he shows that, until our own time, the contribution of Judaism in the area of technology was not significant. Judaism made few significant contributions to human civilization by creating any of the more important physical tools. But, according to Professor Greenberg, it has made invaluable contributions in the vast sphere of the non-physical tools which lie, partially concealed, at the very base of our civilization.

These non-physical tools, useful primarily to the educator in his task of raising children to their highest level of fulfillment, are the Jewish notions of "the basic character of the Universe," "the nature of man" and "the proper goals of life." In a series of brilliant insights, informed with wide reading in Jewish and secular philosophy, Professor Greenberg shows how basic concepts, underlying all modern civilization, ultimately have their roots in the thought of the Prophets and Sages of Israel. Our concept of the physical Universe is far different even from that of the generation before us. But the nature of life as an evolving effort toward spiritual goals remains the same after the discovery of the distant quasars as when the Prophets spoke to a people who believed the Universe geocentric.

Professor Greenberg ends his significant and invaluable work with the essay "Towards a Jewish Version of American Civilization." He denies that Judaism and Americanism are two distinct ways of life, for indeed the whole book shows that much of what is basically American at its best has its roots in Judaism. But he recognizes the existence of a Jewish dialect of American culture, an element in our pluralistic civilization which bears clearly the stamp of Judaism, unchanged throughout the ages. He holds that this element is indispensable to American civilization, as it is indispensable to the world.

Thus, Professor Greenberg in an extremely stimulating and thought-provoking series of essays leads the reader, as he would lead a class, from step to step in his understanding of the role of Judaism in the modern world. The essays (not all of which I have enumerated) were sometimes delivered originally as addresses or lectures. But Professor Greenberg has re-worked them, so that they read beautifully, and constitute a consistent and clear work, as valuable to the theologian and educator as it will doubtless prove to the lay reader. Here, we have a modern "Guide for the Perplexed," a book showing those who wish to be shown why Judaism is as relevant to our day as it was in the time of the Prophets and the Talmud; why it is as important to preserve it in New York, Chicago, Philadelphia, and Los Angeles, as it was in Kovno or Pressburg. This is a book intended to clarify Judaism to those who do not know it well; it also has much to offer to those who regard themselves as scholars in the field.

It would be impossible to close even this brief foreword without alluding to Professor Greenberg's bold and incisive essay on the Seminary itself. Although he modestly introduces this critique of the role of higher Jewish learning with an amusing reference to the difficulties of public self-appraisal, the writer surmounts those problems with apparent ease. In his essay he evaluates the Seminary's goals and achievements with an objectivity which is truly amazing in one who has been an active protagonist in much of what he describes. It is by no means the least of Dr. Greenberg's accomplishments in this volume that he holds the Seminary up for inspection, revealing with a kindly and therapeutic touch both the strengths in its weaknesses, and the weaknesses in its strengths.

The new approaches to Judaism, found in so many chapters of the book, are illuminating as they are inspiring. As one parts from this fine work, one can only pray that its impact on the American Jewish community will be as profound as it deserves to be.

LOUIS FINKELSTEIN

The Jewish Theological Seminary of America
New York City

Preface

Of the areas of Jewish life and thought which have been of primary interest to me—the Jewish religion, the Conservative Movement, Zionism and Israel, and Jewish education—only the first three are represented in this collection. These essays and addresses are here reprinted in substantially the same form in which they first appeared. Changes were introduced in order to achieve greater clarity and to eliminate those matters whose significance depended entirely upon the time and place in which the address was first delivered or the essay first printed. These essays were written over a period of some three decades. They do not pretend to constitute a comprehensive or systematic presentation of a theology or philosophy of Jewish life. If, however, it will ever be given to me to formulate such a philosophy, the convictions and attitudes expressed in them would constitute its basic foundation and be its most significant building blocks.

Among the many irredeemable debts I owe to my dear wife is the one that I incurred by subjecting her to whatever ideas I had when they were in their first raw and unrecognizable state. Whatever clarity and cogency they now possess is due in very large measure to her patience as a listener, her sound judgment and to the unwavering honesty of her reactions.

It is my great pleasure to express my thanks to Dr. Louis Finkelstein, my lifelong teacher and friend, for gracing this collection with his introductory remarks; to Dr. Louis M. Levitsky, chairman of the Board of Governors of the National Academy for Adult Jewish Studies of the United Synagogue of America, and his colleagues for undertaking the publication of this volume; and to Rabbi Marvin S. Wiener, Academy director and Burning Bush Press editor, and his staff for the great care they took in planning the volume and in preparing the manuscript for publication. May it justify their confidence and may it not disappoint those who will turn to it with the hope that it will help them formulate for themselves a satisfying faith for living as a Jew.

SIMON GREENBERG

Heshvan 5728
November 1967
New York City

Contents

CHAPTER I

The Pattern of a Faith[1]

INDETERMINACY AND CONSCIOUS AMBIGUITY IN JUDAISM

Since the days of Moses Mendelssohn, there has been considerable controversy over whether one could rightly refer to Judaism as a faith. It was Mendelssohn's contention that Judaism was a system of revealed law. Observance of the law was obligatory, but one was free to believe almost anything. Extreme as this position obviously is, it had some historic justification in the fact that Judaism never had a creed beginning with the words, "I believe," recitation and acceptance of which was incumbent upon the pious Jew.

This fact becomes the more striking when we realize that Judaism at a comparatively early period in its history obligated its followers to recite twice daily a number of Biblical passages which together constitute the *Shema.* There are three such passages. The first opens with the well-known "Hear, O Israel: the Lord our God, the Lord is one" (Deuteronomy 6:4). The second passage begins with the words, "And it shall come to pass if you shall hearken diligently unto My commandments" (Deuteronomy 11:13). The third passage contains the law regarding the fringes to be placed on the four corners of the garments and includes a reference to the emancipation from Egyptian slavery (Numbers 15:37–41).

As we read these passages, we are inclined to interpret them as confessions of faith—the first, in the unity of God; the second, in the doctrine of reward and punishment. In the third, we find no reference to any doctrine requiring faith.

But the Rabbis do not speak of these passages as confessions of faith. Nor, in explaining the selection of them, do the Rabbis refer to what we would consider to be their doctrinal content. They designate the recitation of the first of these passages as *kabalat ol Malkhut Shamayim,* "the acceptance of the yoke of the Kingdom of Heaven." It is not a confession of belief in God's existence, His unity, or His incorporeality, but rather an expression of our allegiance to God and our readiness to obey Him.

The recitation of the second paragraph the Rabbis designate as *kabalat ol mitzvot,* "the acceptance of the yoke of the commandments." The Jew must declare daily his readiness to assume the obligation to observe the commandments of the Torah.

The third paragraph, which refers to Israel's emancipation from Egypt, serves to remind us that, as a people, we owe our existence to God's mercy in redeeming our ancestors from Egyptian slavery. Therefore we are to wear an outer garment with fringes whose purpose it is to keep us ever aware that we are specially obligated to accept God's sovereignty and obey His laws. The Rabbis thus studiously or intuitively avoid the introduction into their discussion of the *Shema* of the concept of dogma or belief.

Equally striking and instructive is the fact that in the best known passage in the Mishnah in which anything that can be clearly identified as dogma is discussed, the statements are cast in the negative rather than in the affirmative. The first Mishnah of the tenth chapter of the tractate Sanhedrin, after declaring that "All Israelites have a share in the world to come," goes on to say: "And these are they who have no share in the world to come: he that says that there is no resurrection of the dead prescribed in the Law,[2] and he that says that the Law is not from Heaven, and an Epicurean."[3] One may of course infer the positive from the negative and thus draw the conclusion that it is incumbent upon a Jew to believe that the Pentateuch does contain references to the resurrection of the dead, and that the Torah is from Heaven. These are not, however, logically necessary inferences. At any rate, at no time is a Jew required to confess faith in these or in any other doctrines by the recitation of any such affirmatively formulated statements.

The specific forms in which the Rabbinic discussion of the *Shema,* and the statements in the Mishnah in Sanhedrin were cast, reflect a pattern of thinking characteristic of the great spiritual founders of Judaism. Thus Dr. Max Kadushin speaks of "indeterminacy" as "a characteristic . . . of rabbinic theology,"[4] and Dr. Louis Finkelstein has in conversation referred to the apparently "conscious ambiguity" that is often encountered in Rabbinic thought.

There is significant difference between making it obligatory to state categorically that one believes in the resurrection of the dead, or that the Pentateuch refers to it, and forbidding him to declare categorically that he does not believe either the one or the other to be true. In between these two opposite poles there is a considerable area for intellectual maneuverability. It is interesting to note how this characteristic of Rabbinic thought persists down through the generations. We meet it in one of the essays of Solomon Schechter on the dogmas of Judaism:

> The Bible itself hardly contains a command bidding us *to believe.* We are hardly ordered, *e.g.,* to believe in the existence of God. *I say hardly, but I do not altogether deny the existence of such a command* (italics mine, S. G.). It is true that we do not find in the Scripture such words as: "You are commanded to believe in the existence of God." Nor is any punishment

assigned as awaiting him who denies it. Notwithstanding these facts, many Jewish authorities—among them such important men as Maimonides, R. Judah Hallevi, Nachmanides—perceive, in the first words of the Ten Commandments, "I am the Lord thy God," the command to believe in His existence.[5]

Much of the intellectual freedom enjoyed within the framework of Judaism is due to this "indeterminacy" and "conscious ambiguity."

The absence of affirmative formulations of doctrine is in part responsible for the failure of all attempts to fit Rabbinic Judaism into the strait-jacket of the syllogism, the form of thought which has proved so great a boon to science and philosophy and so barren in all areas touching upon religious, ethical or esthetic values.

But if stubborn resistance to the syllogism, indeterminacy of belief, and conscious ambiguity are among the fundamental characteristics of Judaism, what has held the Tradition together and succeeded in giving to it distinctive character and form? The fullest, and to my mind the most persuasive, answer given to that question is found in Dr. Kadushin's volumes to which I have already referred. While formal confession of faith is not indigenous to Judaism and never became an important aspect of its practice, value concepts *implying* faith are of its very essence and substance. They permeate the whole body of its authoritative literature and give it an identifiable organic unity, despite the obvious logical inconsistencies and the oft-bewildering variety of opinions which inevitably abound in a literature that stretches over so long a period of time and reflects so many different historic circumstances and cultural settings.

The number of such value concepts is large, but there are three which are the most nearly ubiquitous, and constitute the main strands of the pattern. They are God, Torah and Israel. Parties, sects, schools of thought within Judaism are based upon differences in emphasis or meaning given to one or the other of these three concepts in the weaving of the overall design. No party or sect remains within the pattern of traditional Judaism at all if it excludes any one of these three concepts or introduces into the overall design another concept as equal in importance to any of these three, or gives to any one of them a meaning that is in essence at variance with that given to it in the main body of the authoritative literature of Judaism—namely, the Bible and the Talmud.

This discussion will be limited to a brief exposition of these three concepts. I hope it may be a helpful introduction to what America's greatest non-Jewish student of Rabbinic Judaism, George Foot Moore, has called Normative Judaism.[6]

THE CONCEPT OF GOD

It is generally acknowledged that Judaism's greatest gift to civilization is its concept of God. The problem of the existence of God is never seriously discussed in the Bible, nor in later Rabbinic literature up to the tenth century. The existence of God was, if you will, an *a priori* category of the Jewish mind. That mind could not function at all without the concept of God. His objective existence was as self-evident to the Jew as the objective existence of space and time was to pre-Kantian philosophy. This was true of all peoples of antiquity. As Schechter so well puts it, "It is as absurd to say that the ancient world believed in God as for a future historian to assert of the nineteenth century that it believed in the effects of electricity."[7] This was true of Judaism long after the existence of God became a very important theological question in Christianity and Islam. Hence Jewish medieval theologians felt the need to defend their activity by adducing Biblical and Rabbinic statements that would indicate one's obligation "to know" God, that is, to be able to prove His existence logically and to grasp His essence intellectually.[8] But the pursuit of anything approaching systematic theology did not, until comparatively recent times, become an integral part of the curriculum of any religiously oriented school of higher Jewish learning.

While the existence of God was not a crucial problem to the Jewish religious mind, His relationship to the world and man was. On that subject, Biblical and Rabbinic literature is prolific and clear and undisturbed by logical inconsistencies. Judaism apprehended the relationship of God to the world and man in terms of three basic concepts—Creation, Justice and Mercy.

The uniqueness and the significance of Judaism's God concept are usually associated with the doctrine of ethical monotheism. Students of the Bible, particularly since the middle of the nineteenth century, applying the principles of evolution to their account of the history of the God idea in Israel, believed that they found in the Bible evidence of a development starting with a parochial, whimsical, desert war God who was accepted as one among many gods, and ending with the one universal God of Justice and of Love.

More recent studies have suggested a radically different point of view. Yehezkel Kaufmann, in his monumental eight-volume Hebrew work on the history of the religion of Israel, summarizes his findings on the nature of the God concept in Israel during the Biblical period as follows:

> The Biblical religion even of the earliest period, reflects a concept of God as supreme above all laws, fate and events. He carries on no wars for supremacy with other divine powers. He has absolutely no association with evil spirits. He practices no divination, brings no offerings. He neither sins nor repents, nor does He celebrate any events in His own life. A divine will absolutely supreme above all other phenomena, that is the essence of Biblical religion, and in that it differs from all other religions upon the earth.[9]

The definitive formulation of the concept of God as the sole and unchallenged Creator of all that exists, is found in the majestic cadences of the first chapter of the Book of

Genesis and in the impassioned pronouncements of Deutero-Isaiah. The Bible opens with the unequivocal statement: "In the beginning God created heaven and earth. . . . And the heavens and the earth and all their host having been created . . . God rested on the seventh day" (Genesis 1:1, 2:1–2). And Deutero-Isaiah, probably having Zoroastrian dualism in mind, proclaims in the name of the Lord: "I am the Lord, and there is none else. . . . I form the light and create darkness; I make peace and create evil; I am the Lord, that doeth all those things" (Isaiah 45:5, 7).

The God of Judaism is not the unmoved Mover, but the uncreated Creator of everything and so there is absolutely nothing independent of His will. Hence any belief or practice which would imply that there is anything independent of God in the universe, whether it be Satan or fate, or eternal matter, or irrevocable eternal natural laws, is foreign to Judaism.

Equally foreign to Normative Judaism is any and every form of monistic thought. There is nothing in the universe which we can identify with God or His essence. God as Creator is absolutely transcendent, differing in essence from anything which He has created. The human soul is no more a spark of the Divine in us, which upon death returns to reunite with God as the original source of its being, than is the body. He has created all out of nothing, and all our efforts to know the essence of this creative act will be of no avail, for to know that is to know God. And man cannot know God, "For no man can see Me and live" (Exodus 33:20).

But while the Biblical, absolutely supreme, uncreated Creator of the universe remains the God of Judaism throughout the ages, He would not have become the God of history and the intimate friend, shepherd and comforter of the individual had He been envisaged merely in these transcendental terms. Judaism bridged the chasm between God the transcendent Creator and the universe which He created, by positing in the first place that the created universe never became independent of its Creator. The daily Morning Service reminds us that "God in His goodness renews every day continuously His creative act." Bearing in mind the inadequacies and dangers of all analogies, one might venture to suggest that God is immanent in the universe as the poet in his poem while the poem is being composed, the artist in his painting while the picture is being painted. But the poem eventually becomes independent of the poet. The world never becomes independent of God. God is constantly sustaining, indeed constantly recreating it.

God's transcendence is further counterpoised by His awareness of and concern for what goes on in the universe. "For though the Lord be high, yet regardeth He the lowly. And the haughty He knoweth from afar" (Psalms 138:6). The wicked are not those who deny the existence of God. They may very well affirm His existence. They deny, however, that He is aware of their acts or that He is in any way concerned with them. The Psalmist repeatedly gives expression to this attitude of the wicked and reacts to it with what only the believer would consider to be an irrefutable argument. He says, "All the workers of iniquity bear themselves haughtily. . . . They slay the widow and the stranger, and murder the fatherless." And they say: "The Lord doth not see, neither doth the God of Jacob give heed. . . . He that planteth the ear, shall He not hear? He that formed the eye, shall He not see?" And having seen and having heard, God gives heed. For he is the Just and the Merciful Ruler of all that He created (Psalms 94:3–10, 16–23).

By conceiving of God as both just and merciful, Judaism posits a logically unresolved and unresolvable paradox at the very core of God's relationship to the world. For justice and mercy are themselves inherently incompatible; yet Judaism finds both of them indispensable to the existence of the universe. The Midrash relates that originally it was God's purpose to create the world with His attribute of justice only.

But He realized that the world could not endure upon justice alone. Hence "He associated justice with mercy and made them to rule jointly."[10]

This paradox is "the way of the Lord in which the just walk and the transgressors stumble" (Hosea 14:10). For out of this paradox arises the most troublesome of all religious problems stated so poignantly by Jeremiah. "Right wouldst Thou be, O Lord, were I to contend with Thee. Yet will I reason with Thee. Wherefore doth the way of the wicked prosper? Wherefore are all they secure that deal very treacherously?" (Jeremiah 12:1). One who does not believe in God's justice and mercy is not tormented by these questions. But neither does he have any ground for hope for the future. It is this paradox which enabled Judaism to look to the future with an *unwavering* but *sober* optimism, shunning both the pit of despair and a Pollyannish confidence.

JUDAISM'S UNWAVERING BUT SOBER OPTIMISM

The world was created as an act of Divine Love. God was not compelled to create it, nor was there any one whom He was obligated to reward. He can destroy it *in toto* or annihilate every living creature upon it. It was Divine Love which after the Flood moved God to "say in His heart that He would not again destroy every living thing" (Genesis 8:21). The prophet reassures his despairing generation that God in creating the world did not create it to be *tohu,* a waste, but He formed it *lashevet*—that it may be inhabited (Isaiah 45:18).

Judaism's optimistic faith in the future reaches its climax in the ecstatic prophetic vision of the "end of days" when "Nation shall not lift up sword against nation, Neither shall they learn war any more" (Isaiah 2:4), when none "shall hurt or destroy . . . for the earth shall be full of the knowledge of the Lord, as the waters cover the sea" (Isaiah 11:9).

Judaism has never faltered in its conviction that the "end of days" is destined to arrive and that mankind will be here to experience its bliss. But it is a tempered optimism. No authoritative teacher of Judaism would venture to predict the day of the coming of "the end of days." That coming was neither automatic nor predetermined for some fixed moment in history. Since that coming is not altogether dependent upon man, but ultimately upon God's love for His creation, man need not despair of the future altogether, because of his sense of his own inadequacies. He may, however, find courage and hope in the faith that he can, by fulfilling the commandments of the Torah, hasten that coming. Therein lies his privilege, opportunity and duty.

This sober but confident optimism is reflected in a Rabbinic comment on the last two (Hebrew) words of the sixtieth chapter of Isaiah. The prophet, speaking on behalf of God, promises: "The small shall be as a thousand, and the youngest as a mighty people. I am the Lord. *B'itah,* in its time, *ahishenah,* will I hasten it." Understood literally, these two words, *b'itah,* "in its time," and *ahishenah,* "I will hasten it," are contradictory. If it is to come in its due time, what can God's promise to hasten it mean? The Rabbis interpret the verse, therefore, as follows: "God said to the people of Israel: 'If you are worthy, I will hasten it—if not, it will come in its time' " (Sanhedrin 98a). Judaism posits a world that was created perfect, that therefore has the potentialities of perfection within it. These potentialities will "in the end of days" become realities. The "end of days" will surely come "in its time." But man has the power through his acts to hasten the coming of "the end of days," or to postpone it to *itah*—to its time.

The nature of "the end of days" has always been a matter of legitimate difference of opinion among the interpreters of Judaism. For some, "the end of days" is to be identified with the *yemot hamashiah*—the coming of the Messiah—when men will continue to be essentially human, will eat, drink, reproduce, and die, except that they will have complete control over all of their evil inclinations so that none will harm or hurt anyone else. The "end of days" will be wholly within history.

Others identify the "end of days" with the *olam haba,* "the world to come," which is beyond history. About its nature the Tradition (Shabbat 63a) speaks in most restrained terms, applying to it the words of the prophet (Midrashically interpreted): "No eye but Thine, O Lord, hath seen it" (Isaiah 64:3).

Are all men destined to a share in the world to come? To that question also, Judaism responds with a qualified optimism. Judaism's faith that man is destined to partake of life in "the world to come" is not rooted primarily in its conception of the nature of the human soul as being in essence immortal, but rather in its conception of the relationship of God to His creatures.

Divine goodness creates the good. Scripture identifies the good with life, and the evil with death (Deuteronomy 30:15). God, being merciful, is the God of life Who does not desire the death of any of His creatures (Ezekiel 18:23, 32). Hence man can have a portion in the world to come, not because his soul *per se* is immortal any more than his body is immortal, but rather because God's justice and His mercy permit human beings to *achieve* immortality. Not every one achieves it. The tenth chapter of the Mishnah of Sanhedrin lists a goodly number who will not have a share in the world to come, nor even be permitted "to stand in judgment." Among them are three kings—Jeroboam, Ahab and Manasseh; four commoners—Balaam, Doeg, Ahitophel, and Gehazi; the generation of the Flood; the generation of the Dispersion; the men of Sodom; and others. Immortality is a blessing to be earned and *the only place one can earn it is in this world.* Hence Rabbi Jacob (one of the great teachers of the second century, Common Era) makes what at first sight seems to be a rather startling statement, namely, that "one hour of repentance and good deeds in this world is better than the whole life of the world to come."[11] But it is only through repentance and good deeds that one can hope to merit a portion in the world to come, and repentance and good deeds can be practiced only in this world. Neither the nature of the soul nor God's mercy make immortality an automatic eventuality for all. Only God is, by His very nature, immortal.

God's mercy sets immortality within the reach of every one of His children. His justice relates immortality to the conduct of the individual. Each is judged on the basis of his own merit. Rabbi Eliezer (first half of second century, C.E.) taught: "The Gentiles have no share in the world to come for it is written 'The wicked shall return to the nether-world, even all the nations' (Psalms 9:18). The words 'the wicked' refer to the wicked Israelites (who also have no share in the world to come)." Whereupon, Rabbi Joshua said to him: "Had the verse ended with the words 'all the nations' I would have agreed with you, but since it continues with the words 'that forget God,' obviously it means to say that the righteous among the Gentiles have a share in the world to come" (Tosefta Sanhedrin, Chapter 13).

Because God is just and therefore also punishes, and is not merely merciful, Judaism does not conceive of man's progress toward his ultimate destiny, whether that destiny be identified with the "Days of the Messiah" or the *olam haba*—the future world—as moving forward inevitably and uninterruptedly in a straight line.

SIN AND EVIL

From time to time man stumbles and brings God's judgment upon himself. Why that happens is one of the eternal mysteries, for surely God does not demand too much from man. Judaism constantly stresses the thought that obedience to God does not require a superhuman effort. In the Garden of Eden all was permitted to man except the fruit "of the tree of the knowledge of good and evil" (Genesis 2:17). Of the Law later revealed to Israel, Scripture says: "For this commandment which I command thee this day, it is not too hard for thee, neither is it far off. It is not in heaven, that thou shouldest say: 'Who shall go up for us to heaven and bring it unto us, and make us to hear it, that we may do it?' Neither is it beyond the sea, that thou shouldest say: 'Who shall go over the sea for us, and bring it unto us, and make us hear it, that we may do it?' But the word is very nigh unto thee, in thy mouth, and in thy heart, that thou mayest do it" (Deuteronomy 30:11–14).

Judaism does not attribute man's constant backsliding to Adam and Eve's sin in eating the forbidden fruit. We are not born with the taint of sin upon our souls. Every morning we say in our prayers: "O Lord, the soul Thou gavest me is pure. Thou didst create it. Thou didst form it. Thou didst bestow it upon me. Thou dost preserve it within me. Thou wilt take it from me, and return it again to me in days to come." Adam was certainly created pure. But he was endowed with the power to choose between alternatives. That power made him uniquely man, set him above all other creatures and made him, as the Psalmist puts it *"me-at me-Elohim,"* "only a little lower than the angels" (Psalms 8:6). Man fails, not because he is born tainted, but because *he is a little lower than the angels.*

God's infinite power has but one limitation. He cannot create another God, and only in God are free will, power and knowledge so related that the free choice always produces the good. Since man is not God, his freedom of choice is not determined by either adequate knowledge or adequate power to result always in the right choice and the good act. He therefore enjoys his freedom at the price of making mistakes and committing sins.

But while man, not being God, cannot possibly progress uninterruptedly toward his highest attainable goal, God in His mercy sustains him in his efforts to achieve his ultimate destiny. For *"midah tovah merubah mi-midat hapuranut"*—"God's generosity in rewarding far exceeds His severity in punishment." The Rabbis find this principle clearly enunciated in the very passage which is so often quoted to prove the severity and harshness of God's justice. The second commandment which describes God as a "jealous God," Who visits the iniquities of the fathers upon the children unto the third and fourth generations, also assures us that God rewards those that love Him and obey His commandments unto the thousandth generation. The accumulation of the good in the world thus proceeds in geometric ratio, while evil grows only arithmetically. God has so ordered the universe that it favors the right and the good.[12]

Moreover, man who was created in the image of God has been endowed with the capacity to know the difference between good and evil. Man's intellectual capacity enables him not only to be conscious of his experiences but also to retain them in memory, to classify them in different categories, and on the basis of these remembered experiences to draw correct conclusions regarding the actions most likely to result in his highest welfare and happiness. It is this capacity that we have in mind when we pray thrice daily: "Thou favorest man with knowledge, and teachest mortals understanding. O grant us knowledge, understanding and insight. Blessed art Thou, O Lord, gracious Giver of knowledge." Man's mental capacities, themselves a gift of God, never become independent of God. Their proper functioning is dependent continuously upon His favor. Hence whatever blessings come to us through the medium of our mental endowments are blessings that are very directly bestowed upon us by God. Just as man is warned against the temptation to say in his hour of triumph, "My own power and the might of my own hand have won this wealth for me" (Deuteronomy 8:17), so also must he be on guard against the temptation to say, "My wisdom, my reason and insight have themselves discovered this truth for me."

THE TORAH

God in His goodness has, in addition, revealed to man through the Torah other truths which are indispensable to his welfare.

What is the Torah? The best brief, authoritative answer to this question is found in a Rabbinic comment on the Biblical passage which states that God renewed with Isaac the Covenant He had made with Abraham "because Abraham hearkened unto My voice, and kept My charge, *mitzvotai*—My commandments, *hukotai*—My statutes, and *torotai*—My laws" (Genesis 26:5).

Mitzvotai (My commandments) is interpreted as referring to those laws of the Torah which, even had they not been directly revealed at Sinai, reason would have enjoined upon us, such as the laws against theft and murder.

Hukotai (My statutes) is interpreted as referring to laws in the Torah which cannot be adequately explained by reason, such as the dietary laws.

Torotai (My laws) is interpreted as referring to the two main divisions of the Torah, the written Torah and the oral Torah.[13]

The written Torah is very easily identified. It is the Hebrew Bible. The oral Torah cannot so easily be identified because it is the living, growing tradition. Originally it was forbidden to commit the *oral* law to writing. But it could not continue in that state indefinitely. At the end of the second century, the vast amount of material accumulated in the oral tradition was for the first time officially codified and became known as the Mishnah. Whether or not it was actually put into writing at the time is still one of the debatable questions. But there can be no doubt that it was memorized as codified under the editorship of Judah the Prince (c. 135–200 C.E.), so that even if it were not committed to writing, it was to all intents and purposes equivalent to a written text.[14] The study of the Mishnah during the ensuing centuries in the schools of Babylonia resulted in the Talmud of Babylon, and study of the Mishnah in the schools of Palestine resulted in the Talmud of Jerusalem. It was the Babylonian Talmud that was destined to become authoritative among Jews.

But Judaism did not end its development with the Babylonian Talmud. The schools of Spain, Northern Africa, Germany, and Eastern Europe, the needs of new situations, the contacts with new cultures, all left their marks in the commentaries upon the Talmud, in the new codes that were formulated, and in the new legal, theological, moralistic, and liturgical literature that developed. This process, which has continued down through the ages with varying degrees of vitality in different countries and eras, is still functioning within Judaism. The oral Torah thus continues to grow and, within limits, to change.

While the Tradition unequivocally declares the truths revealed in the Torah to be far more precious than, and superior to, the truths arrived at by the human mind, the relationship between reason and revelation in Judaism is not as unequivocal as it may at first appear to be. It partakes somewhat of the paradoxical character which we noted in the relationship between justice and mercy. At times the one seems to dominate, and at times the other. The two are constantly interpenetrating and it is impossible to draw a sharp line between them.

Thus in addition to the division between the oral and the written Torah to which we shall have occasion to refer again, the teachings of the Torah are divided by the Rabbis into two main categories, *mitzvot shebayn adam la-havero*—teachings that concern man's relations with his fellowman; and *mitzvot shebayn adam la-Makom*—teachings that concern man's relation to God.[15]

It is ordinarily assumed, both in Rabbinic and in medieval Jewish thought, that the first of these two categories, namely, the laws referring to man's relations with his fellows, could have been arrived at by man through the exercise of his reason. This assumption on the part of those who, like Saadiah Gaon (d. 942), believed that the whole of both the written and the oral Torah was revealed at Sinai, I have always found strange, for it implies that insofar as half or more of the Sinaitic revelations is concerned, God was, as it were, bringing coals to Newcastle. He was telling man what he could have found out for himself through his mental endowments. Jewish medieval philosophers were rather hard put to explain why it should have been necessary for the Lord at Sinai to waste those precious moments of self-revelation by commanding the assembled multitude not to kill, or commit adultery, or steal, or bear false witness, as if He had not already equipped them with the mental powers necessary to formulate these laws.[16]

To me it has always seemed that our theologians were crediting human reason with more than it deserved, because they were overly impressed by the achievements of philosophy in general and of Aristotle in particular. They had surrendered altogether too much to reason when they assumed that by itself it could give us our moral and ethical values. All morality is ultimately dependent upon the concept of the sacredness and inviolability of the life of the individual. That basic premise reason alone cannot arrive at or establish. Nor is there anything in reason *per se* that could validate beyond reasonable doubt the proposition that theft or adultery are intrinsically evil. Plato tried valiantly in his *Republic* to establish logically the nature of justice and then to prove its superiority over injustice. But interesting as his effort is, few would call it successful.

Hence it seems to me that Jewish tradition, in including such prohibitions as those against killing, adultery and stealing in the Ten Commandments revealed at Sinai, is essentially correct. For it implies that ethical values are not the product of human reason alone. They are not deducible from observable facts nor from intellectually demonstrable first principles. Moral values are, and can only be, in their essence, revealed.

THE SEVEN NOAHIDE LAWS

The Jewish tradition does not assume that God withheld the revelation of these fundamental moral laws until He spoke to Israel at Mt. Sinai. Man had not been left completely to his own resources during the long period preceding Sinai. The Torah relates (Genesis 9:1–7) that after Noah and his family had left the Ark, God blessed them and enjoined them to obey a number of laws. Jewish tradition usually speaks of them as being seven in number, namely: prohibition of (1) idolatry, (2) adultery, (3) murder, (4) theft, (5) cruelty, (6) blasphemy, and the establishment of (7) courts of justice.[17] These seven laws represent what was probably the first attempt to formulate a code which might be regarded as universally applicable and as including the basic components of a civilized society.

They are sufficient to enable those who observe them to be called righteous, and to deserve a share in the world to come. But if the observance of these laws is sufficient to make one righteous and deserving of a share in the world to come, what need was there for the later Sinaitic revelation? This question involves the conception of Israel's role in history. We shall return to it later.

REASON AND REVELATION

Let us, however, now return to the question we raised before, in regard to the relationship of reason and revelation in Judaism. If we assume that reason alone could have discovered many of the laws now included in the Torah, we may with some justification ask what is the ultimate sanction for these laws? Is it human reason, or is it Divine revelation?

In regard to the laws found in the Pentateuch, Jewish tradition is unanimous and unequivocal. They are authoritative, not because they conform to the requirements of human reason but because they are revealed. Hence even though in most instances reason can justify the Law, and even though great teachers of Judaism in all generations did not hesitate to attempt to rationalize the Law,[18] by and large there was a tendency to discourage preoccupation with the rational basis of the Law. It was not that the Rabbis feared that reason would invalidate it. They feared the use of reason even when reason would seem to support the Law.[19]

The debate between those who would seek to validate the Law by reason and those who oppose or strongly discourage all such attempts has continued down the ages. There are by now ample precedents in the Tradition to justify either the one or the other attitude. There is general agreement, however, that whether one observes the Law because he can validate it by his reason or because he believes it is revealed truth, is not nearly as important as the fact of his observing it. One of the most remarkable passages in all Rabbinic literature is that in which the Rabbis attribute to God the statement, "Would that they would leave Me but observe My Torah."[20]

Human experience has taught us that when one is armed with reason only, his chance of victory over his passions is none too bright. Nor is faith alone an adequate guide to life. It should be obvious to every one that, just as human life is not livable without a proper mixture of justice and mercy—though the two are in themselves irreconcilable—so are we as human beings lost, if our lives are not properly related to both faith and reason. Judaism is as much beset by this problem as are all great patterns of faith.

At no time would a pious traditional Jew venture to question a law of the Pentateuch because it seemed to him to be contrary to reason. However, when a question arose regarding the application of any of its laws to a given situation, human reason was final and determinative. The circumstances under which this principle was established are related in one of the most dramatic and imaginative passages in the Talmud. The matter in dispute between Rabbi Eleazar and his colleagues was in itself of comparatively little moment. It involved the laws of purity as they affected a stove built in a given fashion. Rabbi Eleazar presented all his arguments, but his colleagues did not find them convincing. Whereupon he said: "If I am right, then let this carob tree testify to it." We are told that the carob tree was uprooted and carried away some hundred yards. But his opponents were not convinced. They said: "One does not appeal to a carob tree in an argument."

"If I am right," said Rabbi Eleazar, "then let this stream of water testify to it." The stream reversed its course, but his opponents said, "The action of a stream of water is not a convincing argument." Rabbi Eleazar then called upon the walls of the house of study to testify. The walls were about to fall, when Rabbi Joshua rebuked them with the words, "What affair is it of yours if scholars dispute a matter of law?" We are told that out of respect for Rabbi Joshua the walls did not fall. But out of respect for Rabbi Eleazar they did not right themselves completely and remained in their inclined position.

Finally Rabbi Eleazar called upon a Voice from Heaven to testify in his behalf. The Voice responded that he was right. Whereupon Rabbi Joshua arose and quoted the Scriptural verse, " 'It [the Torah] is not in heaven' (Deuteronomy 30:12) . We pay no heed to heavenly voices."

The Talmud then goes on to relate how some time thereafter Rabbi Nathan, when visited by the prophet Elijah, asked him, "What did the Lord do at the time when the Rabbis refused to accept the testimony of the heavenly voice?" Elijah answered, "The Lord smiled and said, 'My children have prevailed over me. My children have prevailed over me.' "[21]

UNITY AND DIVERSITY

This extraordinary Talmudic passage requires no elaboration. The great Rabbis throughout the centuries continued their disputations, as have all great interpreters of laws and traditions among all peoples. Some among them appealed primarily to precedent and faith. Others were bolder in their dependence upon their own opinions. Liberal and conservative schools of thought abound, so that today when one who is a stranger to this universe of discourse reads their conflicting opinions, he wonders how he can arrive at any conclusion.

A Rabbinic homily on a verse in Ecclesiastes (12:11) reflects this mood: " 'The words of the wise are as goads, and as nails well fastened (literally: planted) are those that are composed in collections; they are given from one shepherd.' Why are the words of the Torah compared to a goad? To teach that just as the goad directs the cow into the proper furrow so that the world may have food, thus do the words of the Torah guide their students away from the paths of death into the paths of life. But lest you think that just as the goad is movable (and can be carried wherever one wishes) thus also the words of the Torah (can be made to mean whatever one wishes them to mean) the verse says of them that they are (fixed) like nails. But you might think that just as a nail diminishes the space it occupies (*i.e.,* it forms a hole in the area into which it is fixed) so do the words of the Torah diminish without adding. Therefore the verse says of them that they are *netuim*—planted. Just as a plant grows and increases, thus do the words of the Torah multiply. 'Composed in collections' (*baaley asufot*) refers to the scholars that study in groups. Some declare a thing impure, others pure. Some declare a thing forbidden, others declare it permissible. Some declare a thing unfit, others fit. If then one says, 'How can one then study Torah?' (Who can decide what is and what is not Torah?), the verse tells us that 'They are given from one shepherd.' The one God has given all of them, one leader taught them at the behest of the Lord of all creation, as it is written 'and God spoke all these words' (Exodus 20:1). Therefore set thine ear as a funnel and acquire thou an understanding heart to weigh the words of those who declare a thing impure and those who declare it pure, of those who forbid and those who permit, of those who declare a thing unfit and those who declare it fit."[22]

The homily seems to end in mid-air as if to imply that one can then make up his own mind. In the early, formative days of the Tradition undoubtedly much more leeway was given to personal opinions. Unfortunately, the latitude for personal decision has narrowed with the passing of the centuries. But there is at present a great ferment both in the State of Israel and in America for the opening of new avenues of interpretation within the Law. There have always been those who rejected the authority either of the oral Torah or of both the oral and the written Torah. But even within the ranks of those who accepted the authority of both the oral and the written Torah the differences between the liberal and the conservative interpretation of the written text or the oral tradition were many and sharp, even as they are today.

THE STUDY OF TORAH, THE GREATEST OF MITZVOT

However, I would be giving an altogether wrong impression of the place of Torah in Judaism, if I were to conclude my remarks on the concept of Torah at this point, for Torah is far more than Law or ritual. Its study is declared to be the greatest of all the *mitzvot,* the good deeds; and the joy it brings to its students has been described by every superlative available to speech. The Psalmist declares that the Torah refreshes the soul, bestows wisdom, gladdens the heart, and enlightens the eyes.[23] Rabbi Meir, a master of the second century, was wont to say: "He who studies Torah *lishmah*—for its own sake, without hope of winning gain or fame thereby—acquires great merit. The whole world is indebted to him; he is called friend, beloved, a lover of the All-Present, a lover of mankind; it clothes him in meekness and reverence, it fits him to become just, pious, upright, faithful; it keeps him far from sin and brings him to virtue. He is made like a never-failing fountain and like a river that flows on with ever-sustained vigor; he becomes modest, patient and forgiving of insults; and it magnifies him and exalts him above all things."[24] Without an understanding of the passionate love and joy that the Torah, both written and oral, roused in the hearts of its students and followers, one cannot hope to fathom the meaning and glory of Jewish existence.

A generation before the Christian era, Hillel summarized this vast literature for a would-be proselyte who wanted to learn the whole of it while standing upon one foot, by saying, "That which is hateful to you do not unto others. This is the whole of the Torah, all the rest is commentary, go and learn it."[25] Akiba pronounced its core to be the commandment, "Love thy neighbor as thyself" (Leviticus 19:18),[26] while his younger contemporary, Ben Azzai, saw the Torah's message epitomized in the verse: "This is the book of the generations of man" (Genesis 5:1).[27]

Never before had a whole people set its heart and hand with such exclusive, passionate devotion to applying the commandment, "Be ye holy, for I the Lord your God am holy" (Leviticus 19:2), to every conceivable human act. Like the Psalmist, every Jew was to set the Lord always before him (see Psalms 16:8), and at all times to act as if he were in the very presence of God so that every deed might be permeated with Divine sanctity.[28] For the Torah—both written and oral—was that body of instruction that would bring every Jew, at every moment in his life, into proper personal relationship to God and would enable the whole people of Israel to fulfill its role in the unfolding drama of human history.

ISRAEL

We turn now to a brief consideration of "Israel," the third of the concepts which are indispensable to any "pattern of faith" that could be included under the designation of Judaism. If the dynamic quality of Judaism's God-concept is imbedded in the paradox of His being both just and merciful, and that of the Torah-concept in the paradox of its being both reason and revelation, the dynamism of the concept of Israel may be said to reside in the paradox of Israel's being, as it were, both "prince" and "whipping boy," as being both "the beloved chosen" and "the suffering servant" of the Lord. Had Israel conceived of itself as being merely the one or the other, it would have long since disappeared from the annals of history. Had it conceived of itself only as "whipping boy," it might have lost the desire to live. Had it conceived of itself only as a "prince," it might have lost hope and heart in the face of the apparently endless, unequal struggle. But through God's messengers, the prophets, Israel learned to think of itself as both "prince" and "whipping boy," both the "beloved chosen" and the "suffering servant," and in that paradox it could maintain both hope and self-respect in the midst of unprecedented suffering and humiliation.

How did Israel become the "chosen" of the Lord? Other peoples who viewed themselves as the favorites of the deity usually had some myth in which the people or its ruler were described as the actual progeny of the god. Still others would see themselves in the favored position because they inhabited the area over which the god was believed to rule. Gods had favorite cities, or countries, as well as favorite tribes or peoples. But nothing in the known tradition of Judaism even hints at such a relationship between God and Israel. Israel becomes a "chosen people" because of the merits of its ancestors, Abraham, Isaac and Jacob (Deuteronomy 4:37, 7:7–8).

THE COVENANT PEOPLE

The relationship between Israel and God is based on a covenant, a covenant that is entered into between them and God as a reward for the righteous and self-sacrificial action of their ancestor Abraham. "And it came to pass after these things that God tried Abraham. . . ." When Abraham proved his loyalty beyond shadow of doubt, Scripture records that the Lord said, "I swear by Myself since you have done this, since you have not withheld your son, your only son, that I will indeed bless you, I will indeed make your descendants as numerous as the stars in the sky and the sand on the seashore. . . . And in your descendants shall all the nations of the earth be blessed, because you have obeyed My word" (Genesis 22:1–18).

To follow this covenant concept down the corridors of history, to note how it steadily broadens and deepens in meaning, to observe how it decides the destiny of the people who live by it, is in itself spiritually and intellectually among the most fascinating of experiences. Obviously we cannot do more than glimpse some of the most decisive turning points in this long history. Let us start by inquiring who was to be included under the terms of this covenant.

There can be little doubt that in the beginning the covenant was understood to refer exclusively to the physical descendants of Abraham, Isaac and Jacob. The sense of blood kinship was, however, not equally strong in all periods of Jewish history.[29] It reached its highest pitch apparently in the middle of the fifth century B.C.E. when Ezra, the scribe, arrived in Jerusalem and found the small Jewish community on the verge of extinction because of physical and religious assimilation (Ezra, Chapters 9–10). But the very man who laid the greatest stress upon the racial purity of the group also laid the foundation for the ultimate subordination of what he appeared to prize so highly. For he, whom the

Tradition speaks of as having been worthy of receiving the Torah at Sinai,[30] was the moving spirit in the course of events which culminated in the Torah's becoming the distinguishing mark of the people of Israel. He thus ultimately made possible the implementation of the principle announced by Deutero-Isaiah: "Neither let the alien, that hath joined himself to the Lord, speak, saying: 'The Lord will surely separate me from His people'; Neither let the eunuch say: 'Behold, I am a dry tree!' For thus saith the Lord concerning the eunuchs that keep My Sabbaths, and choose the things that please Me, and hold fast by My covenant: Even unto them will I give in My house and within My walls a monument and memorial, better than sons and daughters; I will give them an everlasting memorial, that shall not be cut off. Also the aliens, that join themselves to the Lord, to minister unto Him, and to love the name of the Lord, to be His servants, every one that keepeth the Sabbath from profaning it, and holdeth fast by My Covenant, even them will I bring to My holy mountain and make them joyful in My house of Prayer; their offerings and their sacrifices shall be acceptable upon Mine altar, for My house shall be called a house of prayer for all peoples" (Isaiah 56:3–7).

Thus through the Torah the covenant was transformed from a covenant with an ethnic group into a covenant with servants of the Lord. Israel was transformed from a racial group into a spiritual fellowship. Because Ruth, the Moabite woman, had said, "Thy God shall be my God" (Ruth 1:16), she became worthy of being the ancestress of David (Ruth 4:22) and hence ultimately the ancestress of the Messiah.

The two strains that underlie the composition of the group called Israel, the ethnic and the spiritual, have not as yet completely made peace with each other. The attitude of the average Jew towards proselytes has by and large been ambivalent. But the number of proselytes has been so great and many among them have been so distinguished, that none can any longer maintain that Israel is a racial fellowship only.

For various historical reasons, Judaism during the Christian era has not been—and is not today—an actively proselytizing religion. It has never sought to make conversion easy. The Rabbis give specific instruction to point out to a prospective convert all the difficulties and disadvantages that membership within the Jewish fellowship entails.[31] The ambivalent attitude toward proselytes has often subjected the Jews to accusations of clannishness and haughty exclusiveness. Unquestionably the circumstances which made active proselytism impossible for Jews also at times created a frame of mind which could well be designated as clannish. Now and then voices are raised within the Jewish fold urging positive proselytizing activity, and attempts are made to organize it. But though there have been no large-scale, organized, Jewishly sponsored efforts at proselytizing, it is nevertheless true that the Israel of the Covenant is no longer an ethnic group, either in fact or in theory.

The merit of the Patriarchs which made them worthy of the covenant and made of their descendants a chosen people, bestowed precious privileges upon them. To be chosen by God as Abraham was chosen—"to the end that he may command his children and his household after him, that they may keep the way of the Lord, to do righteousness and justice" (Genesis 18:19)—is indeed a privilege. And what higher distinction can there come to a people than that of being the medium through whom God revealed the Torah to mankind.

But unfortunately not all the descendants of Abraham considered these to be the privileges they desired for themselves as the chosen of the Lord. They thought of privileges far more tangible and mundane. Not many pray to be "on God's side." Most of us pray with the hope that God may be on our side. And while there have always been Jews who feared lest God would repudiate His covenant with them for their failure to fulfill their task in the world, there also always were others who of their own will repudiated it. They did not want to be "God's witnesses" upon this earth, nor to be charged with a responsibility greater than that of any other people to "keep the way of the Lord, to do righteousness and justice."

Since the days of the prophet Ezekiel, Jewish tradition has firmly maintained the conviction that not only will God keep His covenant with Israel, but He will not permit Israel to repudiate it. Individual Jews or even groups of them may successfully reject their divinely ordained destiny. The people as a whole never can or will. More than twenty-five hundred years ago, Ezekiel told the recalcitrant generation that was exiled to Babylonia, "And that which cometh into your mind shall not be at all; in that ye say 'we will be as the nations, as the families of the countries, to serve wood and stone.' 'As I live,' saith the Lord God, 'surely with a mighty hand and with an outstretched arm and with wrath poured out, will I be king over you' " (Ezekiel 20:32–33). The covenant thus becomes the source of both eternal, unwavering hope, and of untold, unparalleled suffering. God Himself has ruled out spiritual suicide as a possible way for Israel to escape from its suffering.

THE SERVANT OF THE LORD

Nor can even obedience to God's law and complete selfless devotion redeem Israel from martyrdom. The conception of the suffering *eved ha-Shem*—servant of the Lord—as portrayed in the matchless fifty-third chapter of Isaiah, and the conception of Israel as the "heart" among the nations suffering for the evil that infects any segment of mankind, as formulated by Yehudah Halevi in his philosophic work *The Kuzari*,[32] raised the concept of the chosen people to the highest level of spiritual insight. To Amos, chosenness made punishment for transgression all the more certain (Amos 3:2). To Deutero-Isaiah, it came to mean that the highest point of suffering comes precisely at the point of the noblest fulfillment of the mission. One suffers most when he is most obedient to the will of God. The suffering of Israel, the true "servant of God," will not cease until Israel fulfills its historic role of being the prime mover in bringing all of mankind to the service of the Lord.

The great physical tragedies that have repeatedly overtaken the Jewish people have frequently resulted in an intensification of the desire on the part of many "to be like all the nations" and to repudiate the special covenant with God. Nothing is further from the truth than the oft-repeated opinion that persecution has kept Israel alive. Every wave of persecution, including the one we have witnessed in our day, is followed by a wave of rejection of the covenant and the Tradition. But in some mysterious manner not all are overwhelmed by the tragedy, and many are made stronger in their determination to remain within the covenant. They find hope and reassurance in it. Consciously or subconsciously they recall that in Egypt, when their forefathers were on the verge of utter annihilation under the yoke of Egyptian bondage, "God heard their moaning and God remembered His covenant with Abraham, Isaac and Jacob" (Exodus 2:24–25). They recall God's promise: "When they are in the land of their enemies, I will not spurn them, I will not abhor them, so as to destroy them entirely and so break My covenant with them; for I am the Lord their God. But I will for their sakes remember the covenant of their ancestors, whom I brought out of the land of Egypt in the sight of the nations, that I might be their God: I am the Lord" (Leviticus 26:44–45). And their faith that God will "hear their moaning and remember His covenant" is renewed.

The miraculous manner in which the Jewish people has been able to rise again and again out of its ruins, is climaxed in our day—after the loss of the most vigorous and devoted third of its members, and in the face of well-nigh universal opposition—by the establishment of an independent Jewish state. This achievement gives renewed courage to the believer and strengthens his faith that Israel is not merely an ethnic group, a racial entity, or some historically conditioned society, but is indeed a servant of God—destined, it may be, to much more suffering, but destined also to live so that it may play its appointed role in establishing God's Kingdom upon this earth.

CHAPTER II

God, Man, Torah, and Israel[1]

INTRODUCTORY REMARKS

I have always opposed any action that would tend to transform the Rabbinical Assembly into anything like a modern version of the Sanhedrin, exercising legislative and judicial power and promulgating authoritative pronouncements on matters of faith and dogma. My opposition was based first upon my fear of sectarianism. Sectarianism does not arise when individual Jews exercise their God-given right to study and interpret the Torah or to decide to whom among the scholars and saints of the past or the present they will turn for guidance in understanding the Torah. It arises when a group unites and issues official pronouncements on dogma and law, drawing up as it were a new covenant and explicitly or implicitly declaring it to be the only or the preferred standard for membership in the religious fellowship of Israel. That danger is ever present and the moment we cease being aware of it, it will overwhelm us.

I was, in addition, always concerned with preserving my own freedom of thought and action. I am ready to abide by majority decisions of any group of which I am a part if those decisions do not require me to violate the freedom of my thought, and do not define for me my obligations to God. As a rabbi, I want to belong to a group of like-minded individuals. But I do not want a like-mindedness achieved by majority vote. It must be a like-mindedness resulting from the free acceptance of common views arrived at by each member of the group after much personal meditation and serious discussion within the group.

Hence, though I agreed to participate in the effort to formulate Guiding Principles for the Conservative Movement in Judaism, I do so with considerable trepidation. I hope that whatever document is finally produced[2] by the Committee will not be presented for formal acceptance by the Rabbinical Assembly, but will be included among its publications as a contribution towards the development of that like-mindedness amongst us which, while inevitably stamping us as an identifiable group within Judaism, will not transform us into a sect.

If, despite my hesitation, I nevertheless heartily welcome this effort, it is because I believe that while the Rabbinical Assembly as a whole should not officially adopt any given set of dogmas or opinions, no member of the Assembly can function effectively unless he has thought through his own position with sufficient clarity to be able to state—at least for himself—what his deepest convictions are. As each one of us thinks through his own theological position and shares his views with his colleagues frankly and sincerely, we shall either develop a broad and satisfying consensus amongst ourselves, or not. If we fail to develop a significant consensus, we shall fail as a significant historic phenomenon in the history of Judaism. If we succeed in developing not merely a consensus amongst ourselves, but a consensus on a high spiritual and intellectual level, one that will contribute towards transforming us personally into significant religious Jewish personalities, then we will have fulfilled our chief task as teachers of Judaism.

This attempt, as I see it, therefore, is first and foremost a necessary stimulus to each one of us to think through his position for himself.

Furthermore, a consensus on the highest possible level arrived at in this manner is becoming increasingly imperative for us as we grow in numbers, lest our Movement fall prey to utter confusion in thought and chaos in action. Our unity, uniqueness and value as a distinguishable group within the religious Jewish community will depend largely upon our ability to demonstrate that freedom of thought and action does not necessarily lead to the disintegration of the group, nor to its deterioration to the status of an organization united primarily by common vested interests rather than by common religious motivations. Our hope to maintain such a significant unity depends not merely upon the preservation of sincere openmindedness and tolerance towards one another, but also upon our maintaining amongst ourselves a constant unflagging dialogue in which we treat one another's opinions, as well as our own opinions, with the utmost of seriousness.

We may differ regarding the principles to which we want to relate our acts, or whether any specific act is properly related to a given principle. Hence, it is possible to accept identical principles and yet vary radically from one another in acts, or to follow identical paths of action and relate them to radically different principles. However, as long as we share at least one of these two basic areas of experience in common, as long as we share either common principles or common acts, we possess the *sine qua non* of intelligible intercommunication and of vital group cohesion. We are not bent upon winning an argument, but upon clarifying those principles upon which we stand ready to stake our own lives and what is more important, the lives of our children. If we feel that anything less than that is involved in what we are doing, then it is not worth the effort.

This statement, even in its present form, is much longer than at first contemplated. To keep it within bounds suitable to its immediate purposes, references, quotations, proof-texts and elaborate argument in support of any specific thesis, were largely eliminated. This statement is neither a bare skeleton outline nor a fully documented and defended thesis. In some sections, a skeletal character predominates and statements are made that are left wholly undeveloped. Hence they are bound to appear rather dogmatic and unconvincing. In some sections, a position is explained at some length. I had to use my own judgment when to do the one and when the other. Skeletons at best are not attractive, and they are even less so when the flesh upon them is unevenly distributed. They can hardly be convincing. But they do suggest possibilities. Perhaps some day I may be able to supply the needed flesh and sinews more attractively and convincingly distributed.

GOD AND MAN

Each man finds God in his own way. The Midrash (Genesis Rabbah 39:1) relates that Abraham's search for God started with the question "Is it possible that a well-ordered, smoothly running castle has no lord?" Some become aware of God by experiencing the sense of "radical amazement" when confronting the mysteries and the majesty of life and the universe. In what follows, I shall indicate the path that led me to God.

It is not enough for a human being to say "I do this because I *feel* like doing it." Human behavior is peculiarly human when it is consciously related to articulated ideas or principles. There is that in man which irresistibly goads him on to "prove" at least to his own satisfaction that what he does "makes sense," that it is "reasonable." We consider an act to be reasonable when we believe it to be reasonably related to a principle whose validity we accept for what we consider to be adequate reasons. The more self-evident the principle and the more universally accepted, the more adequate is it as a standard for judging the reasonableness of an act.

A primary task, therefore, of human thought has been the search for self-evident, universally accepted principles. A principle is self-evident when every term used in its formulation and when it, as a whole, has precise, universally accepted meaning. A principle is said to be "universally accepted" if all who subject it to meticulous scrutiny find it to be valid beyond reasonable doubt.

Unfortunately, however, the American Declaration of Independence notwithstanding, no "self-evident truths" involving value judgments have thus far been formulated. The wide acceptance and "self-evidence" of some moral principles are illusory, for the concepts employed in their formulation are not subject to precise definition and each one accepts the principle on the basis of his own definition of the concepts involved.

The following two principles fulfill the requirements of being self-evident and universally accepted in greater measure than any other known to me. They "justify" more acts to the satisfaction of the doer and the observer than any other principle or principles known to me.

(1) An act is considered reasonable if it contributes towards the preservation of the actor's physical existence upon this earth.

(2) An act is considered reasonable if it helps the actor to avoid physical pain.

The meaning of every word in each of these two principles is clear and is beyond reasonable doubt, as is the meaning of the statement as a whole. Nor are there any goals more universally accepted as reasonable validations of human acts than the preservation of one's physical existence and the avoidance of physical pain.

However, they obviously are not considered as adequate guides under all conditions and circumstances. Not only do all men not act in accordance with them at all times, but few believe that they should. Human beings repeatedly, knowingly and wilfully, perform acts that either terminate or hasten the termination of their physical existence, or cause them physical pain. Men in the thousands have not only willingly suffered physical pain but even risked life and accepted death, believing that in so doing they were acting reasonably. Socrates drank the hemlock as a matter of conscious choice. Rabbi Akiba knowingly risked and accepted martyrdom. Countless numbers of great and humble men and women daily accept physical pain or discomfort and even risk life itself so that someone else may be spared pain or granted life. If asked why they behave as they do, they would not all give the same answer. But they would all try to refer their acts to a principle, in accordance with which the act would appear to be adequately rationalized.

The inevitable question that presses itself upon us then is this: Is there any principle which is at least as nearly self-evident and as nearly universally accepted as the two mentioned, in the light of which actions which are inimical to the preservation of the physical existence of the individual, or which subject him to physical pain, might be rationalized? For this is the crux of the ethical problem that each of us must face. I do not know of any such principle.

I am compelled therefore to choose one of two possible alternatives. I must either declare all acts which an individual willingly performs though he knows them to be both bearers of physical pain and inimical to physical preservation, as irrational, or I must—for what appears to me to be adequate reason—accept as a guiding principle for my action one which is neither self-evident nor universally accepted.

There are those who maintain that all man's acts if they are to be declared reasonable must conform to the requirements of the two above-mentioned, universally accepted, self-evident principles. They implicitly or explicitly declare the act of the martyr, the saint or the hero, to be the act either of a naive, or a misguided, or a foolish individual.

Some reformulate the principles as follows: An act is considered reasonable if it contributes towards the physical preservation of the group (family, people, nation) of which the actor is a member, or of mankind as a whole, or if it helps his group or mankind to avoid physical pain, even though it may not do the same for the actor.

In being thus modified, universal acceptability is obviously sacrificed. For the principle that one should be ready to sacrifice his physical existence and comfort for that of the group, even though he can avoid doing it, is certainly not validated by its mere statement. It has to be proved. I know of no self-evident, universally accepted principle, in accordance with which it is reasonable to assume that when there is a real choice possible between one's own physical existence and comfort and that of any group, be it nation or mankind, one should *prefer the group.*

Moreover, mankind being divided into various distinct and often mutually hostile groups, many individuals in each group have the choice of abandoning their own group and finding greater physical security and comfort through joining another group. If one has the opportunity to do that, is there any self-evident, universally accepted principle in accordance with which such an act could be declared unreasonable?

In addition, in deciding upon acts that would contribute most towards the preservation of the physical existence of the group (whether the group be less than or the whole of mankind), differences of opinion inevitably arise. For the ultimate outcome of any act cannot possibly be foreseen. Hence, in advocating one act over against another, an element of the unknown is inescapably present. Under such circumstances, in accordance with what principle does it become reasonable for one to accept mistreatment, as Jeremiah did, and even death, as Socrates did, at the hands of the very group he seeks to serve, in order to press upon it his own particular version of what will make for its physical preservation and well-being?

Finally, in a world divided among differing groups, what principle should guide the group as a whole in its relations to other groups, or to mankind as a whole? Few who today rationalize the death of the individual in behalf of his group, by the "life" which he thus bequeaths to his group, are ready to rationalize the possible death of the group by the "life" it may thus bequeath unto the rest of mankind. The analogy we so frequently draw between the relationship of the individual to the group and the group to other groups in human society stops short at its most crucial point. And the individual may well inquire why the group which demands of him to sacrifice himself for it, does not at the same time declare its readiness as a group to sacrifice itself for the good of mankind as a whole, whenever mankind may call upon it to do so.

Let us note that this line of thought, which modifies the original two principles by substituting the group or mankind for the individual, continues to justify acts only in terms of physical security and freedom from physical pain. It merely transfers the point of reference of the pain and the security from the individual to a group. But the transfer is purely arbitrary, in no way rationalized by any self-evident, universally accepted principle. Moreover, there is no way of proving that the act of the martyr or saint makes for the physical welfare of his group. Socrates' death did not save Athens nor did Akiba's martyrdom bring physical security to his generation. Indeed, the group is most often of the opinion that the actions of its saints, its prophets and its martyrs are inimical to its own physical welfare, as witness the treatment usually meted out to their contemporaries.

The rationality of one's reverence for qualities which often endanger and even terminate physical security and comfort cannot then be validated either empirically or by any self-evident, universally accepted principle known to me. But everyone who experiences such reverence profoundly and inescapably, must, out of an irrepressible need to preserve his sanity, formulate for himself a principle in the light of which that reverence makes sense.

For what does reverence for the saints, the martyrs and the willing, humble sufferer imply? When that reverence is sincere and is confirmed by reflection, it implies the belief that though the qualities which make for saintliness and enable one to contemplate and serenely accept physical suffering and even martyrdom, may, and most often do, contribute to the physical welfare of the individual, or of his group, it is not that which makes them desirable or gives them significance. On the contrary, the physical welfare of the individual or of the group, be it even the whole of mankind, are of significance only as they serve those qualities, for only they endow life with significance above that of the beast.

What are these qualities and why are they supremely desirable? I found the answer to these questions in the Torah. While all of my childhood experiences and early training predisposed me to my final decision, they did not in themselves determine it. As I matured, I was exposed to other very powerful influences as were all the young Jews who, like me, grew to manhood in democratic America and received their general education from the first grade through the University in secular institutions. The final decision could not therefore have been made without considerable intellectual wrestling and without a large element of conscious choice.

It was the Torah that set before me the doctrine that man's highest destiny is to strive to be Godlike, for only as he approximates God, who is Ultimate Being, does he, as man, have Being. It was the Torah that taught me that not every act that involves physical suffering or death helps man approximate God. Nor do only those acts which involve physical suffering or death help man become Godlike. The Torah taught me that man approximates Ultimate Being only as he "does justly, loves mercy, walks humbly," as he "speaks truth in his heart," as he "loves his fellow man as himself," and as he strives to understand and fulfill the precept: "Be ye holy for I the Lord Thy God am holy" (Micah 6:8; Psalms 15:2; Leviticus 19:18, 19:2). What justice, love, mercy, and holiness require of me, I shall not now discuss. But of one thing I am certain. The significance of the acts they enjoin, and therefore their own significance, may be suggested or foreshadowed in terms of humanly measurable results, but cannot be validated or exhausted by them. Their significance derives ultimately from their association with a realm which transcends man's mundane experiences. Their significance derives ultimately from God.

Thus it was my irrepressible reverence for the saints and martyrs of human history; for the lovers of mankind who ever strive to serve "the stranger, the orphan and the widow"; for the humble who remain loyal to a sick parent, child, spouse, or friend at a painful price of personal physical discomfort; for lovers of freedom who risk and give their lives that freedom may prevail; for the self-sacrificing pioneers of science in search of truth; for the honest artisans and tradesmen who forego opportunities to take advantage of the ignorance or need of others; and my inability to rationalize their acts in terms of the two most self-evident and most universally accepted principles—regardless of how they themselves might have rationalized their acts—it was that which opened for me the only door leading to God which was never again closed even temporarily. Other doors had also been opened that beckoned me on to God. The heavens and their hosts did speak to me of Him. But the doors they opened did not remain as stubbornly resistant to the repeated, irrepressible efforts of reason and self-interest to close them as did the door which the saints, the martyrs and the humble good, had opened.

Though I can never know with an absolute, communicable certainty that what the Torah thus teaches me about God and about the path leading to Godliness is true, I do know with an absolute certainty that if it were not for the

Torah and its teachings, human life generally and Jewish life in particular would for me be bereft not only of all its nobility but of all conceivable meaning.

Man can at best only approximate Ultimate Being, or God. An insuperable chasm separates man from God. Man is a creature and God is his Creator, and man can never be God. For God's omnipotence has but one necessary limitation: He cannot create another God. He cannot bestow upon His creatures the qualities of His own non-creaturehood. But because I believe that He created and sustains His creation in Love, I believe He did bestow upon it the capacity to approximate Him. To the best of our present knowledge, man has been most amply thus endowed. That is what our Bible means to convey to us by telling us that man was created "in God's image" (Genesis 1:27).

I see in the capacity to approximate God the highest expression of God's love for His creatures. To the extent that we exercise this God-given capacity to approximate Him, to that extent do we experience God's love for us. Man may some day achieve that perfection of Knowledge, Power and Will and that perfection of interaction among them which would regularly result in acts conforming to the requirements of justice, love, truth, and holiness. The distance between man and his Creator would thus be reduced to its theoretically minimal proportions. There is, however, no absolute assurance that he will attain such perfection.

Did God then bestow favor upon His creation by bringing it into being even though He cannot endow it with His own perfection? I do not know an answer to that question which is fully communicable and logically beyond all possible doubt. But I do know that for me there is only one answer possible. It is to believe with a perfect faith that in granting me life as a human being, God bestowed His greatest blessing upon me; for what greater gift could He have granted me than the maximum possibility of approximating Him![3]

Inherent in this possibility is the attribute of Freedom,

for Freedom is of God's essence and where there is no Freedom there is no possibility to approximate God in any measure. In stating that God created Man "in His image," Scripture, I believe, is telling us that Man has been so much more abundantly endowed with the attribute of Freedom than any other of God's creatures as to enable him to approximate God in greater measure than any other creature. But Scripture does not deny some element of Freedom to the rest of creation. In comparison to man all the rest of creation, both animate and inanimate, appear to be completely devoid of Freedom and our modern science with its immutable—more recently, not so absolutely immutable—natural laws has reinforced that commonplace observation. For reasons that I cannot here discuss, I believe that every electron—or however else we shall finally designate the ultimate primary component of all observable phenomena—exercises a measure of freedom, however small it may be.[4]

The existence, therefore, of all of the natural phenomena which we observe is in part dependent upon the free cooperation of the infinite number of electrons which compose them. Every cell of the human body exercises its measure of freedom. To that extent, the normal functioning of the human body depends upon the free cooperation of the countless cells which compose it. Thus also every human being exercises his freedom, and the free cooperation of large numbers of human beings constitutes a human society. This cooperation among electrons or cells or human beings is never perfect. Hence the many tragedies and near tragedies in the universe. I see in the travail of God's creation, His travail, in that He cannot bestow upon His creatures the perfection which is His and His only as the non-created Creator of all. Man, who has been endowed with a greater measure of freedom, as well as with a more ample capacity to know, to will and to do, than any other creature as far as it is known to us, must thus strive ceaselessly to approximate God by exercising his capacities to their maximum perfection.

Therein lies his duty and his opportunity. He can find courage in the performance of his duty and in the exercise of his opportunity, in the faith that his Creator is Himself striving to aid him, that He finds divine delight as man succeeds in approximating Him and that He suffers as man fails. *"Bekhol tsaratam lo tsar,"* "In all their affliction He is afflicted" (Isaiah 63:9). The depth of tragedy and degradation into which man can fall is in proportion to the heights of joy and exaltation to which he can climb. God could not offer His creatures the blessings of the heights without exposing them to the dangers of the depths. If He could, He would, for He created them in love.[5]

In man's ceaseless effort to approximate God, the needs of the physical aspect of his being cannot be accepted as the ultimate arbiters of the reasonable. Neither are they to be viewed as its inveterate antagonists. The assumption that man as Being is not identical with his body should not be interpreted to mean that the body is in reality antithetical to man's Being, leading to the conclusion that man achieves his ultimate Being as he denies or destroys the body.

I find meaning in the human experience only as I accept the Rabbinic concept of the essential unity of body and soul. Both are inseparably interwoven in one another's very essence. Both together can strive to approximate God, but can never—either together or singly—become identical with Him. I reject any and all types of monistic philosophy because it identifies the whole of the universe, and man as part of the universe, with God. Nor can I accept any philosophy which posits a fundamentally dualistic conception of man, declaring one aspect of man—his soul—to be in essence divine, and the other aspect—the body—to be non-divine. In all monistic philosophies, man really never loses his essential godliness. Body and soul are merely aspects of the two divine attributes of extension and thought. In all dualistic concepts of man, the soul is, as it were, a divine "spark" imprisoned in a dark cell, destined to return to the original "flame" from which it was but temporarily separated. Hence the soul is really never less than divine while the body can never be anything more than the very antithesis of the divine. No part of me is either God or completely devoid of Godliness.

In praying for life on the High Holidays, we say "The soul is Thine and the body is Thy handiwork. Have mercy upon Thy creature." Both body and soul are God's creations and we ask His mercy upon both of them equally. It is this complete interdependence of body and soul which makes concern for the body's welfare spiritually acceptable and rationally defensible, without making it ultimately determinative. For the martyr, in choosing death rather than physical life, is thus not deciding between body and soul, but between an action which would help him in his totality to approximate God, and one which would seriously impair or completely destroy his capacity to approximate God.

Just as I cannot accept the body's security and comfort as the ultimate guides for my actions, because I would thus identify my essential Being with my physical body, even so do I find it impossible to view what we call death as the utter and irretrievable annihilation of the Being which has its visible presence in the body. For that too would imply an identification of my Being with my tangible, visible body which disintegrates in death. Moreover, if that were so, I see no possible rational refutation of Louis XV's position *"Après moi le déluge"* ("After me, the deluge"). It can be rationally rejected only if we assume that there really is no *après moi.*

What happens to the *moi* after death, we have no way of knowing. Regarding the realm beyond the grave, Rabbinic tradition teaches that even the Prophets were granted no insight into its nature (Shabbat 63a). But I believe that the essential Being of every individual persists in some manner more real than merely as an item in the memory of a descendant or the "race." Moreover, I believe that the *moi* after death is in some significant manner related to the *moi* of before death. To the extent that the body is an integral part of the *moi,* it too must have Being after death. The nature of our Being in the realm "from whose bourn no traveller returns" we cannot know.

Will those who once walked this planet again walk upon it in the form of physical Being that was once theirs? I find no intellectual or spiritual need to deny it or affirm it. I do not find it theoretically impossible because I can think of no necessary limits upon the creative powers of God other than the one I previously mentioned. But I do not affirm it because I do not find it indispensable to a rationalization of my basic belief that my life upon this earth "makes sense" only as I strive to approximate God.

THE TORAH

God, having created in love, sustains His creation in love. The very essence of love is continuous, uninterrupted concern that yearns to bestow blessing upon the beloved. Divine blessing is experienced with utmost poignancy in moments of Divine Revelation and Divine Communication. We should distinguish between the two. Much confusion has resulted in the use of the concept of Revelation for both. They are two clearly distinguishable aspects of God's relationship with man.

The one which we shall henceforth designate as Revelation, man finds to be wholly ineffable. He cannot communicate its essence to another human being by any means at his disposal. The most men have been able to do is to describe in what they feel to be completely inadequate terms, what they experienced either immediately preceding or immediately following upon it. But no one has as yet presumed to be able to communicate to another the essence of the experience itself, nor to give a formula whereby one may achieve it at will.

This ineffable experience, unanimously declared by all who have known it, as the most sublime and the most treasured blessing bestowed by God upon any of His creatures, is not wholly reserved for the chosen few. In its most intense and overwhelming appearance it is indeed relatively rare and never lasts for a very long time. But brief moments of comparative intensity are granted to well-nigh every human being. Dr. Max Kadushin in his *Organic Thinking* has aptly designated this almost universal human experience as "Normal Mysticism" and has given a comprehensive and penetrating analysis of it as it is reflected in Rabbinic thought and action.[6]

It is from such experiences that we emerge with a sense of unqualified conviction that our existence has meaning because we are the creatures of an omnipotent Creator who created us and the whole of the universe in love. If it were not so, we would be far more unpleasant and unhappy beings than we are now. For a self-conscious creature like man cannot know himself and the universe about him without finding himself for a time between the Scylla of self-pity bordering on self-hate and the Charybdis of pride bordering on self-worship. He is saved only as he becomes aware of his Creator. Man's unbearable inner conflict between the depressing sense of his insignificance as compared with the physical universe about him and the intoxicating sense of his superiority as compared with all the other creatures known to him, is resolved only by his experiencing an immediate awareness of the Divine Presence, an experience which enables him to understand the Psalmist's impassioned cry "O Lord, our Lord, How majestic is Thy name in all the earth!" (Psalms 8:2).

Because we experience His presence with ineffable intimacy, we venture to speak of Him in humanly comprehensible terms without feeling that we are uttering blasphemy. But when we become conscious of the blasphemy latent in our speech, we either side with the poets and use words and phrases though we know them to be intellectually incomprehensible and logically indefensible when spoken of God, or we decide with the philosophers that if we are to speak of God at all, we must limit our statements to negatives.

The other aspect of God's relationship to man, we shall designate as Divine Communication. By Divine Communication we refer to that confrontation between man and God which, while it is in itself ineffable, has associated with it a communicable content. Having created man in love, God has not abandoned him to his own inescapable inadequacies. Through Divine Communication, man increases his knowledge, enlarges his power, sanctifies his will, and is sustained in his yearning to approximate his Creator.

God is constantly communicating with man. Insofar as it is given us to discover and express a truth heretofore unknown to man, to create a thing of beauty heretofore not experienced by man, to indicate a path leading us nearer to God heretofore undiscerned by man, we have experienced a Divine Communication, and have thus been blessed by God with a blessing uniquely our own. And insofar as we have the capacity to comprehend and to appreciate Divine Communications granted to others, we share in the blessing which was originally uniquely experienced by another fellow man. We, too, then experience that Divine Communication, not merely in our imagination but in the whole of our being and often with an intensity of awareness of its intrinsic worth and of its ineffable setting which may be only little less than the intensity of the awareness experienced by him to whom the Divine Communication was originally granted.

We know the content of Divine Communication in part with a knowledge which is communicable, and in part with a knowledge which is ineffable. Where the content is largely accessible to the senses, our knowledge is largely communicable. When referring to such content we usually use the verb "know." We say "I know thus-and-so to be true." Where the content is not in large measure or in its most significant aspect accessible to the senses, our knowledge is largely ineffable. To such content we usually apply the verb "believe" and we say "I believe thus-and-so to be true." The indiscriminate use of "know" and "believe" is a source of endless confusion in human communication.[6a]

We hesitate to ascribe to Divine Communication, content which is ultimately completely accessible to the five senses and which is therefore ultimately known with a perfectly communicable knowledge, because we tend to identify the channels whereby we can validate a Divine Communication, namely the senses, with the origin of the communication. But the great scientific insights even like the insights of the great poets, artists and musicians, at first were "flashes of inspiration," *i.e.,* Divine Communication. The completely communicable content of such a "flash of inspiration" is usually verified by communicable knowledge long after the moment of original insight. J. Bronowski, the scientist, notes: "All the discoveries of science, all works of art, are explorations—more, are explosions, of a hidden likeness. The discoverer or the artist presents in them two aspects of nature and fuses them into one. This is the act of creation, in which an original thought is born, and it is the same act in original science and original art."[7] He describes the "act of creation" of the scientist or artist as an "explosion," a concept as recondite as any ever used by a theologian and far more meaningless. For me, the "act of creation" of the scientist or the artist, even as of the prophet is not an "explosion" but a Divine Communication.

There are vital, distinguishable differences between the circumstances surrounding Divine Communications granted the prophets of Israel and those accompanying the Divine Communications granted to any other human beings. Professor Abraham J. Heschel has, with great erudition and with the fine spiritual sensitivity which characterizes all his works, pointed out those differences in his study of the prophets.[8] But I am not at this moment interested in examining this aspect of Divine Communication. My concern at the moment is with the content of the Communication.

A Divine Communication whose content is subject to verification beyond reasonable doubt by communicable knowledge I shall, for want of a better designation, henceforth refer to as Secondary Divine Communication. It includes all of the majestic advances made by man in his knowledge of the world about him which is accessible to the five senses and is subject to formulation in mathematically exact terms. It includes the whole of the realm of the natural sciences. By designating it as the realm of secondary Divine Communication, I do not want to ascribe lesser importance to it. I do so because I want to distinguish it from the realm of Divine Communication whose content is *not* subject to validation beyond reasonable doubt via communicable knowledge accessible to our senses.

The realm of *values,* I shall designate as Primary Divine Communication. Both designations are rather unwieldy, but I could think of no more appropriate terms to use, and I find the division between these two aspects of Divine Communication to be indispensable to the clarity of my thought.

Some inescapable dilemmas

In thinking about Divine Communication, whether in the secondary or primary sense, we face inescapable dilemmas to which we can offer no logically unchallengeable solutions. Each one of us must of necessity struggle with these dilemmas to the best of his ability. In the final analysis, however, he must live the best he knows how, with them, or accept as an act of faith whatever "solution" he prefers. The most one can hope for is to achieve a reasonable integration of his solution into the larger framework of his faith, or his philosophy of life.

In the realm of Secondary Divine Communication, that of the natural sciences and mathematics, we know that much of what previous generations considered to have been proved beyond reasonable doubt has since been disproved. Hence, how can we be certain that that which we now consider validated by our senses will not be invalidated by them in some future time? Why therefore designate such provenly fallible and potentially fallible content as Divine Communication at all? I do so first because if I do not include all that we understand by science, within the realm of Divine Communication to man, we make man independent of God in an all-important and ever-increasing area of his activity. If man can be independent of God in this realm, why can he not be independent of Him in all other realms of his activity? But I believe that man cannot, of his own volition, conceive a truth or even an aspect of it whether it be in science, in art or in morals any more than he can of his own volition grow a new bodily organ. True ideas or ideas that are aspects of truth are communicated to him by God.

Man, however, is not a completely passive recipient. The nature of the communicable content is in great measure, though never completely, dependent upon the physical, spiritual and intellectual condition of the individual who has been chosen to receive it. Our receptivity to, and our understanding of, Divine Communication is in large measure, though never completely, dependent upon the manner in which we had previously exercised our spiritual, intellectual, physical, and aesthetic endowments. An individual's self-preparation cannot compel or necessitate a significant Divine Communication to him, nor can the nature of the communication be predicted by an analysis of the steps taken in preparation for it. Thus Maimonides analyzes the spiritual and intellectual discipline which in his opinion are the prerequisites for prophecy, for Divine Communication on its highest level. But he is careful to point out that no one can exclusively of his own volition attain to prophecy.[9] And what is true of prophecy is true of Divine Communication on all other levels.

In the realm of Secondary Divine Communication, the relationship between the individual's previous preparation and the content of the communication appears to be quite obvious and understandable. A society that never had a Newton could conceivably have had in its midst an individual whose native intellectual capacity was as great as that of an Einstein. But without first having been equipped with all the content originally communicated to Newton and his successors, Einstein would not have been prepared to receive and understand the Secondary Divine Communication granted to him. The majesty of the communication granted him does not detract from the divine character of the communication granted Newton, though the one largely supersedes the other. An atrophied organ of the body is essentially no less divine in origin than a functioning one, and an extinct species was no less the creation of God than a presently existing one. Hence, the possibility that our present scientific knowledge may be superseded does not argue against the Divine origin of whatever is true in it, no more than the possibility that the human race as we know it today may disappear from this earth implies that it therefore has not been created by God.

Nor can we avoid the logically insoluble dilemma which faces us when we think about Divine Communication in the Primary sense, *i.e.,* communications in the realm of values. We cannot establish their validity beyond reasonable doubt by the indisputable evidence of the senses, nor by the irrefutable processes of a mathematically certain logic. How can we ever decide upon the relative merits of the conflicting claims of different Divine Communications which, while they may to some extent be known with communicable knowledge, are known by us in the profoundest sense with a knowledge which is in essence ineffable? I have no solution to offer which I can defend against reasonable challenge. I shall return to this inquiry, under the heading of "The Torah as Divine Communication."

We said previously that Divine Communication, like Divine Revelation, is not the privilege of the chosen few. But just as Divine Revelation is experienced by relatively few, with an intensity that leaves an indelible impress upon them for the rest of their lives, so Divine Communication is experienced by only comparatively few, with a clarity and a weight that bestows upon the communicated content supreme significance not only for him to whom it was communicated, but to others to whom he may later communicate it.

There have been many Divine Communications which have been of *supreme* significance to more than the individual or individuals to whom they were originally communicated. When a Divine Communication takes on paramount importance for a goodly number of human beings over an extended period of time, we have the phenomenon which we designate as a Religion. Judaism is such a phenomenon. It came into being through the Torah. I believe the Torah to be a Divine Communication to man. I believe it to be the perfect Divine Communication to man but, for reasons to be stated later, I prefer to think of it as *a* Divine Communication.

The Divine quality of the Torah is associated not only with its content but with the specific circumstances under which it was communicated to man at a given moment in time and at a given place, namely at Mt. Sinai, "in the third month after the Israelites had left Egypt" (Exodus 19:1). The Torah is thus associated not only with Divine Communication but also with a specific Divine Revelation, whose role in the history of Judaism is central and basic.

Though chapters nineteen and twenty of Exodus appear to be very explicit, there has always been considerable controversy regarding many important aspects of the events therein narrated. We shall not in this inquiry attempt to weigh the merits of the various arguments.[10] But one thing is certain. These two chapters and what they purport to relate occupy a position of primacy and centrality in any definition of the traditional concept of Torah, and no discussion of Torah which fails to give them such primacy and centrality can in any way lay claim to significant relationship to the Tradition.

Let me then be as clear as I possibly can be in formulating my attitude towards these chapters, as I understand them in the light of modern scholarship and thought.

I reject all interpretations of these two chapters which make them out to be sheer figments of the over-exuberant and not altogether innocent imagination of later generations, or which explain them as a case of mistaken identity, in that our ancestors accepted a volcanic eruption, or the rumbling of an active volcano, for a meaningful Divine Revelation and Communication. Nor do I find it necessary to believe that in those chapters we have a concise account of a historic event as it actually occurred. I do not subscribe to the doctrine that one must either accept every word in Scripture in all its literalness or reject the whole of it as a fabric of poetic or sardonic invention. These antipodal approaches to Scripture are both equally destructive of a true understanding of it. In the following sections of this inquiry, I shall return to this most important and difficult problem again. But we might at this point profitably make at least a brief reference to another Biblical account, namely that of the enslavement of the Israelites in Egypt and their subsequent emancipation and exodus. It occupies in the Jewish tradition a position of primacy and centrality almost equal in importance to that of the narrative regarding the events at Sinai.

Modern scholars have for various reasons questioned many details of the Biblical account regarding Egyptian slavery and the exodus. However, it is generally agreed that the memory of Egypt which is so deeply ingrained in Israel's consciousness, has roots in historic reality. There was a period of enslavement in Egypt, if not for all, then certainly for a substantial part of the people. There was an exodus.[11] This core of historic reality has become a central pillar in Judaism. Its memory has served to sharpen the moral sensitivity of our people. It has forever demanded of us to identify ourselves with the oppressed, and to think of God as the defender of "the stranger, the orphan and the widow."[12] But its main role has been that of "evidence beyond reasonable doubt" of the validity of the covenant between God and Israel, and of God's eternal concern for Israel.[13]

Thus also do I believe that the narrative in Exodus, chapters nineteen and twenty, rests upon a firm base of actual historic experience. Sometime, not long after the emancipation of the Israelites from Egypt and while they were wandering in the desert of Sinai, they, *as a group,* experienced with unprecedented clarity and intensity, an ineffable awareness of the Divine Presence. Associated with that ineffable awareness was a communicable content. Whether the circumstances surrounding that experience are accurately recorded in chapter nineteen of Exodus or whether the communicable content of that experience was from the very beginning expressed in exactly the same words now found in chapter twenty of Exodus, or chapter five of Deuteronomy, I do not feel called upon unequivocally to affirm. Neither do I feel a compelling need to deny it. The whole tradition of the Jewish people bears indisputable testimony to the fact that the impact of the original experience was indelible, and that the spiritual resources of its communicated content proved to be infinite. From the days of Moses unto our own day, every generation under the leadership of its own spiritually most sensitive sons and daughters continued to drink from the waters of the original inexhaustible well of inspiration. Moreover, through their own bold spiritual adventuring and through the Divine Communications vouchsafed them, they discovered heretofore untapped veins of living waters in the original well. Thus, they broadened and deepened it, slaking ever more fully their own spiritual thirst and that of those who came after them.

A substantial part of the continuously unfolding meaning which generation after generation has discovered in the original Divine Communication granted our ancestors, has been preserved for us through the inadequate medium of the written word as recorded in the Hebrew Bible, the Talmud, the Midrashim and cognate literature, all of which we now designate by the term Torah. Not all of these records ever exercised equal authority. The Humash was in theory always given a position of primacy. The practical application of this theoretical primacy was, however, increasingly more limited from century to century.[14]

The historic core in the Biblical narrative of slavery and emancipation has been and remains to this day, for the believer, the indisputable validation in history of God's covenant with Israel and of Israel's indestructibility at the hand of external enemies. The historic core in the Biblical narrative of what transpired at the foot of Mt. Sinai and during the forty years of desert wandering is for him the indisputable historic validation that Israel as a people did experience a Divine Revelation and Communication. That Communication forever transformed Israel into a people, the essence of whose being was inexorably and inseparably interlocked not with a specific biologically, politically, sociologically or geographically defined phenomenon, but with a Faith and a Pattern of Life embodied in the Torah. Some of the implications of this fact we shall further discuss in the section devoted to Israel.

THE TORAH AS DIVINE COMMUNICATION

I believe that the Torah is Divine Communication not only because of what transpired at Sinai but also because the prophets whose messages are recorded in the Bible all testify that what they taught came to them from God and was not the product of their own senses, imagination or reasoning power.[15] Had they believed that the validity of their teachings were demonstrable by reason or experience, they would have said so, as did the Greek philosophers. For it is in the very nature of reason to have such profound self-assurance that that which is clear to it beyond reasonable doubt it wants to transmit as its own and in its own terms, not merely as a matter of pride but out of a conviction that that is the surest way of convincing its counterpart in another fellow man of the validity of its own position. The fact that prophets and sages of other peoples also claimed that their messages or teachings were Divinely communicated to them in no way refutes or weakens the claim of the prophets of Israel. The truth of the matter seems to me to be that the recognized sages and prophets of other nations were not imposters consciously fabricating an untruth with the hope that it would bestow authority on their own opinions. I believe that in some real sense, they meant exactly what they said. Lincoln did not ask his fellow Americans to be "firm in the right as we see the right," but "as *God gives* us to see the right." I do not believe that at that solemn moment, Lincoln was merely employing a conventional cliché. I believe he meant exactly what he said—namely, that unless one believes that "the right" to which he holds firm is in some real and experienced sense a "Divinely communicated" right, and not merely one that seems to suit his own mundane purposes, it is the very essence of immorality to hold firm to it, especially when that firmness involves the welfare and the very lives of other human beings.

Moreover, the teachings of the prophets cannot be explained as the necessary logical deductions made by men on the basis of their historic experiences or reasoning power. They remain beyond our power to validate empirically or rationally. What the prophets teach speaks ultimately not to our reason nor to our senses but to that within us which is different from both reason and the senses. It is that most nebulous and elusive of all of our human endowments, our intuition. The Psalmist, I think, refers to it when he prays "Make me, therefore, to know wisdom, *vesatum*"—a rare use of a well-known Hebrew root, and usually translated—"in my inmost heart" (Psalms 51:8). I would translate it "through my intuition" or "intuitively." For it is our intuition which leads us to accept as right or true, that which, while it does not directly contradict reason, or the undisputed evidence of the senses, is nevertheless beyond the power of reason and the senses to validate beyond reasonable doubt. It is, I believe, because we are endowed with the power of intuition that we react with reverential affirmation to the Ten Commandments, or Isaiah's vision of world peace (Isaiah 2:2–4, 11:1–9), or Micah's definition of what it is that the Lord requires of us (Micah 6:8).

From my own reaction to these and many other passages in the Torah, I can at least faintly imagine with what power the ideas and visions expressed in these words must have seized hold of the whole of the prophet's being when they first came to him in all their pristine force and splendor. No human being could have written the addresses in Deuteronomy or the visions of Deutero-Isaiah and feel that *he* was writing them, the way I feel that I write a letter to a friend, or an address for an audience. And even as I write, I rarely feel that *I* alone write them for I know that if ideas ceased "coming," if there were not some channels of communication open between me as I know myself, and sources beyond and outside of me, there would be little I could do to cajole or force an idea to come. That is true for the least amongst us who ever had the experience of "seeing" or "understanding" or conceiving something not seen or understood or conceived by him before. That is why we can all in some measure empathize with the Psalmist's prayer: "Cast me not away from Thy presence; And do not take Thy holy spirit from me" (Psalms 51:13).

We return now to the problem raised at the end of a preceding section—namely: How shall the individual choose between the conflicting claims of Primary Divine Communications? If we knew with absolute certainty the answer to this question, we would be either God or at least among those with whom "He took counsel" (Isaiah 40:14). I find strength in the faith that I am as beloved of God as any other of His creatures and that to the extent that I have sincerely sought to approximate Him in justice, in love, in truth, and in holiness, He communicates with me also and helps me "see the right" in which I believe I should be firm. When He does not guide me, I stand utterly confused and lost, incapable of decision and hence also of firm action. For reasons that I shall only partly indicate in some of the following pages, I decided to accept the Torah as *the perfect* Divine Communication to man, and to the best of my ability to act accordingly.

This decision did not, however, obviate the need to make many another agonizing and heart-searching decision. For while Torah in its most characteristic and eternally significant aspects is Primary Divine Communication, it also contains much which belongs to the category of Secondary Divine Communication. Moreover, its Primary Divine Communications at times are, or at least appear to be, contradictory. I shall return to these problems later.

The Torah describes itself as *the* perfect Divine Communication (Deuteronomy 4:8). I have what appears to me to be very good reason to agree with this judgment. I see the perfection of the Torah not in its completeness, in the sense that it ever was, or is now, or ever will be fixed and final to its last detail. I see its perfection rather in the fact that within the Torah there are found the noblest, literarily the perfect, inherently the most inspiring, and intuitively the most persuasive formulations of the ultimate goals of human life. It is only as man strives to achieve these goals that his life is crowned with nobility and endowed with a spiritual joy that no other creature can experience. In addition to the formulations of these ultimate goals, the Torah indicates the paths whereby they may be attained. This combination of ultimate goals and paths leading to their realization bestow upon the Torah an unparalleled capacity for infinite growth in relevance and meaning as men strive to approximate God and establish His kingdom upon this earth.

Yet though I strive to pattern my own life upon the conviction that the Torah is *the* perfect Divine Communication vouchsafed unto man, I, nevertheless, prefer to think of it as *a* Divine Communication. I do so because the Torah itself negates the assumption that the rest of mankind was abandoned by God. Other nations, too, had their *nevi'im*—prophets (Bava Batra 15a), their *hasidim*—their pious and righteous (Tosefta Sanhedrin 13:2), and their *hakhamim*—their wise men in whose presence one was required to pronounce a benediction (Berakhot 58a).

I find it necessary to distinguish between my belief that the Torah is *the* perfect Divine Communication and my preference to think and speak of it as *a* Divine Communication because that is the only way in which I can formulate in words my conviction that though the Torah is the perfect Divine Communication, I must approach all those who differ from me not only without hostility and condescension, but rather with positive, sincere regard and open-mindedness. It is, it seems to me, the inevitable inner tension with which every one must live, who believes that God loves all men as much as He loves him, and who wants to remain spiritually and intellectually alert to new experiences without at the same time abandoning his anchors, and himself becoming like a rudderless ship driven hither and thither by every stray breeze.

But to accept the Torah as the perfect Divine Communication does not imply that one is henceforth to close his mind, put blinders on his eyes, cease learning anything that is not strictly and narrowly part of Torah, and suspend all judgment in studying Torah. I believe that the Torah should be accepted *knowingly, reverently* and *honestly.*

To accept the Torah knowingly does not mean that one delays committing himself to it until he has mastered the whole of it. It is beyond the power of any single individual to know the Torah with a perfect knowledge not only because the texts which presently constitute it, namely the *Tanakh,* the Talmud, the *Midrashim,* and all their commentaries, the

Codes, the Responsa, the philosophical and theological literature and the moral and ethical literature, are in themselves so vast a library, but primarily because this library does not pretend to have included within it the last book. It is the essence of the perfection of the Torah, as we noted above, that its message to man, being infinite in scope, can never be exhausted.

To accept the Torah knowingly means in the first place that every one who is expected to accept the Torah should be enabled and expected to know it directly by mastering the texts which constitute it, to the best of his intellectual and spiritual ability and to the extent to which economic, political and other external circumstances will allow. This he must do at every period of his life from the earliest dawning of intelligence to the last thought that he thinks.

It means moreover that every community must maintain within its midst the maximum number of men and women who devote themselves as completely as possible to the study of the Torah in all of its aspects and to the making of the results of their studies available in the most easily accessible oral or written form to all others who cannot devote themselves with equal concentration to the study of the Torah.

Moreover, the acceptance of Torah must in no way be associated with or dependent upon ignorance of other humanly available knowledge. On the contrary, to accept the Torah knowingly in the profoundest sense means to accept it in the light of the totality of human knowledge available at any one time or place, insofar as it is possible for any single human being to know it. Knowledge available to man has never been limited only to that which was included in the Torah. There were always zealots who condemned, or looked askance at, the study of anything else but Torah. There were also those who would limit one's mental horizon exclusively to specific portions of the Torah, some looking unfavorably upon the study of Bible, or grammar, or philosophy, others upon the study of Talmud, or Kabbalah. But within the main current of Judaism, whose headwaters are the Bible and the Mishnah, the study of non-Torah literature though it may have been limited, was not forbidden. Professor Saul Lieberman in his two volumes of studies on the relations between the Jews and the Greeks[16] has established beyond reasonable doubt that ancient non-Jewish thought and science was known to the Rabbis. Rabbinic sources repeatedly refer with evident regard to "the wise men of Athens" (Ekhah Rabbah 1:4 ff.). Saadiah and Maimonides knew the Torah in the light of the sum total of knowledge available to them in their day and place. Nor were the intellectual horizons of Rabbi Akiba or the Gaon of Vilna limited to the knowledge available to them in the Torah only.

The sum total of knowledge available to us today is far vaster than that available to them. No one can master all that there is to know either of Torah or of general human knowledge. Every single individual must, therefore, perforce act on the basis of incomplete knowledge most of the time. But that does not mean that we equate "incomplete knowledge" with "no knowledge," and decide that if we cannot know all, we will make no effort to know anything at all. We are in duty bound to know as much as we can in all areas of available human knowledge. For one thing is quite certain at least to me, namely that our knowledge of the Torah today will *not* do justice even to the Torah, if we willfully remain ignorant of all that is not found in the Torah itself.

To accept the Torah reverently means first and foremost to approach it with the conviction that one is to be fashioned by it, rather than it by him. As between me and the Torah, it is not the Torah that has to justify itself before me, but I who have to justify myself before it in whatever area, large or small, I appear to be departing from its precepts. I start with saying "yea" to everything in the Torah. That means that I must make an honest and an heroic effort to live in accordance with the precepts and doctrines of the Torah to their last detail; that I cannot justify any variation from any of its precepts and doctrines by appealing to mundane considerations of personal comfort or economic advancement or even of physical security, except under circumstances which the Torah itself permits me to take into consideration.

Since it is difficult, and often impossible, for even the most favorably situated in our day and society to fulfill all of the ritual and ethical precepts of the Torah, it means that we are compelled to live with an ever-present sense of spiritual failure. That is the inescapable burden of anyone who lives with the consciousness that he is in the constant presence of God (see Job 4:17–19). Such a one will not, in order to lighten his burden or appease his conscience, argue that Torah includes only that which he or the majority of his generation can or have the spiritual fibre to observe. Nor will he condemn as an obscurantist one who makes a greater sacrifice than he does to live in accordance with all the precepts of the Torah, nor as a hypocrite one who observes as much of the Torah as his physical, intellectual, economic, and spiritual resources enable him to observe.

Though one who strives to live in accordance with the precepts of the Torah is never free of the sense of spiritual inadequacy, he is never crushed or broken by its burden because he believes with the Psalmist that "The Lord is full of compassion and gracious, Slow to anger, and plenteous in mercy. . . . Like as a father hath compassion upon his children, So hath the Lord compassion upon them that fear Him. For He knoweth our frame; He remembereth that we are dust" (Psalms 103:8, 13–14).

I *start* with saying "yea" to everything in the Torah, because I believe it to be the perfect Divine Communication to man. But I find it impossible to *end* with saying "yea" to it in every detail. I find that impossible because it is the Torah itself which taught me that "The seal of the Holy One blessed be He is Truth" (Shabbat 55a), that God does not want us to speak "with a double heart" (Psalms 12:3), that He "desires truth in the inward parts" (Psalms 51:8), and that only if I seek earnestly to speak truth in my heart do I have the right even to hope for the privilege of sojourning in His Tabernacle, let alone of dwelling upon His holy mountain (see Psalms 15:1–2). If then I am to preserve my intellectual integrity and my inner spiritual wholeness, if I am to be honest with myself and others in as profound a sense as I possibly can be, as I believe the Torah requires me to do, I find that I simply cannot accept every statement, every precept, every narrative in the Torah, blindly and thoughtlessly. I must accept the Torah with the whole of my mind as well as with the whole of my heart, my soul and my might.[16a] That means the following to me:

1. All statements in the Torah regarding the physical nature of the universe and regarding natural and historic phenomena which, in accordance with our definition, belong to the category of Secondary Divine Communication must be subjected to the test of our senses and of our incontestably established knowledge. Where we possess knowledge which has been validated beyond reasonable doubt, which contradicts the unmistakably clear literal sense of a statement in the Torah, we have no choice but to reject the literal meaning of that passage. If the significance of the passage depends entirely upon its literal truth, and its literal truth is thus irrefutably contradicted by our fuller knowledge, then that passage inevitably loses its significance for us. If the passage has a significance not dependent upon its literal scientific truth, then that significance must be consciously divorced by us from the literal statement. We cannot for example, continue to refer to the heavens as "a firmament," nor to speak of "waters that are above the heavens," nor to conceive of the earth as the center of the universe, as if it were in all literalness, true.

But what happens to the concept of Torah as the perfect Divine Communication if some aspects of it are to be declared as no longer valid?

Let us recall first what was said previously about the nature of Secondary Divine Communication, and then what was said about the nature of the Torah's perfection. I cannot assume that faith in the perfection of the Torah as Divine Communication requires me to deny the incontrovertible evidences of the senses—that it requires me, for example, to believe that the earth is a flat disc or that it is stationary while the sun circles around it. Such an assumption would make sane, normal thought and experience impossible for me.

But why should we continue to include in the Torah that which has clearly been superseded? Its inclusion serves a threefold purpose. In the first place, the unity of the Torah is of so extraordinary a nature that there is no portion of it which does not throw some light on the whole or on part of it. Secondly, we have no way of being certain that that which appears to be completely superseded for us may not have great relevance for those who come after us. That has repeatedly happened in the past. Finally, a statement in the Torah whose content may have been superseded scientifically may, and well-nigh always does, have significance for us in some other way. The Torah conveys its message not only in the literal meaning of its words, but also in the many overtones of meaning that generations have found in the very letters of the text, in the ethical and spiritual assumptions underlying it, or in the illumination it brings to our understanding of our ancestors.

It is for these and other good reasons that we in the United States do not remove from the Constitution any section which has been invalidated by later amendments. How much more reverent then should we as Jews be of any passage that has at any time been a part of the Torah.

2. The miracles related in the Bible are not to be either accepted or rejected *in toto,* nor is one's faith in the Bible as a Divine Communication to be made dependent upon faith in the historic authenticity of the miracles therein related.

The term "miracle" is usually understood to designate an event that is either diametrically contrary to the established course of natural events, or at the very least a unique combination of natural events, a combination which to the best of our knowledge never occurred before and is not expected ever to occur again. The supreme moment of communication of God to man, hence the greatest miracle recorded in all of the Torah, occurred at Mount Sinai.

Assuming for a moment that the events related in chapters nineteen and twenty of Exodus are all the inventions of later generations, we must ask what it was that prompted them to create this myth.[17] Did they hope thereby to validate the contents of the Divine Communication? If so, they obviously defeated their own purpose by associating the incident of the golden calf so intimately with the events at Sinai. Why should they expect a generation that did not itself participate in that event to be more impressed by a narrative about it, than were those who were supposedly actually there! It always seemed to me to be surpassingly strange that in Scripture, the account of every miracle which was apparently meant to impress our ancestors is followed immediately by an account of the further and even greater "murmuring of the people."[18] It is as if Scripture were saying to us: The miracle did occur, and God can and does perform miracles, but he who believes in God, or in the Torah because of the miracles related in it or surrounding its communication, his faith is built on quicksand.

Every event in which human beings are involved is in essence unique, unprecedented and non-repeatable. But some events involve such an amazing, so unprecedented a combination of circumstances, that, even though no single circumstance is in itself contrary to nature, those who observe or participate in the event can find no word whereby to designate it as a whole, other than "miracle." Participants in such events are often so profoundly impressed by them that they will resolve to introduce some significant change in the pattern of their behavior as an expression of gratitude or new insight.

But the effect of the miracle, in the overwhelming majority of instances, wears off very rapidly. Indeed, the Torah itself warns us to be wary of miracles and miracle workers. The ability to perform a miracle of any kind is not to be accepted as proof of the validity of the teachings of the miracle worker (Deuteronomy 13:2–6).

That does not mean that I categorically deny the possibility of miracles which involve a breach of the established natural order. My refusal to deny the possibility of such miracles is in no way related to my acceptance of the Torah as the perfect Divine Communication. It is related rather to the fact that such denial implies that the natural order stands outside of God's jurisdiction. This is a dualism that I cannot accept.

The miracles related in the Bible and the Talmud are not to be accepted or rejected *in toto*. Each narrative must be studied as a separate unit. We have criteria by which to judge the reliability of a narrative. The account of Hezekiah's illness (II Kings 20:1–11), of Balaam's ass (Numbers 22:21–35), of Honi Hame'agel's prowess as a rain-bringer (Taanit 19a) do not belong to the category of Divine Communication but of human reporting. I have a duty to inquire into the circumstances attendant upon the event related and upon the circumstances of its narration, and draw whatever conclusions seem plausible and reasonable to me. My faith in God and in the perfection of the Torah is in no way dependent upon my estimate of the scientific accuracy of any narrative in Scripture, whether it purports to relate history or to record miracle.

Finally, to accept the Torah honestly means for me that whenever I find in the Torah laws or sentiments which in my opinion reflect moral practices or precepts inferior to other laws or sentiments found in the Torah, I am in duty bound to accept what I believe to be the nobler doctrine and reject the less noble one. I must accept what I believe to be the Torah's highest and noblest vision of God and man for my own aspirations and conduct, and reject the less noble even though that too is found in the Torah. Just as much of the content of Secondary Divine Communication found in the Torah has been superseded, thus too does it contain elements of Primary Divine Communication that have been superseded. But while in the first instance, the Torah has been superseded by contents originating in non-Torah sources, in the second instance both the one and the other are found in the Torah. If even the Primary Divine Communication of the Torah were to be superseded by more noble Divine Communication originating in non-Torah sources, then the Torah would become little more than the record of "a glory that is past," interesting perhaps to an antiquarian but irrelevant to the significant problems of life. It would cease to call forth the love and devotion that enabled men to live by it under most adverse circumstances, and to die for it when the occasion required it.

Satan is encouraged and seems justified in his quoting Torah for his own purposes by those who attribute equal authority to every sentiment expressed in it. Those who refuse to use their God-given powers of intellectual and spiritual discrimination are the easiest prey to the disingenuous and the cynic. The Torah puts before us the most perfect formulation of the noblest ideals ever communicated to man. They must become the standards whereby every other aspect of the Torah is judged. Thus those passages which have been designated by our Rabbis as *zeh kelal gadol ba-Torah* (literally: "This is a basic principle in Judaism") such as "Thou shalt love thy neighbor as thyself" (Leviticus 19:18) or "This is the book of the generations of man" (Genesis 5:1) wherein the unity and equality of all men is pronounced, or that unsurpassed statement on the brotherhood of man, his uniqueness and supreme worth, which is found in the Mishnah (Sanhedrin 4:5) or Hillel's dictum that "That which is hateful to thee do not unto others" (Shabbat 31a) or "Be ye holy, for I the Lord thy God am

Holy" (Leviticus 19:2)—these and similar formulations of the ultimate standards of conduct set for man by the Torah, must in all sincerity and intellectual integrity become for us the touchstones for judging every sentiment and law expressed in the whole of the literature of the Torah. Any law or sentiment in the whole of the literature of the Torah which is found in fact and beyond reasonable doubt to contradict these highest spiritual reaches of the Torah should be modified or suspended. If the contradiction is only apparent but not real, then it becomes our duty to indicate wherein it is only apparent.

Every creative period in Jewish history had some bold spirits whose loyalty to the Torah was infinite, who nevertheless did not hesitate to discriminate between one moral sentiment and another. Thus, even though Deuteronomy specifically states that "Unto a foreigner thou mayest lend upon interest" (Deuteronomy 23:21), nevertheless, the verse which depicts the righteous man as one "who putteth not out money on interest" (Psalms 15:5) is interpreted to mean "not even interest from a heathen" (Makkot 24a). The same verse (Psalms 9:18) which suggests to Rabbi Eliezer that the gentiles have no share in the world to come is interpreted by Rabbi Joshua to mean that the righteous among the gentiles do have a share in the world to come (Tosefta, Sanhedrin 13:2).

One of my most precious privileges as a Jew is the right I have to take my stand with Rabbi Joshua rather than with Rabbi Eliezer. I believe that the cause of the Torah is most effectively advanced when we take our stand with the noblest moral purposes and practices it sets before us. Only as we identify the Torah with its own clearly expressed highest goals do we truly revere it and make it increasingly more difficult for Satan and his cohorts to quote Torah for their own purposes. When we fail to speak up clearly and courageously on those aspects of the Torah which are beyond the shadow of all doubt scientifically untenable or ethically vulnerable, we contribute towards the desecration of the whole of the Torah. This is the area to which we can and should apply the Rabbinic dictum *"Makom hinihu li avotai lehitgader bo"*—"My fathers left me an area in which I could exercise my spiritual endowments" (Hullin 7a).

ISRAEL—A TORAH-PEOPLE

There are in the world today some twelve million human beings who, in addition to any other designation, are designated by others and designate themselves as Jews. Since the French Revolution, the question of whether the Jews are a religion, a nation or a people has been heatedly debated among both Jews and non-Jews. The question obviously has more than academic interest. It was immeasurably complicated by the fact that there is no commonly accepted, unambiguous definition for any of the three concepts. All three have common characteristics. The choice one makes from amongst them does not therefore necessarily imply that he excludes all aspects characteristic of the other two.

Nevertheless each concept has a commonly recognized major emphasis. Hence, the choice one makes from among these three concepts serves primarily to indicate the dominant, indispensable quality which he desires to have associated with the term "Jew."

The term "nation," no matter what else it may imply, is associated primarily with statehood and political sovereignty. Hence, those who sought the implementation of the Zionist program adopted in Basle in 1897, always spoke of the Jews as a nation, even though the program, in its preamble spoke of them as a "people." They argued that the Jews needed and were entitled to a state of their own because they were, are and should be a "nation." There are those for whom Jewish nationhood in this political sense is the very core of their philosophy of life as Jews. They do not necessarily exclude religion from the life of the Jewish nation. But no matter what importance they may attribute to it, it is never primary in their thinking of themselves as Jews.

Since the establishment of the State of Israel, the term "nation"[19] has become far less prominent in discussions about the essential character of the Jewish group. And that for obvious reasons. No Jew who is a citizen of a state other than the State of Israel wants to be thought of, nor does he think of himself, as having any allegiance of a political nature to the State or the government of the State of Israel.

Not all of those who in the past or in the present spoke or prefer to speak of the Jews as constituting an essentially religious community meant or mean thereby to exclude statehood as a legitimate and even necessary part of the life of the Jewish people. The hope for the restoration of a politically independent Jewish community in *Eretz Yisrael* is an integral part of the traditional religious conception of the Messianic era. It was only the founders of the modern Reform Movement in Judaism who, by defining the Jewish people as a religious community, expressly intended thereby to repudiate the traditional hope for the reestablishment of Jewish political sovereignty in the Holy Land or anywhere else.[20] But whether statehood may or may not be legitimately included under the concept "religion," it is primarily associated with a concept of God and with a body of sacred literature which exercises ultimate authority in defining the relationship of the individual and the group to others, to the universe and to God.

The term "religious community" as a designation for the Jewish people continues to be in disrepute among many, first because of its association with those who for two generations based—and to this day continue to base—their opposition to Zionism and Jewish statehood on the argument that the Jews are a religion and not a nation.[21] Secondly, the term "religion" is suspect because it is usually associated with a narrow definition of the concept, limiting it to matters of dogma, ethical maxims and ritual. It does not easily lend itself to the inclusion of that vast area of intellectual, aesthetic, recreational and organizational activity usually thought of as non-religious or secular.

The term, therefore, that has become most widely accepted at the moment, as a designation for Jews as a group is "people." The Jews are a "people." The primary guiding principle or principles to be derived from the fact that one is a Jew should thus be related to the concept Peoplehood, rather than to that of Nation or Religion.

I have a great predilection for this concept. I find it indispensable in my thinking about the Jews and about my relations to them. But I also find that in any systematic formulation of my philosophy of life as an individual and as a Jew, I cannot give primacy to it. It occupies at best a secondary position in that it is not or should not be an ultimate sanction for human action, and in that it is descriptive of a situation resulting from other primary factors, without itself being a primary factor. I prefer to think of the Jews not as a nation, or a religion, nor yet as merely a people. For reasons to be stated in what follows, I prefer to think of the Jews as a Torah-People.

Peoplehood is, in some measure, a characteristic of every identifiable group in the world that has a history. Membership in any group that has an extended history can never be completely equated with acceptance of certain doctrines or practices, or with political allegiance or with geographic location. There are factors of a biological, sociological, political, historical, and psychological nature which are integral parts of the relationship between a group and any of its members. These cannot be eliminated at will. The more such factors there are, the more highly they are developed, the more deeply they are rooted, the firmer the bonds that hold the group together. It is these objective, largely uncontrollable factors that bestow upon any group that has maintained a specific identity for a number of generations, the character of Peoplehood.

Because Peoplehood is rooted essentially in factors beyond the individual's control, one cannot during his own lifetime completely dissociate himself from his people, regardless of how persistently he may try, or how often he may officially announce his resignation. When or how does a Scotsman cease to be a member of the Scotch people or an Englishman of the English people or an Irishman of the Irish people? At what point does a "people," as distinguished from a state or a religion, cease to consider one of its former members as still part of itself so that it ceases to feel justified in expecting him to be concerned with the advancement of interests growing out of shared historical, sociological, psychological, or religious factors? An item in *The New York Times* of February 11, 1957, reports that "Irish Patriots Ask Aid of People Here." It then goes on to relate that "A local Irish Republican Army group called upon members of the nation's Irish American community yesterday to besiege the homeland with personally written notes pledging their support of the Republican movement. Wholehearted response by the 5,000,000 persons of Irish birth or descent now in the country would solve our problems completely, a spokesman. . . ."

An individual may resist his "people's" advances, but as long as the memory of his former association with the group persists, the group continues to view him as one of its own and to pass judgment upon his action towards it. He cannot prevent his people from censuring or approving his actions towards it nor, being human, can he remain completely indifferent to its attitude towards him. Nor can he prevent others from identifying him with his "people" and approaching him with the predispositions that they may have towards his people as a whole. Finally the individual himself, try as he will, cannot completely disregard the fact of his once having been a member of a people not only because he will be reminded of it in one way or another by what he hears, reads and sees but, above all, because of the mysterious power inherent in knowledge *per se* whereby any known fact seeks to relate itself to attitudes and acts. No fact known by me is completely isolated from my attitudes and acts. The more intimately associated that fact is with me personally, whether it be knowledge of the state of my health, or my wealth or my ancestry, the more insistent it is to involve itself in my attitudes and acts. The measure of the involvement depends upon the depth and scope of the memory within the consciousness of the individual and that of his contemporaries.

The Jews are a group that has had a continuous recorded history for a longer period of time than any other people in the world today, with the possible exception of some of the peoples of the Far East. Though from the earliest dawn of their history they were associated with a unique conception of God and an identifiable body of religious doctrine and practice, there were always amongst them many variations of belief and practice, dependent upon historic circumstance, regional customs and locally recognized authority. These variations were often so pronounced that they created recognizable sub-groupings within the Jewish group. But these differences did not destroy the sense of kinship among these sub-groups as over against the rest of mankind.

The Jews had enemies whose hostility undoubtedly contributed both to their cohesion as well as to their disintegration as a people. "For average men and average movements, placed under a sudden and unexpected pressure, the following maxim applies: a small and medium pressure increases the power of resistance; a stronger weakens it and the maximum breaks it. Apart from individuals and very glorious exceptions, this law was confirmed within the life and cultural activity of the German Jews under National Socialism."[22] The overwhelming majority of Jews are "average men," and repeatedly in the course of their history, they were subjected to "stronger . . . and maximum" pressures against them. There is no canard more completely discredited than the oft-repeated one that Jews owe their persistence as a group to their persecutors.

The group's cohesion was immeasurably advanced by its political status as a legally recognized community, exercising considerable power of self-government over its inner spiritual and communal affairs. As a group, it could bring immense social and economic pressures to bear upon its individual members to compel them to conform to whatever standards it set. But the opportunity to leave the group was nevertheless always present, the temptation always great. The dominant religion was tireless in its exertions to attract to itself members of the Jewish community. Through marshalled arguments, reinforced at frequent intervals by merciless persecution, it sought to persuade the mind and thus remove the stigma that attaches to one who sells his birthright for a "mess of pottage." But the "pottage" offered was very real and substantial in terms of personal physical security, of political status and of educational, social and economic advancement.

During all periods of Jewish history, there were Jews who either out of conviction or out of desire for advancement left the Jewish community and joined the dominant group. When that happened, how did it affect the status of the individual concerned? He was obviously excluded from the privileges enjoyed exclusively by members of the Jewish group. But the fact of his former membership in the Jewish group did not cease completely to play a role in his life. Within the new group that he had joined, insofar as it was known that he was once a Jew, he could not escape completely the effects of the attitude commonly held within that group towards the Jewish people. Nor did the Jewish people ever cease thinking of him as a renegade. As long, therefore, as one knows himself and/or is known by others to have been born a Jew, the bonds between him and the Jewish people, tenuous as they may be, are not completely severed until all memory of the original relationship is lost.

The tenacious tentacles with which Peoplehood enmeshes the individual have become for some the basis upon which to build a philosophy of life. One is asked to start with the assumption that regardless of what he does, he cannot dissociate himself from the Jewish people. The converse of this proposition is that except for the physical destruction of every individual Jew, the Jewish people is indestructible. The argument runs somewhat as follows. Nazi persecutions have again proved that no matter what one does, he cannot escape the consequences inherent in his once having been a Jew as long as the fact of his former association continues to be known. Hence, to the Jews who consciously or subconsciously acknowledge no guiding principle higher than that of physical comfort and security, Jewish historic experience says, "Since one can never dissociate himself from the Jewish people, elemental enlightened self-interest makes it incumbent upon every Jew to do all in his power to strengthen his people, to increase its spiritual and economic resources, to advance its status in human society, so that through it, his own life may acquire maximum security and dignity." This argument in behalf of remaining a Jew we shall refer to as the "argument from necessity."

Though this position has much to commend it, it cannot be validated, either rationally or empirically. It is an incontrovertible fact that many have left and continue to leave the Jewish group. Even the Nazi persecutions with their purely racist basis did not keep thousands of Jews from seeking escape in conversion to some branch of Christianity. And indeed many who were thus converted were saved and never returned to Judaism. While the Chuetas of Majorca seem to support the argument that one's Jewish antecedents are never forgotten or forgiven, the fact is that the Chuetas have enjoyed greater physical security than their fellow Jews who were not converted. Moreover, tens of thousands of Jews who left Judaism as a result of the Spanish Inquisition and the various expulsions, were completely assimilated, and their descendants permanently severed from even the most tenuous association with the Jewish people. The same has happened in well-nigh every generation. During the nineteenth century in Europe, thousands of Jews dissociated themselves from the Jewish people. From all that is known to us, all but very few among them actually did attain their immediate goal of greater physical security and opportunity for personal advancement. Their descendants have been completely absorbed into the non-Jewish community. The argument, therefore, that one cannot leave the Jewish people even if he tries, and hence its logical converse, that the Jewish people cannot be destroyed except by the physical destruction of every one of its members, is historically simply untrue. Hence, to base one's philosophy of life as a Jew on it is to build on quicksand.

Others start from a diametrically opposite position, namely, that it is self-delusion to think that the Jewish people is "immune to the danger of extinction." Far from being indestructible, it is really in great danger of imminent extinction. ". . . biologically and spiritually, the prospects of an indefinitely continuing Jewish life outside Israel are very dim, and those of Jewish religion anywhere in the world, even darker."[23] But if one then asks why make the effort to preserve the Jewish people, why not permit them to disappear, the answer is found by following a rather circuitous path. "Human beings . . . share . . . spiritual interests [that] have their roots in certain distinctive demands or needs of human nature. Those needs converge upon the need for belonging to some self-perpetuating group, which provides the goals of, and the means to, the fulfillment of human life."[24] For the Jew, this group should be the Jewish people.

This position I find completely acceptable only if it includes the belief that the Torah and the Jewish people can *even now* provide for me "the goals of, and the means to, the fulfillment of human life," or at least possess something which I cannot find in any other group and which *is deemed to be indispensable* to "the fulfillment of human life." But those who build their philosophy of life as Jews upon the individual's "need for belonging" to a group which "provides the goals of, and the means to, the fulfillment of human life" maintain at the same time that, as at present constituted, neither the Jewish people nor the Torah offer an opportunity for self-fulfillment to the individual Jew. Hence, for the time being at least, our "problem . . . is to find, *in the very process of belonging itself,* a valid justification for wishing to maintain" the Jewish people.[25] Thus starting "with the need for belonging," it becomes one's duty "to bend all of one's efforts to render the People to which one looks for salvation, capable of providing it" and thus achieve salvation for oneself.[26] But if the only reason why the individual Jew should be ready to sacrifice security and comfort in order to preserve the Jewish people is because he has a human "need for belonging," what is wrong with belonging to another group, if the group will have you, and will in addition offer you greater physical security and opportunity for advancement?

Moreover, if in addition to not offering me physical security, belonging to the Jewish group *as it is today* cannot offer me the opportunities for self-fulfillment and salvation, and if it is the law of the spiritual life that "the way to achieve salvation is to bend all of one's efforts to render the People to which one looks for salvation capable of providing it,"[27] why should one not "look for salvation" to and "bend all of his efforts" within, the confines of a people within which he can start with the advantage of greater security and opportunity? Why seek personal salvation in striving to transform the Jewish group? Why not seek it in efforts to transform the Episcopalians, or Catholics or Americans or Mankind? This is precisely what Jewish radicals, communists and revolutionaries of the nineteenth and twentieth centuries have advocated and done. Unless, therefore, there are benefits to be derived from belonging to the Jewish people which outweigh the benefits of physical security and larger opportunity offered by belonging to another group, why should one choose to belong to the Jewish group?

Ahad Ha-Am, I believe, was the first to answer the question "Why remain a Jew?" by maintaining that to ask it is in itself a symptom of psychological abnormality. Just as one who asks why he should not commit suicide reveals thereby a state of mental illness, thus one who asks why he should not contribute toward his people's extinction reveals a state of mental illness. The normal reaction is for one to want to maintain his group's identity. And the proposition that one has an obligation to try to remain normal is self-evident and universally accepted.

This argument would be much more convincing if people were not constantly shifting from one religious and national group to another, without thereby revealing abnormality. Vast numbers of individuals have left their original national, linguistic and ethnic groups, determined to become naught but Americans. Members of religious communities are constantly abandoning the one in favor of another. Moreover, the departure of one or more individuals from a people does not and has not in the past caused the people's death. There were others to maintain its identity. Why therefore should one be labelled as abnormal if he leaves a group into which he was born, for one of his own free choice?

But what of one's obligation not to abandon friends and relatives under attack? That can be properly designated as an obligation only by those who accept a principle other than that of personal security and welfare, and only if the path one follows for his own security is not open also to others. But if the path is open to all, then those who do not take it cannot claim that they are abandoned. They have none but themselves to blame for their plight.

But what of those who, like the Jews under Nazi rule, had no choice open for them? Under these circumstances, the obligation resting upon all decent human beings, but especially on other Jews, was that of helping them to escape from Nazi power. One's obligation to help Jews suffering from discrimination and persecution can hardly be made to include the obligation to identify oneself completely with them, or that of helping them in some positive way to preserve their Peoplehood. Indeed, hundreds and even thousands of non-Jews have valiantly fulfilled what they conceived to be their obligation to help the persecuted without identifying themselves with them. Nor did anyone expect them to do so. There are many Jews today who see no inner contradiction between their really self-sacrificing labors in behalf of the State of Israel or of Jewish sufferers anywhere, and the complete absorption of their families into the vortex of the non-Jewish community. Some may even view it as proof of their broadmindedness.

The philosophies of Jewish life based on the concept of Jewish peoplehood thus far discussed do not view Jewish peoplehood as an ultimate goal *per se,* but only as either a fact which one cannot escape, or a situation which might be helpful to the individual in his search for personal salvation. In an address recently delivered at an educators conference by the leading theoretician of the Yiddishist-Secularist schools, Jewish peoplehood attains its ultimate apotheosis. He maintains that Jewish education should set as its central and highest goal, the inculcation in the child of a love for the Jewish people. *"Vos es iz gut fahr Yidden—iz gut fahr der lern-program. . . . Haklal, iber land un moledes, iber shitah un kitah, iber vissen un Torah shtelln mir am Yisrael"*—"What is good for Jews is good for the curriculum. . . . In short, we put the Jewish people above land and birthplace, above principle and party, above knowledge and Torah" (Yudel Mark).[28] This is, it seems to me, the inevitable, logical, ultimate position of any philosophy which accepts as its highest or central concept either nationalism or peoplehood. As formulated by Mr. Mark, I see little to distinguish it from "My people, right or wrong, my people." Mr. Mark quotes the well-known passage of the *Tana d'bay Eliyahu* to the effect that Elijah was of the opinion that love of Israel takes precedence over love of Torah.[29] I do not know exactly what that passage means. But of one thing I am certain. This passage does not sanction a Torah-less Israel, nor can it conceive of a Torah-less Israel as being the object of love except as that love is expressed in a tireless self-sacrificial effort to bring Torah to it. Elijah loved his people even though his generation was one of widespread apostasy. His love, however, is reflected in his efforts to win them back to God and not in celebrating their qualities as he found them. He did not replace Torah by Israel.

Moreover, the decision to remain a Jew because it is impracticable to try to be anything else or because one needs to belong, or because one simply loves the Jewish people *per se* or for any of the other reasons mentioned, is in itself of no help as a guide to positive action as a Jew. With any of these principles as guides, one can with equal cogency defend a secularist or a religious, a Zionist or a non-Zionist, a Hebraic or a non-Hebraic program for Jewish life. Without ascribing to the Torah a place of primacy, centrality and authority in Jewish life, the Jewish people theoretically reverts to the conditions that prevailed amongst them before they stood at Sinai,[30] when almost any path they might have chosen or accidentally stumbled upon would have appeared equally legitimate in their eyes.[31] It is as if one would be advocating a program for the American people without ascribing to the Declaration of Independence and the Constitution of the United States a place of primacy, centrality and authority, thus urging them implicitly to revert to a situation paralleling that which prevailed before July 4, 1776. No people can survive so violent a rupture with its past.

It is therefore my firm conviction that the following elements are indispensable to a logically and morally tenable rationale for the preservation of Jewish peoplehood, whether Jews enjoy political freedom and comparative social equality or whether they face hostility and persecution.

1. There must be conscious, clear and firm rejection of physical security and freedom from pain or any of its more

subtle formulations, as an ultimate validating principle for human action.

2. There must be a conscious, clear and firm belief that human life has meaning only as one strives ceaselessly to approximate God.

3. There must be a conscious, firm and clear belief that the Torah is *the* or at least *a* perfect Divine Communication guiding and aiding man towards the fulfillment of his highest destiny.

4. There must be conscious, clear and firm belief that the greatest blessings that "peoplehood" can bestow upon the members of any people and upon the whole of mankind depend upon the rejection of peoplehood *per se* as an ultimate arbiter for human action. On the contrary, the greatest blessings flow rather from *that peoplehood which comes into being when a significant number of individuals remain, for a significant period of time, loyal to commonly-held principles which reach out beyond peoplehood.* That is the essence of the concept of Israel—of Jewish peoplehood—as presented in the Torah, beginning with the statement in which the peoplehood of the future Israel is first foreshadowed by God—"For I have known him (Abraham), to the end that he may command his children and his household after him, that they may keep the way of the Lord, doing righteousness and justice" (Genesis 18:19) and attaining its climax in the Divine imperative, that Israel "shall be unto Me a kingdom of priests and a holy people" (Exodus 19:6). The ultimate ideal was not peoplehood but beyond peoplehood.

Do I then wish to imply that "peoplehood" is of no importance, or is in itself in any way an evil which should be eliminated? Not at all. Man undoubtedly does have an impelling psychological need to belong which cannot be denied with impunity. Moreover, he apparently does not possess the spiritual, let alone the physical, capacity to feel a warm, satisfying kinship with more than a rather limited number of people, with whom he shares a common language, common historic memories, customs, ideals, etc. This natural, inescapable division into peoples has been the source of much blessing.

A people is like a country into which one is born. It is the setting for one's earliest experiences. If those experiences are pleasant, the bond with the people or the country becomes deep-rooted and strong. These early bonds between an individual and his people, or his native land are rarely if ever completely severed. Even unpleasant memories seem to act as a bond. Modern psychology has pointed out to us, however, the human inclination to forget the unpleasant and cling to the pleasant. Memory dwells on the happy moments, and even the meanest slums, strange as it may seem, often rouse nostalgic yearnings in their former occupants. The Israelites recalled even their Egyptian experience with some gratitude towards Egypt (Numbers 11:5). I recall my amazement at hearing Jews who fled the persecutions of Czarist Russia, speak longingly of their poverty and fear-ridden *shtetl* as *in der heim*—"back home." The fact, therefore, that I was born into the Jewish group and that before I could evaluate events and institutions, I prayed with Jews, observed the Sabbath, read a Yiddish newspaper and laughed at a Jewish joke, undoubtedly predisposed me to love the people and the society into which I was born.

But as I indicated previously, there came a day when the inevitable conflict between the life of this people and the life around it bore in upon me. The mere fact that I was born a Jew was not enough to keep me or to influence me to remain a Jew, though it played a large role in the final decision. Nor did I decide to remain a Jew because I believed Jews *per se* were the finest people in the world, nor yet because I found within the Jewish community all that represented the best and noblest in human life. I remained a Jew because I found in the Torah the path leading to what I believe are the highest reaches of human life. I found among the Jewish people the individuals most ready to cooperate with me in building the kind of a community within which that life could be most fully lived. For a non-Torah-directed life, I, like thousands of my contemporaries, would have had little, if any, need for Jews.

For that reason also I could not find complete satisfaction with the definitions of Judaism as a civilization nor even as a religious civilization, strong as is the attraction they have for me. "Civilization" is a term that is usually descriptive of the totality of the activities of any given group or people. There was a time when idolatry was part of Jewish civilization and there are aspects of Jewish civilization in the State of Israel today that, if they be included in our concept of Judaism, make the concept totally meaningless. And when not used for the totality of the activities of a group, it "denotes an advanced state of material and social well-being," or "a state of social culture characterized by relative progress in the arts, science and statecraft" (Webster's Collegiate Dictionary). It certainly is not ordinarily associated primarily with the religious aspects of a people's activities.

Nor does the concept "religious civilization" help us much, for it is not any kind of religion which can be identified as Judaism. A civilization whose religious element is not rooted in the Torah is not Judaism even though people who practice it may call themselves Jews.

Hence I prefer to think of Judaism not as a religious civilization, but as a *civilizing religion* rooted in the Torah.

I believe that my primary duty in life as a Rabbi is to preserve a knowledge of the Torah among Jews in particular and in the world generally, and to help people live in accordance with its precepts. As long as there will be people who will know the Torah and seek to live in accordance with its precepts, there will be a Jewish people. The reverse is not true. Jews can be and have been as rebellious against their spiritual heritage as were the gentiles. The Maccabees fought a civil war even while fighting the Syrian oppressors. And those who rejected the Torah or even were negligent in its study and observance finally were lost to the Jewish people *no matter where they lived or who their parents were.* On the other hand, those who accepted the Torah, studied it and lived by it, no matter what their ethnic origin may have been, became part of the Jewish people.

Because human beings tend to judge the value of any phenomenon by the satisfaction they derive not only from it, but also from that with which it is associated in their minds or in their experiences, and because the life of Torah is of necessity associated with the life of the Jewish people, I want all associations between the Jew and his people to be as pleasant and as satisfying as possible. Hence, I want the life of the Jewish community to be as rich culturally, as comfortable physically, as attractive aesthetically as it possibly can be.

That does not mean that I agree with the statement that "The assumption that a religion can be made the aim of a group of individuals that have only religion in common is altogether untenable."[32] I disagree with it because on the one hand it sets up an unrealistic "straw man." It is impossible to have only religion in common, if by that is meant only a number of commonly held doctrines and commonly followed rituals. No group can have anything which in its essence is as significant as religion, without having other things in addition to doctrines and rituals in common. They must have some common historic memories, some commonly studied literature, some common problems in relation to their fellow men, etc. Secondly, it is historically not true to say that people who had "naught but religion in common" soon did not have religion in common either. Every great world religion, including Judaism, has demonstrated the falsity of this statement. Every great world religion includes groups and individuals who have "only religion in common" in the sense that they have no other significant cultural element in common, such as language, social institutions, art, music, etc. What beside their religion *and the memories and mores directly associated with it* do the Jews of America and the Jews of North Africa or India have in common? And what do the Catholics in America have in common with the Catholics of Germany, Poland or Asia, except their religion?

In saying this I do not mean to imply that I consider all activities of the Jewish community other than the establishment of schools of learning and of houses of prayer and study as insignificant and therefore not worthwhile in themselves. The development of the human intellect *per se,* of the human endowment for aesthetic expression in art, dance, drama, music, the human impulse to innocent play of all kinds, are ends worthwhile in and by themselves. Not only do they not contradict the pattern of life taught by the Torah, on the contrary, they all can and do help to enrich that pattern. But it does mean that the central and primary concern of the Jewish people anywhere in the world must be the teaching of Torah and the creation of those conditions which would be most helpful to the study of Torah and the observance of its ethical and spiritual precepts. It means that all other activities should be interpreted and understood as the necessary concomitants and the inevitable outgrowths of Torah. All philanthropic activities of the Jewish community, all of its civic activities in behalf of human equality, freedom and justice, our concern for the State of Israel, our ideals for personal and family life, our pursuit of scientific knowledge, our encouragement of aesthetic expression of all kinds, our concern for proper utilization of leisure should all be consciously and clearly related to the teachings of the Torah.

That will not result in uniformity of thought and action in the future any more than it has in the past. The problem of diversity within a larger unity, of maintaining that delicate balance which prevents differences from degenerating into chaos, and unity into conformity, is not a new one within Judaism. Rabbi Eleazar ben Azaryah's remarkable interpretation of Koheleth (12:11) as recorded in Hagigah 3b, obviously reflects his concern and that of his generation (end of first, beginning of second, century, Common Era) with this very problem.[33]

The Jews, therefore, are not merely a people, but a Torah-People. It is the Torah which establishes the basic difference in the relationship between one born a Jew and the Jewish people, and one born as a non-Jew and the Jewish people. One born as a non-Jew, even if he be a citizen of the State of Israel, cannot become a member of the Jewish people unless he consciously rejects any other ultimate spiritual guide which is in opposition to the Torah, and consciously accepts the Torah as his ultimate spiritual guide in life. One born as a member of the Jewish people remains a Jew as long as he does not consciously accept as his ultimate spiritual guide in life a doctrine that is in opposition to the essential teachings of the Torah. One born a Jew who willfully and knowingly rejects the Torah in its totality but accepts no other formulated and concretized doctrine in its place is somewhat like one born an American who has violated every law on the books but has not repudiated his American citizenship. He is still considered an American. But one who consciously and willfully replaces the Torah by another faith and pattern of life has thereby read himself out of membership of the Jewish people, even as one who repudiates his American citizenship is no longer recognized as an American. Thus one born a Jew who has replaced the Torah by the Christian Bible, or by the Koran has thereby put himself outside the ranks of the Jewish people no matter how anxious he may be for recognition as a member in good standing in the Jewish people.[33a] Peoples always exercised the right to decide whom to recognize as members.

The only reason we can be citizens of modern democratic states is because such citizenship does not require us to reject our Torah or to violate any of its basic precepts. If it would, we could not long remain Jews. Ideologically consistent Communism does require that. It is therefore impossible for Jews to be ideologically consistent Communists and Jews at the same time, any more than they can be Christians and Jews or Moslems and Jews.

Because Americanism does not require me to reject the Torah or even to violate it, I do not feel that as a Jew I live in two civilizations in America. I live in America my own version of American civilization, even as the Catholic, or the Methodist, or the Quaker, the atheist, or the artist lives each his own version of American civilization. I am here an integral part of the totality and I do not see myself as one who is constantly shuttling between two civilizations. I may not find it possible to develop for myself or with the help of a group, a personally satisfying version of American civilization. Many American-born artists found it impossible to do so in the United States of the nineteenth century. I am staking my life on the faith that it is possible to develop such an integrated, satisfying, Jewish version of American civilization, and that Judaism can flourish in the United States not as an isolated sanctuary to which one may repair from time to time, as one who commutes between his summer and winter home, but rather as a significant, legitimate, integrated version of American civilization.[34]

The Torah alone offers us the possibility of achieving the *sine qua non* of inherently significant, group cohesion. It alone offers a common central point of reference *which in itself has ultimate meaning* and to which each member of the group is expected to relate himself in some manner significant to him personally. Through such relationship to Torah, the individuals recognize an ultimate relationship to one another which is not rooted exclusively in the accidents of history or biology, but has roots also in personal decisions, which alone give significance to human relationships.

It is the Torah that not only makes it possible but makes it necessary for me to think of the Jewish people as an *am segulah,* a specially favored people. It should not be necessary at this late date to belabor the fact that "chosenness" does not imply innate biological superiority. If that were ever so, then the large number of converts to Judaism during the centuries, as well as the results of repeated wars, pogroms and massacres, have greatly diluted that original biologic inheritance. Moreover, it certainly does not imply privileges denied any other human being. Whatever privileges a Jew may have over any other human being is limited to the fact that being born a Jew, he has a greater opportunity and therefore a greater obligation to study and obey Torah. But the Torah is here for all to accept it, who choose to do so. It is the sense of ineffable awe that we experience when we contemplate the grandeur of the Torah which compels us to say that it was no virtue inherent in us which made us worthy of being the bearers of the Torah. We did not write it. Only God's love for us, or rather for our ancestors, made this unique and supreme distinction possible (see Deuteronomy 7:7–8, 9:4–6). Israel avoided the pride of claiming authorship of the Torah by assuming the responsibility inherent in being chosen to be the bearers of the Torah.

The concept of an *am segulah* is inextricably intertwined with the sense of guilt, of failure as a people to fulfill its God-given destiny, even as the concept of "man in the image of God" is the necessary presupposition to the concept of human sin. The rejection of the concept of human sinfulness is usually associated with the rejection of the doctrine of the *Tzelem Elohim* (man's having been created in the Divine image). In much the same way, the rejection of the doctrine of the *am segulah* is a rejection of the doctrine of the Perfection of the Divine Communication which is Torah, and the rejection of the sense of failure as a people which permeates the whole of our tradition from Moses' heartrending cry "Ye have been rebellious against the Lord from the day that I knew you" (Deuteronomy 9:24) to our own confession, "We have acted wickedly and have transgressed; wherefore we have not been saved."[35] This is not a sickly obsession with guilt, but a heroic obsession with a majestic vision of man's ultimate destiny and our relationship as individuals and as a people to that destiny. We refuse to attribute our suffering merely to mankind's failure and sinfulness. We accept our share in the failure of mankind.

Our generation has demonstrated the infinite spiritual powers inherent in our people by vindicating at the moment of greatest suffering and deepest despair the faith of two millennia that the Jewish people would again be returned to its ancestral soil as an independent people. We prayed for that return all these centuries, and only a small fraction of the whole people during the last two generations labored for it with unsurpassed zeal and selflessness. From what the few have achieved, one can measure what might have been achieved if all had been equally zealous and selfless. The achievements of the few make all the more apparent the sinfulness of the many. But what they achieved dare not be stunted by transforming it into an ultimate goal, into a dead-end. The State of Israel can be the prelude to the fulfillment of human as well as of Jewish history only as it steadfastly and courageously knows itself to be the indispensable condition for enabling the people of Israel to fulfill its historic role in mankind's march towards "the end of days." That role is what bestows meaning upon Jewish peoplehood and that role we can hope to enact triumphantly only as we persist in being a Torah-People.

CHAPTER III

A Revealed Law[1]

For more than three decades, Dr. Boaz Cohen served as the *Rosh Bet Din* of the Rabbinical Assembly and as the recognized authority on Rabbinic law among the members of its Law Committee. In both capacities he was called upon to apply his encyclopedic knowledge of Jewish law to the practical exigencies of life, probably more often than any other member of the Rabbinical Assembly. The activities of these two bodies, their deliberations and decisions, reflect the basic principles that characterize the Conservative approach to Jewish law more tangibly and relevantly than do those of any other constituted agency of the Rabbinical Assembly. In papers prepared for various occasions, Rabbi Cohen formulated his understanding of these principles and how they are to be applied. These papers have been gathered into one volume under the title, *Law and Tradition in Judaism*.[2]

The reader of these papers cannot but be impressed by their author's vast erudition. Rabbi Cohen is a master not only of Rabbinic law and literature. He is also one of the most learned students of the law in general and of Roman law in particular. Hence, he is able to illuminate his subject matter with light from many another source.

The reader's second impression is one of intellectual honesty, struggling boldly if not at all times successfully (at least from this reader's point of view), with the logically intractable problems of change and continuity within a tradition.

Each essay is a complete unit unto itself. Yet such is the breadth of Rabbi Cohen's knowledge and the essential consistency of his philosophic outlook that though these essays were written over a period of three decades there is little repetition or contradiction. Each essay is a fresh approach to the central theme. Rabbi Cohen formulates that theme as follows: Though ". . . traditional Judaism can be fully grasped only in the light of its five-fold tradition" (*i.e.,* Halakhic, Ethical, Theological, Philosophical, Mystical), ". . . the Halakic tradition is primary and takes precedence over the other traditions, when they come in conflict with it" (pp. viii–x). Basic to this Halakhic tradition is the proposition that, "Biblical law is not subject to abrogation, but can only be amended through the traditional method of interpretation" (p. 26). It is to a manifold exposition of "the methods of interpretation" that these essays are devoted.

Rabbi Cohen's erudition serves him gloriously in expounding the methods of interpretation developed by the Rabbis. His paper on "Sabbath Prohibitions Known as *Shebut*" may well serve as a model for the presentation of the history of the scores of legal concepts created by the Rabbis whereby Jewish law was enabled to grow and change while preserving its essential character. Most of these concepts have yet to be studied and presented with such thoroughness, at least in English.

In an extended essay, "Law and Ethics in the Light of the Jewish Tradition," Rabbi Cohen amply demonstrates that "Many interpretations of the rabbis which apparently are a deviation from the letter of the Biblical law, were undoubtedly animated by ethical considerations" (p. 216). It is to be regretted that he does not discuss those instances in which the Rabbis did not deviate from "the letter of the Law" when it would appear that ethical considerations would justify such a step. This, after all, is the crux of the dilemma for many of us.

Similarly, his essay, "The Responsum of Maimonides Concerning Music," includes the remark that "Law cannot arrest the operation of human instincts" (p. 173). Dr. Cohen arrives at this conclusion after pointing out that the Rabbis failed in their efforts to limit music in Jewish life to religious purposes only. Surely music is not the only instance in which "human instincts" proved mightier than Rabbinic or even Biblical injunctions. There must be much that we can learn from a careful, comprehensive study of such instances. It should be made.

Rabbi Cohen does not limit himself to scholarly studies of the past. He also attempts to formulate "Canons of Interpretations of Jewish Law" for our guidance. Ten such principles are presented in one of the essays. Listed among these principles is the proposition that "We should aim to interpret merely for American Jewry, and not for 'catholic Israel' . . . " (p. 61). This seems to be in direct contradiction with an opinion formulated in an earlier essay to the effect that "There must not be, e.g. a Conservative law on Kashrut, the Sabbath, or Gittin, in contrast to the Orthodox law on the same subject. . . . What we must never let come to pass is the origin of a new faction in Judaism" (p. 29). In that same essay Dr. Cohen declares that, "Fundamental to our thinking is the doctrine of *Kenesset Yisrael,* by which we mean that the Jewish people must be regarded as one community with respect to the essential principles of Jewish Law and observance" (pp. 27–28). Perhaps this contradiction is but a reflection of Rabbi Cohen's wise warning to us that in interpreting our tradition, ". . . we must consider whether we should dedicate ourselves to the implacable ideal of consistency . . ." (p. 61).

Rabbi Cohen believes that "The introduction of the historical point of view . . . has revolutionized the whole structure of Jewish learning including the study of the Halakah, with far-reaching effects" (p. 27). He identifies these far-reaching effects with "expending more time and energy on the original sources of the Talmud rather than on the pilpulistic commentaries" (p. 30); distinguishing the sources of the Shulhan Arukh and giving due weight to each (p. 76); discovering the reasoning processes, the rationalizations and motivations that are concealed in the Rabbis' seemingly peculiar and artificial exegesis (p. 12); distinguishing between law, custom and superstition (p. 77); giving due consideration to economic and social conditions (p. 90); and to our sense of propriety and expediency (p. 95).

Dr. Cohen offers three criteria for the interpretation of Jewish law. In order to be valid, an interpretation must be "right, proper, and acceptable. By right, we mean what is deemed valid in Jewish law by a body of scholars that is competent to pass judgment on them" (p. 116). Rabbi Cohen does not indicate how that "body of scholars" is to be organized, though at one point he seems to have felt that "the Palestinian rabbinate" might become that body (p. 35). Unfortunately, the rabbinate as presently organized in the State of Israel does not, by and large, share the historical point of view in its interpretation of Jewish law, nor does it enjoy the confidence of the whole of *Kenesset Yisrael.*

". . . the remedy [interpretation] must be proper so as not to offend our moral sense" (p. 117). But again, Rabbi Cohen does not indicate whose "moral sense" he has in mind. Certainly, we do not all have the same "moral sense." Finally, Rabbi Cohen suggests that an interpretation must be "acceptable to *Kenesset Yisrael,* to the learned as well as to the laity, to the pious as well as to the religiously indifferent" (p. 117). Obviously, few interpretations could meet all three qualifications.

Many of the difficulties which we face in our efforts at adjusting Jewish law to new circumstances while preserving its essential continuity, are faced by all peoples with a long and cherished tradition. However, two factors distinguish the problems faced by Jewish law today from those faced by other systems of law. (1) There is no agency which can exercise effective authority to enforce it. (2) No agency is endowed with the right to legislate new laws or to interpret or abrogate the old ones.

This essay will focus attention upon the problem raised by the first factor, namely, the absence of an agency exercising effective power to enforce the law. This has raised the question whether the concept of law applies at all to the injunctions and admonitions of the Jewish religion. We shall not dwell upon the semantic difficulties which this question raises. For us, the concept "Jewish law" refers to the existence of a well-organized, carefully articulated set of principles and precepts whose purpose it is to direct human behavior in almost every area of human concern. Moreover there are men and women who voluntarily subject themselves to the demands of these principles and precepts and hope that their descendants will do likewise. Jewish law is today a relevant reality because there are such people in goodly number.

The fact that the concept of law is generally understood to imply the existence of an enforcement agency indicates one of the basic characteristics of laws, namely, that obedience to them usually involves the individual in some measure of unpleasantness. The degree of unpleasantness involved is of little moment; once a habit of obedience is established and its compensations experienced, the inconvenience involved in observing the law may be reduced to a minimum or entirely eliminated. In every instance, the very fact that a law had to be enacted and sanctions imposed indicates that even the best-intentioned people are inclined to avoid what is enjoined by the law. Rabbi Judah the Prince probably had this in mind when he admonished, "Reckon the loss incurred by the fulfillment of a *mitzvah* against the reward secured by its observance, and the gain derived from a transgression against the loss it involves" (Avot 2:1). Note that in the case of a *mitzvah* one becomes conscious first of the loss incurred; in the case of a transgression, of the gain. It must be so of necessity. How else could one explain the constant need to exhort people to perform *mitzvot* and to avoid transgressions?

Because obedience to the law so often involves some measure of unpleasantness, effective enforcement agencies are required even in the case of the most obviously beneficial laws, such as those regulating traffic, and even in the most civilized societies. The character of Jewish law and the circumstances of Jewish life made the problem of enforcing the law particularly difficult. Jewish law contains many provisions which, by their very nature, cannot be enforced by any human agency. The code which commands us not to steal and not to deal falsely also enjoins us not to "hate thy brother in thy heart" and "to love thy neighbor as thyself" (Leviticus 19). Moreover, even when there was an effective Jewish government in Jerusalem, some Jewish communities were beyond the reach of its powers of enforcement. Within those dispersed communities a substantial number of people voluntarily subjected themselves to the authority of Jewish law. Since Jewish law calls for the performance of acts involving considerable difficulty and since it contains provisions which under the most favorable political circumstances were beyond the power of the civil authority to enforce, the question of the ultimate sanction of Jewish law was always high on the agenda of Jewish life.

Until comparatively recent times, authoritative expounders of Jewish law agreed that it should be obeyed because it is the revealed will of God. To be sure, Rabbinic literature and particularly medieval Jewish philosophic literature abound in statements pointing to the intrinsic moral goodness and rationality of the Law. However, not even the most zealous rationalist attributed the *authority* of the Law to its moral excellence and inherent rationality. And just as those who stressed the revelatory origin of the Law did not thereby deny its intrinsic goodness and rationality, so those who preferred to stress its rationality in no way desired to imply that its authority rested on any basis other than *revelation.*

It is the Law which has established the pattern of Jewish life, with its religious, educational and philanthropic institutions, dietary laws, family relations and ethical obligations. Hence, the question facing those who are committed to the preservation and enhancement of this Jewish pattern of life is whether it can be done without the concept not merely of Law but of a *revealed* Law.

Those who today are thus committed are divided into three camps. The first camp rejects not only the concept of a revealed Law but even of Law *per se* as applicable to the Jewish pattern of life. Since the concept of Law inherently involves the performance of acts which one may find unpleasant, those who would eliminate the concept completely from Jewish religious life tend to take the position that only those aspects of the traditional pattern of Jewish life which people readily delight to observe should be preserved. As for the rest, it not only may be, but it will and should be discarded.

Those in this camp who do not reject the concept of Law, but only that of a revealed Law, argue that every custom, practice, or precept must stand or fall on the basis of its intrinsic rationality. Hence, those practices which are not amenable to satisfactory rationalization not only may, but should, be discarded. Since proponents of this attitude have no generally accepted standards for "satisfactory rationalization," the violence that this approach has done to the historic pattern of Jewish life is too well known to require elaboration.

The second camp is made up of those who retain the concept of a revealed Law, but insist upon interpreting it in the narrowest possible sense as to time and place and in the broadest possible sense as to its provisions. They maintain for all practical purposes that "In the third month after the children of Israel were gone forth out of the land of Egypt"

(Exodus 19:1), the Law, as embodied in the latest edition of the traditional code, was revealed at Sinai.

The third camp consists of those who are equally insistent upon retaining the concept of a revealed Law, but would interpret the concept in the widest possible sense as to time and place, and in the narrowest possible sense as to its provisions. They would apply to the legal codes those methods of discriminatory study referred to by Dr. Cohen. They would scrutinize the provisions of the codes in the light of modern historical, psychological and philological studies. But, however broad their interpretation of revelation might be, they would nevertheless insist upon its indispensability to any system of Jewish thought which would lay claim to authenticity and meaningful continuity. No matter how niggardly they might be in applying this concept to the specific contents of the codes, or how widely they might differ in regard to the specific content to which it should be applied, they nevertheless would insist that it is significantly applicable to a substantial core of those codes. This, it seems to me, is the position of Dr. Cohen, a position which in essence I, and I believe the main body of the Rabbinical Assembly, share with him.

One who presumes to speak of a revealed Law cannot avoid questions regarding the time and place of the revelation. Did it occur as a "perceptible event in the external world" or was it, as Dr. Cohen seems to feel, "the internal experience of the prophet permeated by the divine spirit" (pp. 23–24)? Elsewhere I have struggled with that question and shall not now return to it.[3] I want here to indicate why I believe that the concept of a revealed Law must be maintained not as the empty shell of a once firmly held conviction, but as the expression of a conviction indispensable (a) to the meaningful continuity of Judaism as a philosophy and pattern of life, (b) to the existence of the Jewish people and (c) to the moral life of man.

It will help us understand why the concept of a revealed

Law is indispensable to us today if we understand why the concept came to occupy so central a position in Jewish thought. Note that we are not inquiring how the concept came into being. If we reject *in toto* the tradition that at Sinai the Israelites experienced an overwhelming event at which time a Law was revealed to them, then we have no way of establishing with any degree of certainty why the Israelites alone among all the known people of history, attributed direct divine origin to both their civil and religious law.[4] The most that we can hope to do is to try to explain how the concept functioned, that is, to what need it responded. The exposition of how a concept functioned is not equivalent to an explanation of how and why it came into being. Nor does the manner of its functioning validate its cognitive content. It indicates merely what psychological, intellectual and emotional needs of the individual or of the group the concept served. Those needs were undoubtedly very real and urgent or else the concept would never have assumed so central a position in Jewish thought. If those needs still exist today, we must ask whether they are being served or can be served by a concept more acceptable to us.

Among the most deeply-felt needs of our ancestors was that of appropriately expressing their sense of overwhelming awe when they contemplated the grandeur and the majesty of the contents of the Law. "See, I have imparted to you laws and norms. . . . Observe them faithfully, for that will be proof of your wisdom and discernment to other peoples, who on hearing of all these laws will say: 'Surely that is a great nation of wise and discerning people.' . . . What great nation has laws and norms as perfect as all this teaching that I set before you this day?" (Deuteronomy 4:5–8). The ecstasy and admiration and hence the love and loyalty which the Law called forth in the hearts of our fathers is mirrored in Psalm 119 and in hundreds of other passages in Biblical and Rabbinic literature. Our fathers could rationally attribute the perfection which they found in it only to its divine origin.

Our ancestors' frame of mind is movingly reflected in a comment made to me by Professor Ernst Simon as we left a synagogue in Jerusalem on the Sabbath. "When I read some of the stirring passages in Deuteronomy," he said, "I cannot understand how anyone can believe that they were written by a human being."

But far more universally experienced and more deeply felt was the need for a logically and emotionally compelling rationale to buttress a pattern of life which included socially "offensive" institutions such as the Sabbath and the dietary laws, personally demanding injunctions such as those regulating the most intimate relations between the sexes, and intellectually and spiritually burdensome chores, such as the study of an unspoken language and attachment to a land one often neither lived in nor saw. The concept that the Law which established this physically burdensome and spiritually taxing pattern of life was revealed, has proved over the centuries to be more effective than any other in offering a rationale equal to the task of making this pattern of life acceptable even under the most trying circumstances, not to all Jews, to be sure, but to a number large enough to assure the preservation of the pattern and with it of the Jewish people itself. For it can hardly be gainsaid that before the modern era in Jewish history only those Jews remained Jews for whom the concept of revealed Law had vital relevance and significance.

There are two reasons for this. In the first place, no one could possibly produce a fully comprehensible and acceptable rationalization for all elements in the traditional pattern of Jewish life. Ingenious thinkers have rationalized the Sabbath, the dietary laws and the civil and ethical laws of the Torah, but it is beyond the power of the most ardent apologist to formulate a satisfactory rationale for the *hukim*—laws of the red heifer, of cloth made from a mixture of wool and linen, of the sacrificial system and similar laws. Secondly, it was obvious from earliest times that while rationalizations in completely comprehensible human terms were undoubtedly of great importance in sustaining one's determination to observe the Law, *in themselves* they rarely, if ever, were able to move the nonobservant to observe, or the observant to persist in his observance in the face of long and burdensome hardships. Moralists and psychologists have wrestled with only indifferent success in their search for an answer to the question why Reason, when appealing only to those factors which are completely within the scope of its comprehension, is rarely adequate to the task of moving men consistently to observe even precepts which involve only a modicum of discomfort in comparison to the obvious beneficial results their observance entails. We shall not presume to be able to do what they have failed to do. We shall point only to those aspects of the question which are relevant to our purposes.

One of these aspects is reflected in the Rabbinic discussion of the cause that led to King Solomon's defections from the Law. Among the laws rationalized in the Torah, two refer to the conduct of the king. He was not to keep great numbers of horses, because that might lead to traffic with Egypt and the Lord had warned that "You must not go back that way again." Nor was the king to have many wives, "lest his heart go astray" after foreign gods (Deuteronomy 17:16–17). Since the purpose to be served by both these laws is thus clearly indicated, Solomon—the Rabbis say—decided that he could fulfill the purposes without obeying the laws.

A rationale implies that the law is subsidiary to the purpose it is intended to serve. This inevitably leads to the conclusion that it should be permissible to disregard the law if there appears to be an equally effective but less burdensome way to serve the indicated purpose. Very few human beings, from the very young to the very old, are so utterly bereft of ingenuity that they cannot envision achieving a desirable goal in a manner that appears less burdensome than the one suggested by teachers, elders or group experience. And very few people will refrain from choosing the easier path if there is nothing to prevent them from so doing.

Moreover, our most elaborate rationalizations of a law limit its significance to consequences already experienced or anticipated. But the consequences of any act are potentially infinite in number, and the nonforeseeable consequences of any act far outnumber the experienced and foreseeable ones. One of the fundamental components of the religious life is the faith that the beneficial but nonforeseeable results of an act which religion enjoins are far greater than any foreseeable results. Hence, when even the most ardent rationalist of the past insisted that the authority of the law rested not upon its humanly comprehended rationality but upon its divine origin, he was in effect saying that the authority of the law rested not upon our reason but upon divine Reason, that the rationality which we are able to attribute to the law is too narrow in scope to contain the divine Reason.

Our collective experience, in many crucial instances, has vindicated this position. All the beneficial consequences which resulted from the institution of the Sabbath for both Jews and mankind at large could not possibly have been foreseen two thousand years ago, when Jews were mocked for maintaining so "obviously foolish" an institution. The practice of circumcision, now almost universally adopted, was declared to be a relic of barbarism even by some of the founders of Reform Judaism. Jewish laws concerning relations between husband and wife are only now being rationalized as physically and psychologically sound. The overtones of infinite meaning which our observant fathers subconsciously and intuitively experienced and which everyone who faithfully observes the Law experiences in a measure, can never be fully and cogently verbalized. The concept of revealed Law expresses an awareness of the reality of these intuitively experienced but nonverbalized meanings, and transmutes them into a conscious source of inner strength indispensable to the observance of the Law over a long period of time and in the face of ever-present obstacles.

I repeatedly refer to the presence of obstacles, of immediate unpleasantnesses involved in the observance of the Law and to the need for each Jew to face up to them throughout his lifetime, because I believe this to be basic not only to the problem of Jewish existence, but also to that of living the good life. To be sure, one should, when expounding the Law, stress primarily its inherent rationality as reflected in the readily comprehensible beneficent consequences following upon its observance. However, an exposition of the Law which does not take into account the sacrifices which its observance often entails, reflects neither honest thinking nor sound pedagogy. The greatest harm we can do to anyone—child or adult—is to give him the impression that being an ethical person and a good Jew is easy, that it will involve him only in pleasant experiences. It is simply not true, and no one matures ethically and religiously until the unpleasant experience is faced triumphantly.

Unpleasant experiences are inherent in the demands of the logically most acceptable laws, whether they be the laws requiring us to deal honestly in business transactions or those enjoining upon us abstention from work on the Sabbath. One must be naive indeed to imagine that resisting temptation of any kind is always a pleasant experience for anyone but the tried and tested saint.

Nor can all of our rationalizations of the traditional Sabbath as an invaluable boon to one's physical and spiritual welfare convince one that he ought not to harvest his fields or keep his place of business open on that day. These rationalizations undoubtedly help those who for other conscious or subconscious reasons are committed Sabbath observers, to persist in their observance. However, after more than four decades of rather intimate contact with thousands of Jewish laymen I cannot name a half-dozen who were moved by these rationalizations to become traditional Sabbath observers.

The intelligent, intellectually honest observer of the traditional pattern of Jewish life was always conscious of the sacrifice, the immediate hardships which it involved. He was always equally conscious of the fact that he could avoid them by rejecting the Law. Moreover, as Dr. Cohen points out, there is no acceptable "remedy within the Law" for some of the unpleasantnesses which at times are inevitably involved in its observance, even as there is no morally acceptable "remedy" for the unpleasantness involved in returning found money when the owner is known and the finder can be discovered only by his own admission.

The Law was not intended to be either the lackey of our mundane physical needs and passions—though it is in no way their enemy—nor even of our nobler impulses and aspirations, though it unquestionably buttresses and sustains them. Its purpose is to make us servants of the Lord. This attitude which is repeatedly expressed by the Rabbis is perhaps most pointedly reflected in the injunction that "he who says 'have pity upon us even as Thou dost pity the bird' (Deuteronomy 22:6–7) is to be silenced" (Berakhot 33b). No one has been more consistent than the Rabbis in teaching that God is a merciful and loving Father. Why, then, did they reject so appealing a rationalization of the Deuteronomic law? Because, as one of the Rabbis in the Talmud there puts it, "This would rouse jealousy among God's creatures" since God seemed to have favored one creature, the mother bird, above others. If the laws of the Torah are to be understood in terms of God's mercy, how explain the fact that the Torah permits us to slaughter animals for food? (see Maimonides, *Commentary on the Mishnah, ad loc.*). Did God's mercy fail Him when He permitted us the flesh of sheep? Above all, was it merciful of God to demand that Jews choose to live lives of poverty and persecution, rather than to violate the Sabbath or accept baptism?

The historic experiences of the Jewish people have always compelled them to grapple with the paradox that the God of mercy commanded them to perform acts which, from the human point of view, all too often proved not to be merciful either to the actor or those acted upon. The concept of revealed Law enabled our fathers not only to live with this paradox but also to accept both terms of it as valid. It matured them as men and sustained them spiritually in their heroic efforts to live ethically as Jews, even though being Jews and living ethically often involved great sacrifices.

This, then, is the second vital need which the concept of a revealed Law served in the life of our fathers. It was the ultimate rationale for the hardships which being a Jew and living a moral life inevitably and under the best of circumstances entail.

The third, universal human need profoundly experienced by our fathers which the concept of revealed Law helped to satisfy was the need to feel that human life had ultimate significance, that man was not created to "labor in vain nor to bring forth confusion" (Isaiah 65:23), that their mundane concerns as well as their noble aspirations had cosmic significance. The quality of one's life depends not merely upon his recognition that he is not God, but equally upon his conviction that he is, as the Rabbis put it, God's partner in the universe, and that God looks to him for aid in completing His creation. In obeying a natural law discovered by science, we avoid physical pain and frustration. In obeying the revealed Law of Judaism, our fathers undoubtedly experienced the *simhah shel mitzvah,* the joy in the performance of *mitzvot.* But when obedience involved pain, they were sustained by the conviction that they were acting as the partners of the Creator of the Universe.

Man cannot possibly feel that his actions are of cosmic significance if he can relate them all to a purpose satisfying his immediate, mundane, completely comprehensible needs. Man cannot escape a sense of futility and meaninglessness unless he transcends his biologically felt and rationally comprehended wants. This inevitably involves the subjection of oneself to demands that contradict one's immediate, biologically rooted personal satisfactions. Subjugation to such demands makes sense only when those demands are given cosmic significance. It was the concept of the revealed Law which alone was capable of transmuting the mundane suffering involved in living as a Jew in the here and now into transcendent spiritual joy not only in contemplation of future rewards but in the actual here and now.

These, then, were the psychological and emotional needs of the individual Jew to which the concept of a revealed Law proved heretofore to be intellectually the most adequate, and emotionally the most effective response. But, in meeting these needs of the individual Jew, the concept simultaneously performed an indispensable service to the Jewish people. *By bestowing finality and irrevocability upon the basic pattern of Jewish life, it became the most important single factor in the preservation of the Jewish people.*

Every people which becomes conscious of its identity as a group associates its self-identity primarily with one or all of three factors: (a) the territory it occupies, (b) the language it speaks and (c) the pattern of life which distinguishes it from other groups. These three factors are not of equal importance in the life of any one group; nor does any one of the three factors play an equally important role in the lives of all groups. By and large, territory has been the strongest single factor bestowing self-consciousness upon a group as long as it occupies that territory and is determined to defend it. Severance of a whole people or of significant segments of it from the native soil, whether voluntary or compulsory, usually has been followed by disintegration of the exiled group's self-identity. If a significant portion of the group continued to live on its native soil, nostalgic attachment to the land of origin would continue to bind the dispersed segments to that group. But such nostalgic attachment usually has never persisted beyond the second or third generation, after which the dispersed segments either were completely assimilated within the larger community of which they were a part, or, like the French Canadians and South African Dutchmen, began to think of themselves as a distinct entity having no particular allegiance to any other large group. Immigrant groups in America maintain only the most tenuous ties with their country of origin beyond the second generation.

In comparatively recent times, language has become an unprecedentedly important factor for conscious group identity. Attachment to language today rivals attachment to soil in intensity. Many leaders consider it to be the most significant factor maintaining the self-identity of their groups. Hence, the desperate attempts of the Irish to revive the knowledge and use of Gaelic among the Irish everywhere, and of Jews to revive the knowledge and use of Hebrew among Jews everywhere. But no people thus far has succeeded in maintaining a widespread knowledge and use of its language among those of its members living as a minority in societies where they are free to mingle with the majority group.

The factor bestowing self-consciousness upon a group that seems to have the greatest vitality and the greatest power of adaptability is the group's pattern of life. Though the pattern as a whole is usually discarded, some aspects of it linger long after attachment to land or language has disappeared. Scotsmen who never have visited Scotland and no longer speak Scottish will, on set occasions, sport their bagpipes and kilts. Dutchmen who do not know their language and have never visited Holland will adorn their communities and their homes with miniature models of windmills, with wooden shoes and with tulips. Irishmen who have no knowledge of Gaelic and no particular attachment to Ireland will continue to delight in the green on St. Patrick's Day.

This attachment to a distinctive group pattern of life or some aspect of it, universally tenacious as it is, was never as pervasive and determinative of the group's destiny as it proved to be in the case of the Jewish people. Moreover, the Jewish pattern of life was so marvelously constructed that both land and language were an integral part of it and continued through it to function as vital factors in the life of the people. Thus the Hebrew language was preserved because it was an indispensable element in the pattern of life established by the revealed Law. The Torah had to be read publicly in Hebrew. Public prayer had to be recited in Hebrew. The earliest Jewish Diaspora communities retained their attachment to the land only insofar as it played a significant role in the pattern of life they continued to live, that is, only insofar as it was the goal of a religious pilgrimage or played a part in the celebration of a festival or in the prayers of the Synagogue. When they lost interest in that pattern of life, their interest in the land also inevitably ceased. Hence, while the land and language continued to play an important role in the life and thought of the Jews, they did so until recent times only because they were part of a pattern of life believed to have been established by a revealed Law and therefore possessing ultimate, irrevocable significance. When, in the past, faith in the ultimate significance of that pattern of life died, concern for the language and the land withered and died with it.

The concept of a revealed Law has fallen into disrepute among Jews in our day, resulting in widespread disaffection from the Jewish pattern of life and ultimately from the Jewish people. This fact has caused a widespread search for a substitute. A number of substitutes have been offered; chief among them are: (a) Jewish nationhood or the more innocuous concept of Jewish peoplehood,[5] (b) the Hebrew language and (c) concern for the State of Israel. Undoubtedly these have been the most powerful antidotes to Jewish group disintegration within the last three generations. Nor have they yet run their beneficent course. Fortunately they still have, and for a long time may continue to have, considerable vigor and vitality.

Each of these three factors has inherent virtue which everyone concerned with the preservation of the Jewish people is in duty bound to cherish and to nurture. But neither history nor contemporary experience offers cogent reasons leading us to believe that any one or all of them can displace the authentic pattern of Jewish life as established by the Law, as the bond of meaningful Jewish self-identity either for the individual or for the community. Each one of these factors—significant as it unquestionably is—will, when separated from the authentic pattern of Jewish life as established by the Law, at best flourish but briefly like a flower separated from its roots. I believe, therefore, that the preservation of the Jewish people anywhere in the world depends upon the preservation of the basic pattern of Jewish life as established by the Law. I believe, moreover, that it was the concept of the revealed Law which sustained our fathers in their allegiance to the pattern of life established by the Law, and that neither we nor our descendants will remain loyal to it unless we set at the heart of our philosophy of life either the concept of the revealed Law as conceived by our fathers or some acceptable but equally cogent, modern version of it. Whether such an "equally cogent, modern version" can be formulated is the question which should be at the very heart of the concern of all those who are interested in the future of the Jews and the Jewish religion. I believe that it can be done.

To those who look to the State of Israel and to the Hebrew language as the future substitutes for the traditional Jewish pattern of life as established by the Law, and who not only reject the traditional version of the concept of a revealed Law but also do not believe that a modern, cogent version of it can be formulated, I venture to offer an analogy which, though imperfect as all analogies of necessity are, I find helpful and suggestive. I hope they, too, will find it helpful.

The relationship of the Jewish people to the pattern of life established by the Law is analogous in four essential aspects to the relationship of the Jewish people to the Hebrew language and the land of Israel. The relationship in each case (a) is final and irrevocable; (b) its origin is beyond the reach of reason; (c) it *can* be tampered with but only to a limited extent, without dangerously impairing the vitality of

Judaism and the Jewish people; (d) its maintenance involved repeated and serious sacrifices.

The Zionist Movement, against all considerations of "common sense" determined early in its career that the relationship between the Jewish people and the Hebrew language and *Eretz Yisrael* is final and irrevocable. There was no rationally compelling argument against the position of the Territorialists in 1900, or against that of the Yiddishists when more than three-quarters of the Jewish people spoke Yiddish, or against those who advocated the use of a European language for the Technion in Haifa in 1913. But Zionists based their contention upon the logically unprovable conviction that there can be no significant sense of continuity and self-identity for the Jewish people except as it is related to the Land of Israel and the Hebrew language. The relationship of a people to its language is not, in its origin, a matter of conscious choice. It belongs to the eternal mysteries which surround all of human life. Nor does the Tradition envision the origin of the relationship of the Jewish people with the Land of Israel as having been a matter of the people's conscious choice. The Tradition attributes the establishment of that relationship to a Divine act of grace. There are Zionists who prefer another explanation for the origin of the relationship between the people of Israel and the Land of Israel. They agree, however, with those Zionists who do accept the Tradition in this—that this relationship once having been established assumes a finality and an irrevocability whose validity can not be successfully challenged by an appeal to reason. It is a relationship whose essential quality is beyond the reach of reason. Reason plays only a secondary role in determining whether one accepts or rejects the irrevocability of that relationship.

But the finality and irrevocability of the relationship do not imply fixity and rigidity in the related factors. The related factors undergo constant change. The Jewish people is, as a biological entity, certainly not the same today as it was two thousand years ago. No one at all acquainted with the vicissitudes of Jewish history can deny the obvious fact that the Jewish people has over the centuries received large admixtures of so-called non-Jewish blood, through proselytization, intermarriage, and the ravages of pogroms and wars. And yet those admixtures were never at any time so great as to destroy the sense of ethnic kinship among the people. This biological admixture is continuing today for the same reasons and with the same effects as in the past. The new elements made their impress but did not destroy the people's sense of essential biological continuity. There are those who like to believe that the Jewish people represent a "racially pure" group and who look askance at the acceptance of any non-Jew into the fellowship of the Jewish people. And there are those who would open the doors wide to admit anyone at all into that fellowship without requiring any more of the newcomer than a statement that he would want to be counted as one of us. And there are those who are ready to accept non-Jews into the fellowship of the Jewish people but only on condition that it would not lead to the destruction of the essential character of that fellowship. They, I believe, represent the mainstream of Jewish historic continuity.

Nor is the Hebrew language the same today as it was two thousand or even a hundred years ago or as it will be a generation from now. The prevalent differences of opinion regarding changes in the Hebrew language are substantially the same as those regarding changes in the Jewish pattern of life. There are purists who would preserve the vocabulary and grammatical structure intact as it came to us from the past, using only old Hebrew roots and combinations of them to express new terms. Others would introduce foreign elements with almost reckless thoughtlessness. Some would even change the script. There are those who would have the people at large, rather than the Hebrew Language Academy, determine the proper grammatical structure and vocabulary. However, the overwhelming majority seem to acknowledge the inevitability of linguistic change and want merely to control its frequency and character so that there will be no radical break with the inner genius of the language. They differ only in what would constitute a radical break.

The land, too, is undergoing change. The State of Israel today is neither the country of David nor of the Maccabees. New "holy places" are appearing. The country is being industrialized and mechanized. One can no longer experience there the very sights, smells and sounds that our ancestors experienced in the days of King David or of the Maccabees or even in the days before the rise of the State of Israel. Some people refuse to be reconciled to the changes in the land's borders. Some bemoan its complete modernization. But even those who welcome some or all of the changes agree that Jerusalem as capital could not be replaced by any other city, even as Uganda never could have become a new *Eretz Yisrael*.

Similarly, the pattern of Jewish life will undergo change, as it has in the past. But its essential character must be preserved. What that essential character consists of will remain subject to discussion among those interested in its preservation. To me it seems certain that the Synagogue, the Hebrew language, the Sabbath, holy days and festivals, the dietary laws, the laws of Jewish marriage and divorce, and vital concern for the Jewish autonomous community in *Eretz Yisrael* are among its indispensable elements. There may be variations of emphasis in regard to each one of these elements. But whoever would set a pattern of Jewish life which completely omits any of these is, in my opinion, striking a blow at the vital center of the whole pattern.

Can this pattern be maintained without some version of the concept of revealed Law? At one time I blithely might have answered, "Yes," though intuitively I always had very grave doubts. Today I am as convinced as it is possible for a human being to be in such matters, that it cannot. And since I am equally convinced that with the disintegration of the

Jewish pattern of life the Jewish people will disintegrate, I believe that every thinking Jew—if he is to remain a *profoundly committed* Jew regardless of where he lives—must come to terms intellectually and emotionally with the concept of a revealed Law, either as formulated by the Tradition or with some version of it which is more acceptable to him and serves his intellectual and emotional needs as effectively as the traditional concept served our fathers. The fundamental task of Jewish spiritual and intellectual leaders of every generation is to help their generation to come to terms with this concept in a constructive, positive manner.[6] Dr. Boaz Cohen's volume, *Law and Tradition in Judaism,* is a very important contribution to the all-too-meager literature on this subject.

CHAPTER IV

Judaism and the Democratic Ideal[1]

Although the concept of democracy has a long history, all attempts to formulate a universally accepted definition of it have failed, as have attempts to define other concepts such as liberty, justice and love. However, the search for definition has not been fruitless. It has deepened our understanding of the concept of democracy and it has enlarged the area of its applicability in three major realms of our concern—forms of government, goals of the state and interpersonal relationships.

A form of government is said to be democratic to the extent to which each person governed exercises equal control over the machinery of government. Absolute equality has never been attained; it is even theoretically inconceivable. Nevertheless, it remains valid as an ideal to be ceaselessly pursued.

A democratic form of government does not necessarily imply democratic goals. These are said to be democratic to the extent to which they seek to eliminate inequalities of opportunity, enabling those governed to live free and satisfying lives. Not only ignorance, selfishness and bigotry but also pressing administrative considerations and sincere moral convictions have moved majorities to limit a minority's opportunity to live a fully free and satisfying life. Thus, for example, in the United States we generally recognize only one official day of rest per week, and there is but one official language. We forbid Mormons and Moslems to practice polygamy. During World War II we moved one hundred and fifty thousand Japanese Americans from their homes purely as an administrative measure, because the military authorities deemed it necessary for the safety of the country.

However, we have advanced beyond this negative formulation of the goals of democratic government. We now seek not only to remove man-made inequalities from among our citizens but also to reduce to a minimum the unhappy consequences of those natural inequalities to which man is heir, by making special facilities available to the physically, mentally, socially and economically handicapped.

No government can control the attitudes which determine the personal relationships between husband and wife, parent and child, teacher and pupil, client and professional. But the concept of democracy is also applicable to those relationships. It demands that each of us constantly be on guard against the temptation to take advantage of our superior strength, knowledge or wisdom, either to use another human being as a mere tool, even with his own consent, or to cause someone else physical or spiritual suffering. It is because many individuals have fulfilled this democratic ideal in their own lives that we have the courage and the faith to look hopefully towards man's future on earth.

DEMOCRACY IS NOT ENOUGH

The concept of democracy *per se* directs us to establish the relationships between one individual and another upon the basis of equality. But equality is not enough. The relationship between one human being and another must also be governed by love, compassion and devotion. Moreover, the concept of democracy does not help us to understand our relationship to God and the universe; nor can it serve as a guide in our relationship to ourselves in our solitariness.

These limitations are not noted in order to derogate the significance of democracy. No single concept is universally applicable and all-sufficient for our moral life. The limitations are noted precisely because the concept of democracy is so important and so widely applicable that we are often inclined to set it up as the adequate touchstone for a complete philosophy of life. When we try to make a part carry a load designed for the whole, it not only fails to perform its own unique task but is itself warped and disfigured in the process. The concept of democracy cannot achieve its own fulfillment without the aid of a number of other concepts to supplement and buttress it. Those who have tried to build societies based on the concept of democracy alone have not only failed in their efforts to build a truly democratic society but have most often ended with political tyrannies of one kind or another.

Athens, under Pericles, is generally pointed to as the ancient state in which the democratic ideal received its fullest possible philosophic formulation and political embodiment. Yet Athens was a city-state inhabited by a comparatively small number of free citizens and a much larger number of slaves. In modern times, the democratic ideal became a mighty force in the political affairs of men when the United States of America came into being. Nevertheless, within the bounds of the authority of the established government there remained a large number of people who were held as slaves and an even larger number who, because of sex, property requirements or religious convictions, were deprived of full participation in their own government. This flaw in the application of democracy to the political structure of our government led ultimately to the tragedy of the Civil War, and is the root of the present widespread and serious challenge to our "domestic tranquility."

Not long after the Declaration of Independence was

signed, the French Revolution issued its call to liberty, equality and fraternity. Revolutionary France was fortunate in having no complicated problem of slavery or color to face. But there were Jews in France at the time, and the call to fraternity, liberty and equality did not, *ipso facto,* include them. A long and acrimonious debate preceded the partial political emancipation of French Jewry. Even the most ardent defenders of Jewish emancipation based their arguments either on the proposition that the Jews must renounce their national aspirations and characteristics before being admitted to citizenship, or on the hope that such a change would inevitably follow their emancipation. Only thus would they finally qualify for the blessings of equality and fraternity.

Obviously, then, good and wise men have been able sincerely to proclaim their devotion to democracy and liberty while advocating the inherent justice of slavery, or of other oppressions and discriminations which may be physically less painful but which are spiritually no less burdensome and obnoxious.

Many factors contribute to the creation and maintenance of a chasm between an ideal and the reality: external obstacles actually or apparently insurmountable, the failure of human will power to rise to the noblest human vision, and the widespread psychological phenomenon of departmentalized thinking. All of these have played a part in democracy's failure to fulfill itself in life. But all of these together do not present the entire explanation. We must add to them the proposition that democracy needs the support of a number of other valuational concepts if it is to fulfill its own highest ethical potentialities. Before democracy can become the successful bearer of our noblest moral and social aspirations, our minds must be equipped with, and our hearts sensitized by, those valuational concepts which are democracy's indispensable allies. What are those concepts and where are they meaningfully explicated?

MANKIND INDIVISIBLE

The first of these indispensable allies is suggested by the *obiter dicta* of one of the most famous decisions ever written by a Chief Justice of our Supreme Court. In his Dred Scott decision of 1857, Chief Justice Taney raises the question whether Negroes were included under the concept of "Men" in the Declaration of Independence, and of "People" in the preamble to the Constitution. He concludes that the terms "people of the United States" and "citizens," as used in the Constitution, refer only to "every person, and every class and description of persons, who were at the time of the adoption of the Constitution recognized as citizens in the several states." Only these, Justice Taney maintains, "became also citizens of this new political body, and none other; it was formed by them and for them and their posterity, but for no one else. . . . In the opinion of the Court, the legislation and the histories of the time, and *the language used in the Declaration of Independence* (italics mine, S.G.) show that neither the class of persons who had been imported as slaves, nor their descendants, whether they had become free or not, were then acknowledged as a part of the people, nor intended to be included in the general words used in that memorable instrument." Samuel Eliot Morison, in his widely hailed *Oxford History of the American People,* agrees with Justice Taney's position: "Did Jefferson think of Negroes when he wrote 'All men are created equal'? His subsequent career indicates that he did not, that in his view Negroes are not 'men' " (p. 222). These views, right or wrong, point up a basic prerequisite to a proper understanding of democracy.

If a Chief Justice of the United States in 1857 and a Harvard Professor of American History in 1964 could maintain that, when Jefferson wrote "all men are created equal," he and those who signed the Declaration with him really meant only "white men," how can we censure lesser men for using the words "men" and "people," when referring only to Protestants, or Aryans, or proletarians? Hence, we arrive at the inescapable conclusion that the moral quality of one's faith in democracy, and the extent to which that faith holds out hope for mankind's future, depends largely upon how the concept "man" is understood.

Where can we turn for a concept of man adequate to the highest needs of the democratic ideal? We suggest that the Biblical-Rabbinic tradition has a contribution of unsurpassed importance to make in this area. It is obviously impossible within the limits of this paper to present a complete record of Biblical-Rabbinic thought on this subject. But we hope to give a large enough sampling to indicate its extraordinary depth and relevance.

We do not want to leave the impression that there are no passages in the Biblical-Rabbinic tradition which fall short of the nobility of sentiment and high purpose reflected in the sources about to be quoted. No religious or cultural tradition has remained uniformly true to its own highest spiritual insights. But the potentialities inherent in each tradition are projected in its *noblest* spiritual reaches. It is these that serve as the conscience of the tradition. The tradition as a whole stands constantly under their judgment.

The basic characteristic of the Biblical-Rabbinic concept of man is its *indivisibility*. The concept cannot tolerate any limiting modifiers. There are no such concepts as Black Man, White Man, Jewish Man or Pagan Man. There are men who are black and men who are white. There are men who are Jews and men who are not Jews. But all are men. Ben Azzai, a contemporary of Rabbi Akiba, had so profound a comprehension of this basic characteristic of the Biblical concept of Man and of its supreme importance that he was moved to differ with the universally revered Akiba who maintained the most important passage in the Bible to be the commandment "Love thy neighbor as thyself" (Leviticus 19:18). Ben Azzai maintained that the most important passage in Holy Scripture is the statement, "This is the book of the generations of man . . . in the likeness of God made He him" (Genesis 5:1).[2]

The profundity of Ben Azzai's insight becomes all the more apparent when we recall that the passage most frequently quoted as the Biblical rationale for the brotherhood of man is Malachi's rhetorical question, "Have we not all one father? Hath not one God created us?" (Malachi 2:10). To be sure, all ethical values in Judaism find their ultimate rationale in the doctrine of the One just, merciful, omnipotent Creator and Sustainer of the universe and all its component parts. This doctrine compels even its least thoughtful and sensitive adherents to expand their intellectual horizon and ethical sensitivity. It establishes at least one fundamental relationship between the individual and all phenomena that he observes around him, namely that he and they are the creatures of the same Creator. Ethics begins with the discovery of some area of identity between oneself and the other, whatever or whoever that other may be. The larger the area of acknowledged identity, the larger the scope of the ethical involvement.

One of the main sources of ethical confusion and moral failure, even among many who sincerely profess their faith in democracy, is this: they limit its application to their "own kind." The denial of legal or social equality to another is invariably associated with a denial of essential identity with that other. He is declared to be in some way significantly different and "inferior," and therefore not worthy of the consideration one extends to one's "own kind."

The fact that "the fish of the sea, the birds of the sky, and all the living things that creep on earth" (Genesis 1:28) are also creatures of the One God who created man, does establish a very important area of identity between them and man. God created them also in love and is concerned with their welfare even as with the welfare of man. "He sendeth the springs into the valleys which run among the hills. They give drink to every beast of the fields; the wild asses quench their thirst. By them shall the fowls of the heaven have their habitation. . . . He causeth the grass to grow for the cattle, and herb for the service of man" (Psalms 104:10–14). God's concern for the cattle is thus expressly equated with His concern for man. This is most impressively reflected in the Fourth Commandment, which includes one's cattle as well as one's sons and daughters in the category of those who are to rest on the Sabbath (Deuteronomy 5:13). It is most movingly expressed in the closing sentence of the Book of Jonah, "And should not I have pity on Nineveh, that great city, wherein are more than sixscore thousand persons that cannot discern between their right hand and their left hand, and also much cattle?"

Moreover, God's concern for the welfare of all of His creatures imposes ethical limitations upon man's relationship to all the nonhuman components of the universe, whether animate or inanimate. He too must, to the best of his ability, be concerned with their welfare. They may not be wantonly abused to satisfy human greed, sadism, whim, or childish fancy. They may be used only when man's welfare is thereby directly and significantly advanced, and then only with care to inflict a minimum of pain.

The common element of creaturehood is, however, not sufficient in the Biblical-Rabbinic tradition to establish parity or equality among the creatures. Indeed the Biblical narrative expressly distinguishes between man as a creature of God and all other creatures created by Him. Man alone is made "in the image of God." The Biblical-Rabbinic doctrine of the equality of man is rooted, therefore, not in the Fatherhood of God but rather in the common descent of all men from Adam. *Actual consanguinity is thus assumed for men of all races and creeds.*

In a Talmudic passage which is the most comprehensive and unequivocal formulation known to me of the doctrine of the essential equality of all men, the Rabbis ask, "Why did

God create only one man, Adam?" And they answer, "So that no man should be able to say, 'My ancestor was greater than yours' " (Sanhedrin 37a). The narrative in the first chapter of Genesis does not attribute any specific color, or race, or religion to Adam. It thus responds to the deepest inner need of every individual to feel that he and the racial group to which he belongs are biologically and intellectually the equals or at least the potential equals of every other individual or racial group. The authors of the American Declaration of Independence apparently sensed this need of every man, not merely to enjoy the same inalienable rights that others have, but also to be considered the equal of all others. Hence the first of the truths which they held to be self-evident was that "all men are created equal." Only then do they declare that all men "are endowed by their Creator with certain unalienable rights." This principle of the essential biological kinship and therefore of the equality of the endowments of all men, the Rabbis did not find in the faith that God is the Creator of us all, for He also created the animals and the inanimate world. The Rabbis root it rather in the Biblical narrative which traces all of us back to one ancestor, Adam. The differences that exist are not inherent but peripheral and accidental.

The acceptance of the doctrine that all men, regardless of race, color, creed, or present status of intellectual or social development, have all been fashioned in the same mold and are therefore physically and psychologically basically the same, is a prerequisite for the development among men everywhere of a sense of brotherhood that is more than an attitude of condescending benevolence. There will be no lasting and significant world peace based upon justice until men feel a sense of *biological* and psychological identity with all other men, a sense of *blood kinship* which leaves no room for any thought of inherent biological superiority of one group over another. This sense of identity with all men is nurtured among the adherents of Judaism by the narrative in the first chapter of Genesis as unequivocally interpreted by the Rabbis in the Talmud, and by the highest moral reaches of Biblical and Rabbinic law.

How far mankind still has to travel to accept this religious value even in theory, let alone in practice, is evidenced by the hold that the Nazi race theories obtained on the scientifically most advanced nation of the West; by what is happening in South Africa today; by the long and difficult struggle to change the racially rooted immigration laws of the United States enacted in the early nineteen twenties; and by the daily experiences of the Negro population in our country.

Though the Constitution of the United States did not at once implement the bold pronouncement of the Declaration of Independence that all men are created equal, it could not remove from the conscience of America the "proposition" to which the Republic was "dedicated." Robert Frost phrased it perfectly when he wrote: *

"That's a hard mystery of Jefferson's.
What did he mean? Of course the easy way
Is to decide it simply isn't true.
It may not be. I heard a fellow say so.
But never mind, the Welshman got it planted
Where it will trouble us a thousand years.
Each age will have to reconsider it."

Thus also the doctrine of human equality rooted in the Biblical idea that all men, of all colors and all ethnic characteristics, are the descendants of one and the same man and woman, both of whom were created by the One just and merciful God, can never be eradicated from the conscience of men. It will remain as a spiritual goad, giving neither rest nor peace to man until the ethical truth it teaches has been fully embodied in human society.

THE INVIOLABILITY OF THE INDIVIDUAL

This insistence upon the essential indivisibility of the human race has a most important bearing on yet another problem of democratic society. For there is an inescapable intellectual dilemma at the heart of the democratic process. On the one hand, the written Constitution guarantees certain rights to the individual citizen. On the other hand, the will of the majority must ultimately prevail. The Constitution itself may be amended without the unanimous consent of all the citizens. History and daily life have repeatedly demonstrated that the tyranny of the majority can be as ruthless as that of any despot.

By means of the first ten amendments to our Constitution, and by subsequent legislation, we have done much to protect the rights of the individual against the encroachments of the majority. But important as this legislative protection is, it is not enough. The effectiveness of the law ultimately depends upon what is in the minds and hearts of men, and the rights of the individual must be buttressed not only by legal statutes but by appropriate ideas and convictions, systematically inculcated from early childhood.

The Biblical-Rabbinic principle of the essential indivisibility of the human race implies not only that men cannot be divided on the basis of biological differences, but that, except for the most indispensable administrative purposes, men cannot be divided into minorities and majorities, with the minority subjected in all matters to the will of the majority. Before our Creator, the dignity and worth of human souls do not depend upon any mathematical relationships which may exist at one time or another. The will of any number of souls cannot give them the right to violate the dignity and the rights of any one soul. Indeed, the destruction of one soul is viewed as equal in tragedy and sinfulness to the destruction of the whole world. The Talmud provides that a witness testifying in a capital case is to be admonished in the following words:

> For this reason a single man was created: to teach you that if one destroys a single person, Scripture imputes it to him as though he had destroyed the whole (population of the) world, and if he saves the life of a single person, Scripture imputes it to him as though he had saved the whole world (Mishnah Sanhedrin 4:5).[2a]

Nor is this mere rhetoric. It is, I believe, the metaphysical basis for the Biblical prohibition of human sacrifice. A majority, be it ever so large, is no more justified in sacrificing an innocent person in its behalf than an individual is. The legal formulation of this attitude may help to clarify it. Jewish law prohibits a beleaguered city from delivering to the enemy even one of its innocent inhabitants, chosen by lot or arbitrarily, in order to secure its own relief.[3]

The full implications of this attitude for our own day are obvious. Tyrannies, whether of the right or of the left, have invoked the principle of the greatest good for the greatest number to justify their wanton destruction of individuals and groups who sinned only in being different from the majority, racially or religiously or even only economically. We shall disregard for the time being the absolute impossibility of proving that the present or future happiness of any group is advanced by the annihilation of individuals who differ from the majority in ethnic origin or religious belief. But even assuming that this could be proved, the Biblical-Rabbinic doctrine of man would nevertheless condemn the act, because that doctrine rejects the division of mankind into majorities and minorities, and rejects the notion that the world is the exclusive possession of the majority. The world belongs to each individual just as much as it belongs to all the rest of mankind. No order of society can characterize itself as democratic if it does not ceaselessly strive to incorporate this principle to the greatest possible extent into its administrative apparatus.

French civilization never showed itself to better advantage than when it produced men who rose to the defense of Dreyfus, even though the ruling clique and many others deemed his condemnation to be necessary to safeguard the honor of the army and the stability of the state. The "finest hour" of English culture and civilization was distinguished not only by the heroic physical defense of hearth and home against the Nazis, but by the treatment accorded to conscientious objectors at a time when the very existence of the nation was at stake.

This principle, moreover, applies not only to matters affecting the physical life of an individual. As we advance in our understanding of life, we recognize that violence to a man's mind because of his honest convictions, is as reprehensible as violence to his body because of the accidents of his birth. For the differences in men's opinions—like the differences in their physical appearances—in the Biblical-Rabbinic tradition, are not due to the accidental, meaningless formations of atoms. Nor are they to be interpreted as indicative of an implied hierarchal order among men. They are rather revelations of the infinite power and glory of the Creator. Adam was created alone, the Rabbis teach, in order to reveal to us the greatness of the Almighty, blessed be His name.

> For man, in minting coins, makes one mold, and every coin minted in that mold is an exact replica of all the others. Whereas the Almighty made one mold—Adam—and formed all men in that mold; nevertheless, no one of them is exactly like another (Sanhedrin 37a).

Nor is one man different from all others merely in physical appearance. The Rabbis have formulated a blessing that is to be recited when one sees a large crowd of people to express the sense of awe and wonder at the fact that "just as men's faces differ one from the other so do their opinions differ one from the other. Each one has his own mind. . . ." Hence Moses in asking for the appointment of a successor pleads with God. "You know that there are no two among your children who think alike . . . hence I beg of you appoint a leader for them who will bear with each one of them." That is why Moses in this instance addresses the Lord as "the God of the *spirits* of all flesh" (Numbers 27:16).[4] Just as men, inevitably and *by divine purpose,* differ one from the other in their physical appearance, so too, the Rabbis say, do they inevitably and *by divine purpose* differ in their mental attitudes and outlooks. Any attempt to eliminate or suppress these spiritual differences is both sinful and futile, for it runs counter to the will of God.

Honest differences of opinion and biological differences of appearance are not, therefore, merely to be tolerated. They are to be respected as the inviolable revelation of God's greatness. Therein lies the ultimate rationalization of the basic democratic freedoms of speech and of the press. Milton might have had this in mind when he wrote his historic plea for the freedom of the press:

> Books are not absolutely dead things, but do contain a potency of life in them to be as active as that soul whose progeny they are; nay, they do preserve as in a vial the purest efficacy and extraction of that living intellect that bred them . . . as good almost to kill a man as kill a good book. . . . Who kills a man, kills a reasonable creature, God's image, but he who destroys a good book, kills the image of God, as it were, in the eye.[5]

Though the concepts of the indivisibility of man and the inviolability of each individual man are indispensable to the complete implementation of the democratic ideal, they might well have become the metaphysical basis for a doctrine of anarchism and social chaos, had they not been counterbalanced by the Biblical-Rabbinic concepts of man's responsibility and man's true glory.

"FOR MY SAKE THE WORLD WAS CREATED"

The Rabbis place the destiny of the whole universe literally in the power of every single individual. Because God created only one man and not a hundred million, and because no two descendants of Adam are exactly alike, the Rabbis conclude that it is incumbent upon each one of us to say "For my sake the world was created" (Sanhedrin 37a). Adam was the crown of creation. All that preceded him found ultimate meaning and justification in him, only *one* man. Each one of us is, as it were, Adam, who represents the end-purpose of all creation. So exalted is the Rabbinic view of the individual's status in the universe that it places upon each one of us the awesome responsibility of justifying God in creating the world, for even if only one human being lives up fully to his potentialities as a creature made in the image of God, God's wisdom and mercy in creating the world are vindicated.

But that is not all. The Rabbis maintain that in a very real sense the destiny of the universe may be determined by every single individual. This Rabbinic conception of the power latent in each one of us to affect all the rest of us for good or evil, extravagantly unrealistic as it may have appeared before the dawn of the age of nuclear fission, is now becoming a self-evident truism. Indeed, it is the vast power now available to one man or to a handful of men that is the sword of Damocles suspended precariously above mankind. However, the Rabbis did not need the nuclear age to corroborate their conviction. For physical power, no matter how great, is never as great as the power that the spirit can wield. The Rabbis never wavered in their conviction that the ultimate arbiter in the affairs of man is the divine spirit which moves in him and through him. "Not by might and not by power but by My spirit, saith the Lord" (Zechariah 4:6). Rabbinic tradition created the well-known legend that the universe is sustained by thirty-six righteous men who are to be found in every generation among the humble and the meek.[6]

Moreover, we cannot avoid wielding this spiritual power which dwells within every one of us, whether for good or for evil. Willingly or unwillingly, by what we do or fail to do, we make our contribution to the sum total of good or evil in the world. Hence, willingly or unwillingly, we bear direct responsibility not only for our own individual fate, but also for the fate of the universe. An active awareness of this awful sense of individual responsibility, not merely for one's own destiny but for the destiny of all of creation, must inform every deed regardless of how insignificant we may deem it. Any one deed, the Rabbis say, may determine the fate of the whole universe, for its existence depends upon the preponderance of the good over the evil in it. Therefore, the Rabbis admonish us always to act as if the good and the evil were in exact balance, and as if the next deed which any one of us performs might weight the balance in one direction or the other. If it is a good deed it will weight the scales to the side of merit and save the world, and if it is an evil deed it may condemn the world to destruction (Kiddushin 40b).

It is this sense of "awesome responsibility" for every act, that underlies the imposing structure of what is usually referred to as Rabbinic "legalism," a structure which may appear hopelessly bewildering and unbearably oppressive to the outsider. The Rabbis, as artists of the ethical life, never wearied in their search for the right act, even as the poet never wearies in his search for the correct word, or the artist for the appropriate stroke of the brush.

Nothing is more ancient or more universal than the tendency to reject responsibility not only for the evil that may befall others, but even for the ill that befalls us. We always blame God or nature, or another creature. The Bible (Genesis 3:12) attributes this weakness to the first man. Perhaps many of the woes of our generation can be attributed in large measure to the fact that the sense of personal responsibility which was at the root of many of the phenomenal triumphs of Western civilization, has for some time now been systematically undermined. This has been done by sociologists who tended to shift all blame from the individual to his environment; by psychologists who have pictured man as the plaything of dark powers inhabiting his subconscious; by the phenomenal and blessed advances in medical science resulting in an enormous increase in population, so that it is very difficult even for a member of a politically democratic society to feel that he counts; by philosophies of government that set up the state as the final arbiter of right and wrong and the ultimate master to whom all are subservient; and by dual ethical systems that differentiate between what is appropriate to actions performed by the individual as an individual, and by the same individual when he acts as the head of a state, a business corporation, or any other group.

There is no problem more basic to the successful functioning of any democratic society, and hence to the future of mankind, than the problem of the responsibility that each individual is to bear for that future. Unless men develop a keen sense of awareness of their individual responsibility in whatever role they be cast, no organizational structure, no matter how well conceived, nor how universal in scope, will function effectively. For all organizations must be run by individuals; and organizational machinery, however well-conceived and skillfully set up, cannot compensate for failure of the sense of responsibility on the part of those who administer it.

The high point of the religious calendar in Judaism—the ten day period starting with Rosh Hashanah and ending with Yom Kippur—is devoted to nurturing in its adherents this concept of man as inescapably responsible. He cannot avoid the consequences of his acts, either for himself or for mankind. The belief in life after death, in some kind of experience beyond the grave, is motivated in part by the need to be sure that there is no ultimate escape from the consequences of one's acts. In a passage of the *Ethics of the Fathers* (4:29) man is admonished:

> Let not your evil impulse beguile you to believe that the grave will prove to be a refuge for you. For despite your will you were conceived, despite your will you were born, you live, and you will die, and despite your will you shall be called upon to *give an accounting* before the King of Kings, the Holy One, blessed be He.

Democracy needs as an indispensable ally this sense of responsibility which Judaism seeks to inculcate in its adherents, a responsibility which is and should be ours, not merely as employees in a business establishment, nor as servants of the state, but as citizens of the world, upon whose thoughts and acts the fate of the *universe* depends.

Moreover, Judaism spelled out in considerable detail the exact nature of that responsibility for Jew and non-Jew alike. The responsibilities of the Jew are spelled out for him in the Torah, particularly in the five books of Moses and their commentaries. The Rabbis also find formulated in the Torah the basic responsibilities of the non-Jew. They consist of the Seven Laws for the Descendants of Noah.[7] This concept of the Seven Laws of the Descendants of Noah is of more than parochial or academic interest. It helped solve a very real ethical dilemma for Judaism, and may point a way out of an ethical dilemma for our own day as well.

The fellowship of Judaism, as is well known, is open to everyone, regardless of the accident of birth.[8] But Judaism never considered itself the exclusive path to salvation. The Rabbis were not insensible to the human goodness prevailing outside their own ranks, or to the human wickedness within their own ranks. They recognized the existence of "righteous men" among all people of the earth. Authoritative Rabbinic teaching has always maintained that these "righteous among all men have a share in the world to come."[9] Who are these righteous? They are those who obey the Seven Laws enjoined by God on the descendants of Noah forbidding idolatry, blasphemy, murder, adultery and incest, robbery, and cruelty to animals, and enjoining the establishment of courts of justice. To the extent that one accepts these laws as divinely ordained and obeys them does he become worthy to be classified among the righteous.[10]

MAN'S TRUE GLORY

In the final analysis, what can or should motivate one to want to be among the righteous? What is the ultimate rationale for treating our fellow men as equals, for believing in the sanctity of the individual as a physical and spiritual entity, and for acting on the conviction that the destiny of the universe may well be determined by what any one of us does? The answer most frequently given is that the democratic ideal is the response made by man's enlightened self-interest to the situation in which he finds himself. No individual can act wholly in accordance with his own whims or wishes. The whims and wishes of other individuals are as real and powerful as his. If men do not learn to "live and let live," to curb their own desires when they conflict with the desires of other men and to arrive by consensus at an equitable distribution of rights and privileges, human life will become a nightmare for everyone. There can be no doubt that the concept of "enlightened self-interest" has been a very powerful ally of the democratic ideal, but the history of mankind proves beyond a shadow of doubt that it is not adequate to serve as the ultimate cornerstone of a truly democratic society. For in the final analysis everything depends upon what an individual or a people conceive their "self-interest" to be. Would the "self-interest" of Europeans, or of the White Man, have been better served had he granted to the American Indian the same right to determine who should enter his territory as the White Man claimed for himself? Would the self-interest of the United States have been better served had the Mexican War never taken place and had we not forcibly annexed the whole of our southwest area? Enlightened self-interest failed to abolish slavery without a Civil War, to grant equal civil rights to Negroes without violent agitation, nor did it win equality of treatment for native Africans in the Union of South Africa or for the Jews in Nazi-dominated countries.

Hence, to assume that the democratic ideal can best be advanced by the concept of enlightened self-interest is not only to court frustration but even to encourage the very opposite of what is sought. For "self-interest," no matter how enlightened, tends inevitably to nurture self-centeredness. It dwells primarily upon one's rights rather than upon one's duties, and becomes the final standard for judging the rightness or goodness of an act.

The concept of self-interest can become a basis of the democratic ideal only if it is rooted in an adequate concept of the self. What in the final analysis is the self? What in essence is man and what is his true self-interest? The answer to this question involves a response to one of man's basic instincts, namely the need for status. Man has an instinctive need to think well of himself, to "glory" in his endowments and achievements. Men have sacrificed life itself in order to achieve in their own eyes and in the eyes of others what they believed to be honorable status.

What is the honorable status appropriate to man? Wherein is man's true glory to be achieved? In the answer given by the Biblical-Rabbinic tradition to these questions we find the ultimate rationale of the democratic ideal as it applies not only to the areas of human life subject to government, but also to those human relationships which are beyond the scope of government or of any other social agency.

There are many passages which one might quote from both Rabbinic and Biblical sources which define for man the nature of his true glory. The one that I have always found most meaningful is the one upon which Maimonides bases the homily which concludes his *Guide for the Perplexed.* It is the passage from the book of Jeremiah wherein the prophet proclaims:

> Let not the wise man glory in his wisdom,
> Neither let the mighty man glory in his might;
> Let not the rich man glory in his riches;
> But let him that glorieth, glory in this,
> That he understandeth and knoweth Me,
> That I am the Lord Who performeth acts of loving-kindness,
> Justice and righteousness, in the earth.
> For in these things I delight, saith the Lord (9:22–23).

In the first chapter of Genesis, Scripture speaks of man as having been created in the image of God. This is man's glory and distinction, for therein is he differentiated from all other creatures. But Scripture does not there specify how that "image" is reflected in man. Man is created God-like. But how is that God-likeness made evident? The prophet answers the question by saying that man's glory consists in the knowledge that God "delights" in performing acts of loving-kindness, justice and righteousness in the world. Man has been endowed by God not only with the ability to *know* that God delights in these acts, but also with the power to perform such acts himself and to experience the delight that God takes in the performance of such acts.

The prophet knows the spurious status symbols that men have created for themselves—the symbols of wealth, might and human wisdom. They do not represent man's true glory, nor do they symbolize the noblest status attainable by man. Only acts of loving-kindness, justice and righteousness crown man with true glory; only they endow him with status appropriate to his true nature.

If, then, the democratic ideal is to find its noblest fulfillment in human society, we must nurture among men a conception of themselves which will in the first place restrain them from committing "inhumanities" to their fellow men, not because their fellow men have rights, but because in acting unjustly and unkindly they dim their own glory and reduce their own status. Negro slavery was wrong, not only because the Negro had inalienable rights, but because it lowered our conception of what being an American meant. Those who advocated the abolition of Negro slavery on the basis that the Negro was actually or potentially the equal of the white man were performing a useful service; but they were not touching the heart of the matter. For the heart of the matter consisted, not in what we thought of the spiritual and intellectual capacities of the Negro, but rather what we thought regarding the character and distinction of Americanism.

But we must not stop there. Man's conception of himself must be such as to nurture in him the conviction that the glory of his life consists not only in the great privileges and opportunities God has bestowed upon him but even more so in the responsibilities which these privileges and opportunities place upon him; not in acting always as if he were God's pampered favorite but in being ever conscious of his duty to be God's obedient and, when necessary, even His suffering servant.

The democratic ideal has a long, difficult path to traverse before it shall have been realized in society. The universe of moral and ethical discourse which has been developed within the framework of the Biblical-Rabbinic tradition, if properly utilized, can be the democratic ideal's great stay and ally and help it traverse that long path more easily and rapidly.

CHAPTER V

Some of Judaism's Eternally Relevant Contributions to Civilization[1]

The aim of this paper is expressed as precisely as possible in its title. It is not our purpose to present *all* of the contributions of Judaism to civilization. Nor shall we attempt an exhaustive treatment of those contributions which shall here be presented.

We shall not be concerned with the contributions of individual Jews, nor even of the Jewish people as such, but rather with the contributions of *Judaism* to civilization. Judaism came into being through the medium of the Jewish people, but not everything which Jews did became part of Judaism. Nor were Jews as individuals or as communities always themselves loyal to, or guided by, Judaism. From the days of the prophets to our own day, Jews had to be admonished regarding their own backslidings from Judaism.

Any number of attempts have been made to define Judaism. No one of them has been successful. We shall not offer another definition of it. We shall merely indicate that the teachings, doctrines, ideas, and ideals of Judaism are found primarily in the books of the Bible, the Prayer Book and in that vast ocean of literature, the Talmud. Judaism's contributions to human civilization are formulated in these writings.

We shall accept as a contribution to civilization anything which helps to make the life of human beings physically more pleasant, esthetically more beautiful, spiritually more purposeful, and ethically more just and merciful.

Why should we be interested in Judaism's contribution to civilization? Is it because we want to prove the superiority of Jews over other peoples? That proposition can not be proved. Is it in order to justify our right to existence as a people? No human group, nor any other of God's creatures, has to justify its existence!

I am interested in Judaism's contributions to human civilization only because I find that as a human being they have a supreme relevance to my attitude towards the universe and my fellow-men and to my estimate of my own position as one of the infinite number of living creatures upon this earth. I feel that they have made a vital difference in my own behavior as a human being. I know that they have made vital differences in the behavior of an untold number of human beings both in the past and in the present. And I believe that those differences were and are not only for my good or that of the Jews, but for the good of all mankind.

These contributions have something to tell me—as a Jew—of the duties and obligations which my historic heritage places upon me, which I may choose to accept or reject. They are indispensable to me as guides in my relations to my Jewish ancestors, contemporaries and posterity. Insofar, therefore, as I desire to be something more than an animal that eats, plays and reproduces, these contributions have an immediate relevance to me both as man and Jew.

Moreover, as far as my knowledge and understanding can instruct me, I believe that these contributions are eternally relevant. I believe Jews and non-Jews alike, insofar as they will retain the human qualities that characterize them today, will find these contributions as immediately relevant to them and their problems a thousand generations from today as they are today.

THE TOOLS MAN USED TO BUILD HIS CIVILIZATION

Man is the only creature on earth who makes and uses tools. Human civilization, as we know it, is the product of man's use of tools.

Man's tools are essentially of two kinds:

1. *The Physical Tools* are those made of stone, wood, metal or some other materials. They are tools which man creates and manipulates with his hands.

2. *The Non-Physical Tools* are those which are neither made nor manipulated by human hands. Chief among these tools is human speech. Words are man's most useful tool, far more useful and indispensable to him than any of the tools his hands create or manipulate, for without language, human society, as we know it, would not be possible.

But among the words of human speech some are more important than others. The importance of a tool depends upon the number and the significance of the things that can be done with it. The most important words in any language are those that stand for large, comprehensive ideas, because these ideas are the tools by means of which we understand and give some meaning to our lives upon this earth. Among all of men's ideas, those whereby we judge what is right and what is wrong, what is bad and what is good, are the most important to us, for it is the implementation of these ideas that constitutes our superiority to the beast.

Judaism made no significant contributions to human civilization by creating any of the more important physical tools. Individual Jews may have been inventive in that area also. But as a group we did not distinguish ourselves by creating the tools that helped man to increase his food supply, or to protect himself, or to travel more rapidly from place to place, or to communicate one with another over great distances. But through Judaism and its spiritual offsprings, Christianity and Islam, there came into the lives of hundreds of millions of people some of those spiritual and intellectual ideas, concepts and values which alone can lead mankind out of its present morass of suspicions, hates and wars into the broad places of peace, freedom and justice. Through Judaism, Western man came to know the ideals and ideas that were and are the most powerful tools for social progress ever known to man. We shall touch upon some of them as they impinged upon three areas of human thought, namely:

(1) The basic character of the universe.
(2) The nature of man.
(3) The proper goals of life for the individual.

We shall indicate briefly the bearing the ideas and ideals of Judaism have upon our actions and the reasons why they remain to this day vital and relevant to Jew and non-Jew alike.

Indeed, in each one of the above-mentioned three areas there was a time in human history when Judaism stood alone against the whole world of paganism and idolatry. Today it has, thank God, many allies at its side. But it continues to hold a very important sector of the battle line.

THE BASIC CHARACTER OF THE UNIVERSE

Man looks out at the universe about him and whether he wants to or not he must pass some kind of judgment upon it. His mind restlessly searches for some answer to the question: "What is the nature of the universe?" That is still the most important question for man to answer. We have discarded many answers suggested by previous generations. We no longer look upon the universe as the habitation of demonic, whimsical powers that are to be appeased, or as the arena within which two or more hostile powers carry on an endless struggle for supremacy with man as the chief victim of their combats. But Judaism stood alone for centuries against all of these primitive conceptions of the universe. Its own answer was given in the incomparably majestic opening sentence of the Bible: "In the beginning, God created heaven and earth." The universe was created by one God, and that one God was just and merciful. Man is not surrounded by an infinite number of ruthless, unpredictable, irascible demons, nor by jealous, greedy, power-hungry gods. He is rather the creature of a loving, righteous Creator, Who, "in His mercy gives light to the earth and those that dwell thereon, and in His goodness daily continuously renews the work of creation" (The Daily Morning Service).

To look out upon the universe and see it as the handiwork of evil spirits or of gods dominated by all of the moral weaknesses of men, is to grasp the universe with a spiritual and mental tool which, like the broken reed, not only gives no support but pierces the palm of him who would lean upon it (Isaiah 36:6). Such a mental tool could not and did not serve men in their search for justice, nor in their longing for peace.

While by and large Western man no longer includes this view of the universe in his conscious attitudes and thoughts, vestiges of it are easily identified in the myriad superstitions that still haunt him, in his continued recourse to fortune-telling and soothsaying, to knocking on wood and crossing fingers.

This pagan and idolatrous view of the universe has in our day been superseded by "philosophic" atheism or "scientific" purposelessness. The two are morally and religiously synonymous. Bertrand Russell formulated this position a generation ago in his now classic essay "A Free Man's Worship."[2] "Such in outline, but even more purposeless, more void of meaning, is the world which Science presents for our belief. . . . Blind to good and evil, reckless of destruction, omnipotent matter rolls on its relentless way. . . ."

In our own day, W. T. Stace has restated the same thesis even more forcefully. With terrifying clarity he points to the inevitable conclusions that followed upon the widespread acceptance of this assumption of a godless, purposeless universe. "Along with the ruin of the religious vision there went the ruin of moral principles and indeed of all values. If there is a cosmic purpose, if there is in the nature of things a drive towards goodness, then our moral systems will derive their validity from this. But if our moral rules do not proceed from something outside us in the nature of the universe—whether we say God or simply the universe itself—then they must be our own inventions. Thus it came to be believed that moral rules must be merely an expression of our own likes and dislikes. But likes and dislikes are notoriously variable. What pleases one man, people, or culture displeases another. Therefore morals are wholly relative. . . . The widespread belief in 'ethical relativity' among philosophers, psychologists, ethnologists, and sociologists is the theoretical counterpart of the repudiation of principle which we see all around us, especially in international affairs, the field in which morals have always had the weakest foothold. No one any longer effectively believes in moral principles. . . . This is the inevitable consequence of the doctrine of ethical relativity, which in turn is the inevitable consequence of believing in a purposeless world."[3] It is the *inevitable* and not merely the possible consequence.

Ideas are tools for the fashioning of personal lives and human societies. A godless world implies a purposeless world. A purposeless world implies a world whose ultimate arbiter is sheer physical force. Hence, atheistic philosophies such as Marxist-Leninist Communism, Italian Fascism and German Nazism, when applied to the practical task of founding human societies, had of necessity to depend primarily upon the ruthless application of maximum tyranny, force and violence. If blind, indifferent, amoral matter is the core and essence of the universe, its source and its goal, then hesitation to use force to the limit is naught but either stupid statesmanship or squeamish sentimentality.

The fathers of the American Revolution used other spiritual tools with which to fashion their great adventure in independence. They did not set their activities in a purposeless, morally indifferent world. They acted out of a faith that certain truths were self-evident, namely, that a Creator who was obviously just and kind brought the universe into being, for He created all men equal and endowed them with certain inalienable rights such as life, liberty and the pursuit of happiness. The opening sentences of the American Declaration of Independence would be utter nonsense to a pagan idolater even as it is to a modern Communist, Fascist and Nazi, and as it must be to a logically consistent modern philosopher-scientist of the Russell school.

Inscribed on the walls of the majestic Lincoln Memorial in Washington are the two greatest utterances of any statesman of the nineteenth century: the Gettysburg Address and the Second Inaugural. Within the framework of a purposeless universe, both of these addresses make no sense. The Gettysburg Address relates the Civil War to the proposition that all men are created equal. The war is seen as something more than merely a clash of blind forces. It is viewed rather as another phase of the endless self-assertion of the spirit of liberty and equality which are of the very essence of the universe, of God's self-revelation in history.

The Second Inaugural, reading almost like a chapter out of Isaiah, grapples with the problem that touched every heart and hearthstone in the land. Why had all this slaughter come upon the country? Why had the country been gripped for such an abnormally long time by this madness to shed its own blood? In a purposeless, morally indifferent universe, the very question itself is a mockery. No one asks reasons for the actions of forces devoid of reason. Where life has no purpose, death is no tragedy.

The American Civil War became more than a mere blood

bath because of the meaning Lincoln gave to it by means of the intellectual and spiritual tools derived from the Jewish tradition. Lincoln was far too wise and humble a man to believe, or to try to give the impression, that he knew for a certainty the whole of the answer. But he could get some glimmer of light and hope only by applying to the tragedy that engulfed America, the principle that a just God was operating in the affairs of men. Hence Lincoln suggested that "if God wills that it [the war] continue, until all the wealth piled up by the bondman's two hundred and fifty years of unrequited toil shall be sunk, and until every drop of blood drawn with the lash, shall be paid by another drawn with the sword, as was said three thousand years ago, so still it must be said 'the judgments of the Lord, are true and righteous altogether' [Psalms 19:10]."[4] It was not a matter of revenge but of elementary justice. A society cannot go on indefinitely to live on unrequited toil and by the shedding of innocent blood. Such a human order, if it could continue with impunity indefinitely, would be the most irrefutable proof of a godless and therefore an immoral universe.

Economists, sociologists and historians have given their reasons for the Civil War and its violent destructiveness. America wisely chose to inscribe upon the walls of its great national shrine, the interpretation that Lincoln gave to it with the aid of the concepts derived from the Jewish tradition. To justify God is ever the path not only of saintliness, but of morality and hope. To justify man is the path to spiritual and, ultimately and inevitably also, to physical death for society. Perhaps if there had arisen in Europe, after the first World War, a statesman of the stature of Lincoln who would have told the truth to Europe as Lincoln did to America, namely that the twentieth century is paying the price for Europe's ruthless imperialism of four hundred years, there might be greater hope for the future of Europe today.

If the universe, as a whole, has no meaning then certainly

human history can have no meaning, no goal towards which it should strive to move, no purpose it should seek to achieve. This point of view, which was well-nigh universal in antiquity, found expression in the Bible in the well-known passage in Ecclesiastes (1:2,9): "Vanity of vanities, saith Koheleth; vanity of vanities, all is vanity. . . . That which hath been is that which shall be, And that which hath been done is that which shall be done; And there is nothing new under the sun."

But Judaism does not view the universe as a meaningless accident, nor human history as a monotonous, purposeless cycle. There is a goal towards which human life can successfully strive. That goal was envisioned some twenty-seven hundred years ago. "And it shall come to pass in the end of days. . . . And they shall beat their swords into plowshares, And their spears into pruning-hooks; Nation shall not lift up sword against nation, Neither shall they learn war any more" (Isaiah 2:2,4). "And the wolf shall dwell with the lamb, And the leopard shall lie down with the kid; And the calf and the young lion and the fatling together; And a little child shall lead them. . . . They shall not hurt nor destroy In all My holy mountain; For the earth shall be full of the knowledge of the Lord, As the waters cover the sea" (Isaiah 11:6,9).

This vision of a Messianic age of universal peace has become one of mankind's most cherished hopes. But we too frequently delude ourselves into thinking that universal peace is an ideal either universally approved or generally believed feasible. The two attitudes are in a way different sides of the same coin. To believe that universal peace is inherently not feasible is to declare that the very nature of the universe and of man makes war inevitable. And that which the nature of the universe makes inevitable must in the final analysis be declared desirable.

That is what has actually happened. Not only has universal peace been rejected by respected philosophers as an intrinsically impracticable ideal, it has also been adjudged by them as ethically undesirable. No one has stated the case in behalf of war more persuasively or more authoritatively than the man whom no less a philosophic critic than Morris Raphael Cohen has called "the greatest philosopher of the nineteenth century," Georg Wilhelm Friedrich Hegel.[5] He maintains that "War is not to be looked upon as an absolute evil and a purely external accident which has its accidental cause in whatever it may be, in the passions of the rulers, or of the nations, in injustices etc. . . . War has the higher meaning that through it . . . the ethical health of nations is maintained . . . just as the motion of the winds keep the sea from the foulness which a constant calm could produce—so war prevents a corruption of nations which a perpetual, let alone an eternal peace would produce."[6]

The intensification of the horrors of war may make men hesitate longer before plunging into it, but it will not necessarily abolish it. The fear of death has never kept men from courting it in the hope of thus gaining honor, finding adventure, or enacting what they believed to be grandiose or noble roles. We were ourselves witnesses to the grave evils suffered by the most "advanced" and "civilized" peoples of the earth because of the megalomaniacal visions of men determined either to usher in an egalitarian utopia in their day or to place all of mankind under the heels of a "superrace" of men. In both instances large numbers of all classes and walks of society zealously followed their leaders, willingly accepting untold suffering and even death itself.

Universal peace as a supreme positive value, and not merely as the period of "moral stagnation" between wars, is an ideal we have not as yet really made our own. Nor should we close our eyes to the fact that few of the world's great philosophers, ancient or modern, have set universal peace as the ultimate and highest goal of the moral life of man. The prophets of Israel were the first to conceive of it, not merely as a desirable but as an altogether possible goal. They were the first to maintain that human life does not of necessity have to be a futile cycle of rise and fall, of growth and decay. It can move forward. It does have an achievable goal.

The faith that a Messianic age may be ushered in was the most important single faith for the preservation of Israel in the past. It continues to be equally indispensable for any thoughtful Jew today. For if human history is but a monotonously repetitious cycle, then the building of the third Jewish commonwealth is essentially a wasted effort for it too will meet the inescapable fate of the previous Jewish commonwealths. And if history always repeats itself, then our fate in America will—as we are often told—be but the fate of previous Jewish communities in Babylon and Spain, Poland and Germany.

Nor is it only as a Jew that I am affected by this idea. I must meet it and deal with it as an American and as a human being. If history is only an endless cycle, then those Americans who believe that the next century should be made the "American Century" are right. English world hegemony which lasted about a century and a half is now at an end, even as the previous Spanish and French hegemonies have ended. For the next century or two it is going to be either America's or Russia's turn. That kind of thinking has its own foreign policy for America and its own plans for internal American policy. But if as an American and as a man I do not believe that history must repeat itself; if, on the contrary, I believe that it need not and should not repeat itself, I can work with profounder fervor and firmer faith for the establishment of a world in which no one nation exercises hegemony, but rather a world in which a United Nations assures for all an equal opportunity to enjoy the blessings of peace and freedom.

As a Jew and as a man, therefore, I find the concepts of a universe created and governed by a just and merciful Creator, and of human history having a possible goal towards which to move, to be indispensable tools to my thinking about the future. In a purposeless, amoral universe, with its senseless cycle of human history, I can see no sense in Jewish survival nor in making any sacrificial efforts to assure that survival. As a human being I can see no reason why in a universe other than one conceived by Judaism some version of the philosophy of "Eat and drink, for tomorrow we die" (Isaiah 22:13) should not be gladly embraced by all wise men.

The truth of the matter seems to be that Western civilization is still largely pagan at heart, with its young and immature scientific notions serving as rationalizations of its untamed impulses. For how else can one explain the fact that twice in one generation the culturally most advanced nations of the world consumed their substance in senseless mutual slaughter, and scientists calmly went about the task of exterminating millions of innocent men, women and children, non-Jews as well as Jews?

I find therefore that the concepts of a universe created by a just and merciful God and a goal-oriented human history are still vitally relevant to me as a Jew and as a human being in the twentieth century. Nor can I envision the day when mankind will outgrow the need for these mental and spiritual tools.

THE NATURE OF MAN

Equally important to the progress of civilization has been Judaism's concept of the nature of man. On that question also Judaism "stood on one side and the rest of the world on the other." "All modern views of human nature," says Reinhold Niebuhr, "are adaptations, transformations and varying compounds of primarily two distinctive views of man: (a) the view of classical antiquity, that is of the Graeco-Roman world, and (b) the Biblical view."[7] Plato, Aristotle and the Stoics, whose conceptions of the nature of man are among the noblest ever conceived, viewed man as a composite of an immortal soul imprisoned in a short-lived body. The body was the seat and source of physical decadence and moral corruption; the soul, the embodiment of the eternal and the pure. Modern biologists find no evidence of the existence of the soul. They reject the dualistic concept of the nature of man, and make the mind or the intellect little more than another one of the endowments which the blind evolutionary forces of nature bestowed upon man in his struggle for existence. While it may appear to be different in character, its purpose and its origins are essentially the same as the purposes and origins of the eyes, the teeth or the nails. Like these, mind is but a tool of the body in its blind, intuitive urge for its self-preservation. Man, therefore, is essentially nothing but an animal. The Darwinian exposition of evolution and particularly that of many of his immediate followers "evolved what T. H. Huxley called 'The Gladiatorial Theory of existence' and concluded that the revolutionary ethic must be, first, every man for himself, then every tribe, every nation, every class and so on for itself in the 'struggle for existence.' "[8]

"Darwin did not invent the Machiavellian image that the world is the playground of the lion and the fox, but thousands discovered that he had transformed political science. Their own tendencies to act like lions and foxes thereby became irresistible 'laws of nature' and 'factors of progress,' while moral arguments against them were dubbed 'pre-scientific.' The only text they would heed was 'Go to the ant, thou sluggard,' because ants waged wars."[9]

It did not require all of modern man's detailed researches to discover that there is a relationship between man and the animal world around him. The law of the jungle that "might makes right" was defended "philosophically" and "scientifically" in all periods of human thought.[10] Nor was the Greek-philosophic, dualistic conception of man ever completely abandoned. Until comparatively recent times it was the accepted view of all branches of Christianity and found a ready welcome within Jewish thought as well.

But within Judaism it was confronted with a view of man which denied both the sharp distinction between body and soul, as well as the reduction of the soul or the mind to a mere function of the body. The Bible affirmed that despite man's manifold resemblances to the animals, he was in essence different because he was created in the "image of God." Whether this description of man implies an anthropomorphic conception of God or not, is for our immediate purposes of little moment. It certainly does imply a conception of man as a creature endowed with the qualities of his Creator, "knowing the difference between good and evil" (Genesis 3:22). In that, man was in essence different from all other of God's creatures. Though the Biblical-Rabbinic tradition did not completely resolve the problem of the relationship between body and soul, or between body and mind, it did in the main reject the conception of an irreconcilable antagonism between them, with the body being the source of all evil and the soul as the source of all good. The idea of reducing the soul or the mind to but another handmaiden of the body never as much as occurred to the teachers of Judaism. Nor did the conception of the body as the prison of the soul go unchallenged in Judaism.

It was the conception that man was made in the image of God which, I believe, was responsible for the staunch and successful resistance of what George Foot Moore so felicitously designated as Normative Judaism, to the alluring concept of the body as the jailer and the corrupter of the soul. Normative Judaism became the soil in which there developed an extraordinarily healthy attitude towards the body both as the host of the soul as well as its inseparable partner. The body was to be meticulously cared for because it was the seat of the soul,[10a] and since it could not function independently of the soul, it could not be held responsible for the sins committed by the human being. Thus there developed within Rabbinic Judaism an extraordinarily healthy attitude towards all the normal functionings of the human body. None of them was in essence evil, shameful or indecent.

True to the character of Rabbinic thought, the attitude towards the relationship between the body and the soul was formulated by the Rabbis not in philosophic propositions but in a parable. When, the Rabbis say, an individual will come before the Judgment Seat on High and will be asked why he sinned, the soul will say "I did not sin. I am pure. The body sinned." The body will say "I did not sin. I can make no decisions. The soul does that." Thereupon God will, so to speak, reenact the parable of the lame man, the blind man and the vineyard. "A man hired a blind man and a lame man to watch his vineyard. When he returned he found his grapes were gone. The lame man protested his innocence since he could not possibly have gotten around to the grapes. The blind man offered his blindness as proof of his innocence. The owner then placed the lame man upon the back of the blind man and demonstrated for them how they had both together committed the crime" (Sanhedrin 91b). Thus too are body and soul interrelated. They are not identical and one can not be reduced to the other, nor are they independent of one another. The essence of their interrelationship we do not know and most likely never shall know, but in its reality we have firm faith.

Secondly, the concept that man was created in the image of God fostered within Judaism the closely related concept of man as *shutafo shel ha-Kadosh Barukh Hu,* as "the co-worker of the Holy One blessed be He," in the work of completing and perfecting the universe. God did not complete the whole of the universe in every detail during "the six days of creation." Much remained for man to perfect. Thus the Rabbis teach that the world could not be perfected until the world will be as "full of the knowledge of the Lord as the waters cover the sea" (Isaiah 11:9). But in the achievement of that ultimate perfection, man has a role to play, not as a passive onlooker, but as an active participant. "Every judge who exercises his prerogatives honorably is, as it were, a partner of God in creating the world" (Shabbat 10a).

"Can man improve on God's work?" a pagan philosopher asked Rabbi Akiba in a discussion apparently involving the law of circumcision. "To be sure he can and he does," Rabbi Akiba responded (Midrash Tanhuma, *Tazria,* par. 5). "Do you eat wheat as God prepares it? Do you walk about dressed as God dressed you?" Every aspect of human life offers a myriad of examples to prove that man is God's partner in bringing to ever higher perfection His creative activities in the universe.

Finally, and perhaps most important of all, the concept of the absolute inviolability of the individual person, of his supreme significance not merely as a member of the human species, or of a particular nation, or of a particular group within the nation, but purely and simply as an individual, was rooted by Judaism in the proposition that man was created in God's image. Neither all of our philosophy nor all of our science have been able to provide us with an intellectually sound and spiritually persuasive reason for considering an individual's life sacred. That was provided for Western civilization by the Bible. The Bible declares murder to be the cardinal crime because man was made "in the image of God" (Genesis 9:6). And Rabbi Akiba declared that the murderer *mema'ayt et ha-demut*—diminished, as it were, the presence of the Divine in the world.[11]

Of the many roots that Judaism has supplied to democracy, none is more important than this: its unequivocal emphasis upon the supreme, inviolable sanctity of the individual. There is no passage in all of world literature which formulates that attitude as clearly, as forcefully and as movingly as the Rabbis formulated it in the midst of one of their supposedly dry, uninspiring, legalistic discussions on the court procedures for a case involving capital punishment. They record the manner in which the court is to admonish those who were to testify in such cases. After being reminded that they are not to testify on the basis of hearsay, but only on the basis of what they personally saw and heard, the witnesses were to be addressed as follows:[12]

"Know then that capital cases are not like monetary cases. In civil suits, one can make monetary retribution and thereby effect his atonement, but in capital cases a witness is held responsible not only for the blood of him against whom he testifies but also for the blood of all his [potential] descendants unto the end of time. For in the case of Cain, who killed his brother, it is written 'the voice of the bloods of thy brother cry unto Me' (Genesis 4:10). It is not written 'the blood of thy brother,' but 'the bloods of thy brother' to indicate that both his blood and the blood of his descendants is included. . . . For God created but one man to teach us that whosoever destroys a single soul,[13] guilt is imputed to him as though he had destroyed the whole world, and whosoever saves a single soul, merit is ascribed to him, as though he had preserved the whole world" (Sanhedrin 4:5).

Judaism's affirmation of the absolute sanctity of every one of the descendants of Adam, of the equality of all of them before the Lord, of their right to life, to justice and mercy, is the only adequate hypothesis for all that we associate with the ideals of political, social and economic democracy. I know no more satisfactory philosophy to undergird my faith in democracy than that offered to me by Judaism and I cannot foresee an age when democracy will be grounded in firmer spiritual soil.[14]

THE PROPER GOALS OF LIFE FOR THE INDIVIDUAL

We shall refer to but one more area of civilization to which Judaism has made eternally relevant contributions, namely that of setting before the individual the goals he should strive to achieve as a human being.

We shall not discuss the goals that have in all ages appealed most irresistibly to the average man, goals not set by him as a thinking, reflective creature, but as a creature moved by profound instincts, emotions and passions. Successful living in all ages—and, alas, in our age as well—was gauged by most people by the power over others that an individual exercised, either by virtue of his native physical strength, or his wisdom, or his wealth, or his social position. Power, in turn, was the highest good because by means of it man could satisfy his pride, his greed, his passions. He could command the means that made for mundane pleasures. The highest goal of life, therefore, was the acquisition of power.

To be sure, the philosophers of the Graeco-Roman world had visions of the good life that rose beyond that of mere power. Plato conceived of the attainment of a state of inner peace and harmony as man's highest good. To Aristotle, the good life was the life of intellectual contemplation achieved through the practice of moderation in all things. The Epicureans considered a wise enjoyment of pleasure, and the Stoics, a noble emotional detachment, as life's finest fruit. Judaism set the pursuit of justice and the practice of mercy as man's crowning achievements.

The test of the good life is not in terms of the power one exercises over his fellow men nor in one's ability to rise above all passions and to disengage himself completely—emotionally and intellectually—from involvement with his fellow men. On the contrary, the good life is impossible for Judaism without some commitment to one's fellows, and that commitment must be in terms of justice and mercy.

Justice and mercy are not passive principles calling upon us to do no harm to anyone. Nor are they to be activated only when one's own welfare is at stake. They are positive principles requiring an active allegiance for their own sake. In commenting on the verse "Seek peace and pursue it" (Psalms 34:15), the Rabbis note that all other commandments are to be observed only when the occasion offers itself. In the case of this commandment, we are enjoined to go forth and search out the occasion for its fulfillment.[15] We must do as Job claimed he had done: "I delivered the poor that cried, the fatherless also, that had none to help him. . . . I was eyes to the blind and feet was I to the lame. I was a father to the needy and the cause of him that I knew not I *searched out*" (Job 29:12, 15–16). Moses had set the pattern for us long before Job. Scripture relates that when Moses grew up, "he *went out* unto his brethren and contemplated their servitude" (Exodus 2:11). Moses, the greatest teacher of the Jewish people, was one who could not "mind his own business" when injustice was abroad.[16] Repeatedly he "searched out the cause of him he knew not."

Nor are we to remain emotionally uninvolved in the cares and suffering of our generation. God Himself is pictured in Scripture as being not merely detachedly concerned, but in actual travail, as it were, because of the suffering of His creatures. "In all their affliction, He was afflicted" (Isaiah 63:9).[17]

The prophet, Judaism's noblest and unique contribution to the galaxy of distinguished human personalities produced by mankind, is one who is most completely identified with the woes and sorrows of the world.[18] He, too, on occasion cries, "Oh that I were in the wilderness, in a lodging-place of wayfaring men, that I might leave my people, and go from them, for they are all adulterers, an assembly of treacherous men" (Jeremiah 9:1). However, the dominant mood of the prophet is one of infinite distress at the suffering and the evil that he sees about him. "For the hurt of the daughter of my people am I seized with anguish; I am black, appallment hath taken hold on me. . . . Oh that my head were waters and mine eyes a fountain of tears, that I might weep day and night for the slain of the daughter of my people" (Jeremiah 8:21, 23). The prophet was charged by the Lord with a mission that would make him "A man of strife and a man of contention to the whole earth," and one whom everyone would curse (Jeremiah 15:10). Judaism expects that each one of us be in a measure a prophet, "sticking his neck out," raising his voice whenever injustice shows its ugly countenance, thus "sanctifying God's name." The Rabbis point out that the Torah commands us in thirty-six different passages to practice mercy and justice toward the stranger.[19] A life that is not involved in some specific, identifiable manner with the problem of alleviating human suffering either by correcting patent injustices or supplying crying needs, is, from the viewpoint of Judaism, lacking the most important ingredient of the good life. Thus Judaism brought to mankind new goals for the personal life. Not power over others, but service to others; not the conquering hero, but the "suffering servant," were God's delight.[20]

Abraham was chosen by God not because he was to be the conqueror of the world, nor its greatest poet nor profoundest philosopher, but because he was going "to command his children and his household after him that they keep the way of the Lord, to do righteousness and justice" (Genesis 18:19). Literally hundreds of passages could be quoted almost at random from Biblical and Rabbinic literature that formulate succinctly these goals in an endless variety of expression but with uniform clarity of intent.

One could point to the Ten Commandments culminating in the admonition "Thou shalt not covet" (Exodus 20:14) or to the nineteenth chapter of the book of Leviticus, the chapter that to many is the greatest in all of Scripture, with its commandment (verse 18) "Love thy neighbor as thyself." One can point to Amos' cry, "Let justice roll down like the waters, and righteousness like a mighty river" (5:24), or Isaiah's plea to "seek justice, relieve the oppressed, judge the fatherless, plead for the widow" (1:17). Perhaps no prophetic passage is more frequently quoted as epitomizing the good life, than Micah's surpassingly beautiful statement, "It has been told thee O man what is good and what the Lord doth require of thee, only to do justly, to love mercy and to walk humbly with thy God" (6:8).[21]

Maxims, dicta, proverbs do not constitute civilization. But the spirit of a people and the character of a civilization are epitomized in less than a half-dozen concepts that dominate the thought and the aspiration of any given human society at any one time. "Life, Liberty and the Pursuit of Happiness," "Liberty, Equality, Fraternity," "Honor," "Gentleman," "Classless Society," "Success"—these words and a handful of others like them have destroyed and built civilizations. They create the mood of a society. Consciously or subconsciously, they direct the overt acts of the individuals who comprise that society and fashion their innermost being.

The goals set by Judaism for the individual human being have fashioned the lives of countless men and women throughout the centuries and millennia. These were the humble, unsung members of the race through whom mankind was constantly spiritually renewed. Such renewal is rapidly becoming long overdue for Western civilization. A very substantial number of the peoples of the West must accept for their personal lives the spiritual goals first set for man by Judaism, if Western civilization is to escape the abysmal collapse with which it appears to be imminently threatened.

CONCLUSION

These are but a few of Judaism's eternally relevant contributions to human civilization. Meditating upon them and striving ever to live in accordance with their teachings would help us understand why we have been able to triumph over unprecedented difficulties in the past and why we can hope to continue to live triumphantly in the future. This is so, not because we have had and will have common enemies, but rather because we have shared and will continue to share a common spiritual heritage at whose core is a philosophy of life which is applicable in and relevant to all climes and ages and which teaches us how best to serve ourselves and serve mankind by being loyal and understanding servants of God.

CHAPTER VI

The Multiplication of the Mitzvot[1]

INTRODUCTION

The most significant and pervasive concept used in Judaism to evaluate human action is Mitzvah.[2] An act designated as a Mitzvah is thereby given ultimate approbation. "The Holy One blessed be He, because He was minded to grant merit[3] to Israel, multiplied for them the Torah and the Mitzvot" (Makkot 3:16). This paper will concern itself with an inquiry into the history of the concept Mitzvah and into the process by which Mitzvot were multiplied, so that almost every non-sinful act could potentially be a Mitzvah.

THE TERM MITZVAH IN THE BIBLE

The term Mitzvah is the noun form of the Hebrew root *TzVH* which means "to command." This root in its various forms is among the most prevalent in the Bible, since it refers to one of the most common aspects of the ubiquitous relationship of superior to subordinate.[4] The term is used in reference to man as *mitzvat anashim* (Isaiah 29:13), "the commandment of men" or in reference to God as *mitzvat Ha-Shem* (Joshua 22:3), "the commandment of the Lord."

When the verb is used, its subject indicates the source of the command. In all the books of the Bible, with the exception of Proverbs and Ecclesiastes, the source of the Mitzvah is indicated also when the nominal forms are used. Only in these two books does the term Mitzvah stand alone as an abstract concept so that one cannot, from the context, determine its source.[5] Hence commentators, both modern and medieval, differ on whether it refers to a human or a divine Mitzvah. One thing is certain. The term Mitzvah in these books is a term of unqualified approbation. It is always associated with the admonition to hearken to Mitzvot and to obey them. It would seem that the reason why one is urged in Proverbs and Ecclesiastes to obey Mitzvot is to be found in the high virtue associated with obedience *per se,* whether it be obedience to God, to the king, to a parent, to a teacher, or to any other superior,[6] rather than in the substance of the act itself.

Wherever the term Mitzvah stands alone, the commentators seek its point of reference in the general context. But the context is never an unfailing guide. Thus the maxim "(a) commandment (Mitzvah) is a candle and (a) teaching (Torah) is a light" (Proverbs 6:23), is understood by Rashi as "certainly referring to the commandments of one's father and mother,"[7] though at first he interprets the verse as referring to "the commandments of the Torah." Ibn Ezra and Ralbag see it as a reference to the Torah only. Toy,[8] knowing that many interpret the verse in the light of the verses preceding it as referring to the commandments of one's parents, seems nevertheless to be quite certain that "the discourse here turns from parental instruction to the idea of instruction and law in general."

While in this instance the term Mitzvah may be interpreted in the light of the larger context in which the passage occurs, a later verse containing the term cannot thus be related to either what precedes or follows it. It is the maxim "The wise in heart will receive the (Mitzvot) commandments" (Proverbs 10:8).[9] Ibn Ezra interprets the verse as an admonition to the individual to hearken to what others teach him. One commentator explains it as a reference to "the commandments of the Torah *or* to the laws that society evolved."[10]

Ecclesiastes (8:5) is also of the opinion that "whoso keepeth the Mitzvah shall know no evil." Many commentators, basing themselves on the context, assume that the author refers to the royal command.[11] Barton questions that interpretation because "the word for command is usually applied to commands of Yahweh and the thought contradicts verses six and seven." He concludes that "McNeile is accordingly right in regarding the verse as from the Chasid Glossator."[12] Barton says this despite the fact that in his critical notes he states that "Mitzva may be used either of a king . . . or of man . . . or of God."[13] He obviously experiences a difficulty in the use of the term Mitzvah when it stands alone, which he cannot resolve.

Similar difficulties are experienced by the commentators in their discussions of the verse "He that keepeth the Mitzvah keepeth his soul; But he that despiseth His ways shall die" (Proverbs 19:16). Greenstone comments thus[14] "'*His ways*': is careless about his conduct and does not make it conform to the divine law (13:13). It is also possible to refer the word *ways* to the conduct of man, and not to the ways of God as implied by the capital H in our rendering. 'Man's ways' means proper conduct (16:17)." Note that Greenstone refers to Proverbs 13:13 as if there were no doubt that that verse refers to the divine law.

This consistent equivocation by the commentators on these verses is due to the fact that as used in the Bible, the term Mitzvah does not derive its valuational quality from being associated with a divine source nor with a quality inherent in the act commanded, but rather from being associated with a superior. A Mitzvah was to be obeyed because one owed obedience to a superior.

THE USE OF THE TERM MITZVAH IN RABBINIC LITERATURE

The root *TzVH* loses none of its vigor and variety in Rabbinic literature either in its verbal or nominal forms. But there can never be any doubt as to what the Rabbis refer when they use the term Mitzvah alone. It always designates the unequivocally and the ultimately approved act. But to the Rabbis the commands or teachings of human beings, regardless of their station, are not *ipso facto* assumed to be good. Nor do they consider obedience to a superior, whether he be king or parent, always a virtue. On the contrary, disobedience was among the greatest of virtues, when the commands of a human superior involved violations of the laws of God. That is already explicitly taught in the Bible itself. In contrast to Proverbs and Ecclesiastes who seem to counsel unquestioning obedience to the king, the parent and the teacher, the heroes of the book of Daniel defy the King's ordinances (Daniel, chapter 3). The story of Purim centers around Mordecai's defiance of Haman's orders (Esther, chapter 3). Rabbinic literature is likewise replete with stories of insubordination to secular authority when it is in conflict with God's commands.[15] Even the commands of parents were to be disobeyed if they were contrary to the teachings of the Lord, though the honor due to parents is compared by the Rabbis to that due to the Lord.[16] Therefore the unequivocally approved act was never associated by the Rabbis with the will of anyone other than God. Hence commentators need never equivocate in interpreting the significance of the term Mitzvah when found standing alone in Rabbinic literature. It always refers to an act which is unqualifiedly approved by the Rabbis, not because in their opinion it is a virtuous act, but because they believe it to be in accordance with the will of God.[17]

THE WILL OF GOD

But how was one to know God's will? Judaism's answer to that question was given in the canonization of the Pentateuch[18] and in the acceptance of the authority of the Oral Law. The authority of the Laws of the Pentateuch—the Written Law—was based upon the faith that it was revealed by God to Moses at Sinai. The basis for the authority of the Oral Law is not quite as clear. There is, to be sure, the tradition that the whole of the Oral Law was also revealed to Moses at Sinai (Berakhot 5a; Megillah 19b), and that large sections of it were forgotten (Temurah 16a; Megillah 3a, 18a), and only gradually recovered by the Sages. However, even if we accept this tradition as literally true, the question regarding the manner of recovery of the forgotten enactments, still remained. The Sages could not merely announce that they have somehow miraculously recalled the laws which were forgotten. The authority of the Sages to enact ordinances and laws not specifically formulated in the Pentateuch had, therefore, itself to be rooted in the Pentateuch. The laws they enacted had to be related to the Pentateuch in some acceptable manner.

According to Maimonides, there is a threefold bond between the Oral Law and the Pentateuch.[19] (1) The authority of the Sages to enact laws that would serve as a fence around the Torah is based upon the Biblical verse "You shall keep my charge" (Leviticus 18:30), which was interpreted by the Rabbis to mean "Set a watch around my charge" (Yevamot 21a). (2) The authority of the courts in every generation to enact laws and to interpret Scripture is based upon the commandment "You must not deviate from the verdict that they announce to you, either to the right or to the left" (Deuteronomy 17:11).[20] (3) The authority of some laws and enactments which were not received directly from Moses was based on the fact that they were derived by the

Rabbis from the Torah in accordance with the accepted exegetical principles for the interpretation of the Torah.

Though there is general agreement that the authority of the Oral Law is in the final analysis dependent upon its relationship to the Written Law, not all agree with Maimonides' formulation of that relationship. Thus, Ramban is of the opinion that (a) the injunction "You must not deviate from the verdict that they announce to you, either to the right or to the left" is the basis for the authority of those Rabbinic enactments which are derived by applying the accepted thirteen exegetical principles in accordance with which the Torah is to be interpreted; as well as of the Rabbinic decisions regarding the literal meaning of the text of the Torah; and also of those laws which have been transmitted from generation to generation but which originated with Moses though not specifically included in the Pentateuch, the so-called *Halakhot le-Moshe mi-Sinai*.[21] (b) The authority of the Rabbis to institute new Mitzvot such as the law of kindling the Hanukkah lights and reading the Megillah on Purim is based upon the verse "Ask your father and he will inform you, your elders and they will tell you" (Deuteronomy 32:7).[22] (c) The authority of the Rabbis to enact laws whose purpose it is to serve as a fence around the law and to keep a person far from sin is based on the verse "You shall keep my charge."[23]

The Pentateuch itself designates its laws as Mitzvot.[24] The question of whether laws not specifically formulated in the Pentateuch may also be designated as Mitzvot was for a time a subject of lively controversy. Thus, the author of the *Megillat Esther* in his defense of Maimonides against the strictures of Ramban argues that "we do not find that any ordinance of the Rabbis was ever spoken of by the Sages of the Gemara as a Mitzvah, but only as a *Takanah* or *Gezerah*. . . . Thus the Rabbis speak of the Ten *Takanot* promulgated by Ezra . . . and though they are, to be sure, Mitzvot, yet the Rabbis do not say that Ezra enjoined Ten Mitzvot."[25]

Like all over-zealous champions of a cause, he undertakes to prove far more than the situation requires. Maimonides nowhere maintains that the term Mitzvah has been and may be applied only to the Pentateuchal legislation. In his *Sefer Ha-mitzvot* he uncritically accepts the validity of the frequently quoted statement that 613 Mitzvot were revealed to Moses at Sinai (Makkot 23b).[26] His critical faculties were however deeply aroused when he approached the task of listing those 613 Mitzvot. He rejects the previous, widely accepted lists because he can find no logical principle that governed their compilation. Before drawing up his own list therefore, he formulates fourteen general principles to guide him. His first two principles state:

(1) None of the Mitzvot that are of Rabbinic origin are to be included.

(2) Nothing that was deduced by the Rabbis by applying the thirteen exegetical principles or the principle of *Ribbui* to the Pentateuch is to be included.[27]

Thus Maimonides, in the first of the above principles, obviously does not hesitate to apply the term Mitzvah to non-Pentateuchal laws. In his introduction to his *Mishneh Torah,* he states with his customary clarity and positiveness, "These are the 613 Mitzvot that were revealed to Moses at Sinai—they, their generalizations, particulars and minutiae. All those generalizations, particulars and minutiae that explain each Mitzvah constitute the Oral Torah that one *Bet Din* received from its predecessor. And there are other Mitzvot that came into being after the Torah was given which the Prophets and the Sages established and then were universally practiced in Israel as, for example, the reading of the Scroll of Esther, the Hanukkah lights, the fast of the ninth of Av, the *Eruv* and the washing of the hands. Each one of these Mitzvot also has explanations and particulars."

But the problem at once arises that if the Pentateuch has only 613 Mitzvot and the enactments of the Prophets, Sages and Rabbis also have the status of Mitzvot, does it not violate the injunction "Thou shalt not add thereto" (Deuteronomy 13:1)? That dilemma Maimonides solves by interpreting this verse to mean that "no prophet has the right to make an innovation and to say that the Almighty revealed this Mitzvah to him and commanded him to add it to the Mitzvot of the Torah. But if the court or the prophet at any time added a Mitzvah in the form of a *Takanah,* or a decision, or a *Gezerah,* it is not considered an addition. For they did not say that the Almighty commanded us to have an *Eruv* or to read the Megillah. Had they said so that would have been making an addition to the Torah. But we say thus: the Prophets and the *Bet Din* established these in order to recall the praises of the Lord, the help He gave us and how He heard our cry in order that He be blessed and praised, and to make known to future generations that what He promised us in the Torah is true, namely, 'For what great nation is there, that hath God so nigh unto them, as the Lord our God is whensoever we call upon Him?" (Deuteronomy 4:7). And thus is every post-Pentateuchal Mitzvah to be understood."[28]

Hence there is no doubt that though the Rabbis always conceded a position of high priority to the Pentateuch, they nevertheless—very early in the history of Rabbinic Judaism—extended the use of the concept Mitzvah to include far more than was specifically included in the Pentateuch.[29] Any number of illustrations may be cited. But the use of the term Mitzvah by Hillel, as reported in the following anecdotes, should be sufficient.

Hillel, upon leaving the house of study, was once asked where he was going. He replied, "I am going to perform a Mitzvah." When asked what the Mitzvah was, he answered "To take care of my bodily needs." When further questioned whether that can be designated as a Mitzvah, he answered "Yes, for the body is thus preserved from decay." On another occasion he answered that the Mitzvah he was going to perform was that of going to the bath. When asked whether that was a Mitzvah, he explained by saying that if men considered it a virtue to keep the marble statue of the Emperor standing in the market place clean, as a sign of respect to the Emperor, how much more so should a human being out of respect to the Almighty keep his own body clean for "man is made in the image of God."[30]

While, therefore, there can be no doubt that the Rabbis extended the use of the term Mitzvah far beyond the limits of the Pentateuch, it was never applied by them capriciously or arbitrarily. The closing words of Maimonides in the passage quoted above can, we believe, help us understand the Rabbinic method in this regard. Maimonides says "and thus is every post-Biblical Mitzvah to be understood." What does he mean? If we understand him correctly, what he is saying is that post-Biblical enactments were Mitzvot not because their authors claimed them to be revelations to them from God, but because *they were associated by them with the Pentateuch, in an acceptably legitimate manner*. Thus Maimonides points out that the practice of reading the Megillah assumes the status of a Mitzvah for two reasons. In the first place, it is an enactment of an authoritative court and as such is subsumed under the Pentateuchal Mitzvah of "You must not deviate from the verdict that they announce to you." Secondly, because it serves as an historic corroboration of a statement made in the Pentateuch.

That, then, is the touchstone by which an act not specifically commanded in the Pentateuch may be designated as a Mitzvah; not by what Hillel or anyone else says or does, nor by whether anyone claims to have had a direct communication from God declaring it to be a Mitzvah, but only by relating it in some identifiably logical and legitimate manner with the Pentateuch. For the revelation of God's will was found only in the Written Torah and in the authoritative Oral Torah. Hence, Hillel must justify his designation of his concern with his body as a Mitzvah not by some purely humanistic argument that health is desirable and cleanliness is in itself a virtue. Care of the body is justified by him as a Mitzvah because the body is associated with God *as indicated in the Torah.* Only thus can an act become a Mitzvah. Thus also the study of astronomy was adjudged a Mitzvah (Shabbat 75a), not only because it had direct bearing upon the fixing of the calendar and the dating of the Festivals, but also because it was one of the pursuits which revealed the glory of Israel's "wisdom and understanding before the eyes of all men" (Deuteronomy 4:6). And it was God's will to have that wisdom revealed.

The first step, therefore, in "the multiplication of the Mitzvot" beyond those specifically formulated in the Pentateuch was the elaboration of all of the implications of the Pentateuch and the exercise by the Rabbis of all of the authority granted them by the Pentateuch.

THE PROPHETS AND THE WRITINGS

The Pentateuch continued to hold its uniquely authoritative position in Judaism. The other books of the Bible, however, gradually took on increasing authority. While a proof-text from the Pentateuch was always to be preferred, verses from the other books of the Bible came to be more and more readily used as proof-texts, particularly if the subject under discussion did not deal with matters of criminal, civil or ritual law, but only with what might be described as good manners and human decency generally.[31] One instance taken at random, out of many readily available, will illustrate our point. The Rabbis interpret a *mishnah* in Yoma by stating that it is a Mitzvah to be one of a crowd doing honor to a king or high priest (Yoma 70a). The text offered to prove that this is a Mitzvah is taken from Proverbs (14:28): "In the multitude of people is the king's glory."[32]

The addition of the other books of the Bible to the Pentateuch as a source for the validation of Mitzvot was apparently not readily accepted by all.[33] There were those who did not consider it necessary, for they believed that there is nothing contained in the Prophets and Writings which is not already specifically included or at least hinted at in the Pentateuch itself (Taanit 9a), the difference being that the Prophets and the Writings made explicit what was only implicit in the Pentateuch.[34] Perhaps this very belief helped to establish the authority of the other books of the Bible. Be that as it may, the base for validating acts as Mitzvot was thus immensely broadened without, however, becoming boundless.

The extent to which the other books of the Bible gradually assumed a position of equality with the Pentateuch in all nonlegal matters can be noted from the fact that Rabbi Simlai—a Palestinian Amora of the second generation—in choosing the passages that represent the essence of the whole Torah, does not turn to the Pentateuch for his source as did Hillel (Shabbat 31a),[35] Akiba (Yerushalmi Nedarim 9:4) and Ben Azzai (*ibid.*) before him, but turns rather to the Prophets and the Writings. To him (Makkot 24a) the most inclusive and therefore the most significant verse in all Scripture from which all else derives is Amos' cry (5:4), "Seek Me and live." Rabbi Nahman bar Yitzhak (*ibid.*), a fourth generation Babylonian Amora, prefers a verse from the prophet Habbakuk (2:4), "The righteous shall live by his faith."

It was, however, Bar Kappara, a younger contemporary of Judah the Prince, who highlighted the non-Pentateuchal verse which more than any other became the basic proof-text to justify and stimulate the multiplication of the Mitzvot. Bar Kappara designated the verse in Proverbs (3:6), "In all thy ways acknowledge Him, and He will direct thy paths," as the "small passage upon which *gufay Torah*—the whole body of the Torah—depends" (Berakhot 63a). Rabbi Jose, a pupil of Johanan ben Zakkai, had taught, "Let all thy deeds be done for the sake of Heaven" (Avot 2:17). He, however, offered no Biblical proof-text for his teaching. Hence this injunction was merely a personal opinion, being neither legally nor morally binding. The statement that "it is a Mitzvah to obey the wise" (Yevamot 20a) refers only to those instances in which "the wise" were acting under the authority derived from the Pentateuch and in relation to some specific law of the Pentateuch. In the beginning it certainly did not refer to their own Biblically-unsupported opinions.[36] Hence it was not Jose's statement, but the verse quoted by Bar Kappara which in time became the ultimate validation for that irrepressible drive in Judaism to sanctify life to its smallest detail and to elevate every normal human act into a Mitzvah.[37]

The injunction to "acknowledge Him in all thy ways" did, in time, indeed become in many ways the one on which "the whole body of the Torah came to depend." It served a twofold purpose. (1) It helped to explain a number of theological problems. (2) It became the Biblical authority for the validation of an infinite number of new Mitzvot.

One of these theological problems involved the content of the Sinaitic Revelation. Why did God deem it necessary to reveal laws forbidding murder, adultery and stealing when the human mind was capable of arriving at these laws by its own logical powers as was proved by the laws of the heathens and the writings of the pagan philosophers? The Rabbis answered that God's love for Israel was evidenced in His revealing those laws to them because opportunities to perform Mitzvot were thus multiplied. The Israelites were able to observe these laws not because they satisfy a human need or meet the demands of human logic or emotion, but because *God commanded them.* Moreover, in this apparently unnecessary revelation God not only displayed His love for us, He also indicated to us that He can be served through actions that might otherwise have been considered as purely human and therefore completely unrelated to Him. He thus taught us that we can "acknowledge *Him* in all *our* ways."[38]

The other theological problem involved the relationship of God to the gentiles. God has no favorites. God said to

Moses, "Do I then have favorites? If one performs a Mitzvah, whether he be an Israelite or a gentile, a man or a woman, a male slave or a female slave, it is rewarded."[39] Moreover, logic would seem to indicate that he who performs the good deed out of the goodness of his own heart is superior to one who performs it in obedience to a command. Hence the gentile who is not obligated to observe the Ten Commandments and yet honors his parent should be more abundantly rewarded than the Jew who does the same thing. The Jews would then seem to be at a distinct disadvantage. That apparently logical conclusion was rejected by Rabbi Hanina on the basis of his oft-quoted paradox that "he who is commanded and fulfills the commandment is more virtuous than he who is not commanded and fulfills it" (Kiddushin 31a). Nor is that statement as paradoxical as it, at first sight, appears to be. For what moves one to do something which he is not commanded to do? Obviously only his own pleasure. But what one does merely to please himself, whether it be to satisfy an emotional impulse or a logical necessity, cannot in essence be considered a virtuous act. Since it is only a matter of his own pleasure, he can refrain from doing it when it does not suit his purposes.[40] The essence of the Mitzvah, however, resides in the conscious purpose of the performer of it to fulfill *not his own will,* inclination or desire, *but the will of God.* For a man is not to say "I refrain from forbidden food or from committing adultery because I find no particular pleasure in them." On the contrary he should say "I find great delight in them but I refrain from them because they were forbidden me by my Father in Heaven."[41] God's will, not man's, determines the quality of an act.

For every act can be judged from two points of view. It can be judged in and by itself as an entity that has its own being and therefore its own evil or beneficent quality. And it can be judged on the basis of the motive which inspired the actor. An act can be in itself good regardless of the motive that inspired it. But it cannot be a Mitzvah unless it is associated by the performer with a desire on his part to fulfill the will of God. Hence, no act is in reality a Mitzvah, even though it is commanded in the Pentateuch, unless he who performs it consciously intends thereby to fulfill God's commands. The difference between the Jew and the gentile who both perform the same good deed consists therefore in this: the Jew does it as a Mitzvah, to please God. But the gentile who does not believe in the God of Israel or in His Torah does it merely to please his own whim. Hence while the act performed is in itself virtuous and therefore worthy of the reward of the Almighty, it does not have the same quality of perfection which it achieves when it is performed by a pious Jew out of his desire to do God's will. Hence the teaching of the Rabbis that *mitzvot tzerikhot kavanah,* that one must perform a Mitzvah with an awareness that what he is doing is being done with the intent to fulfill the command of the Lord.[42] Therein is man "a partner of God" in transforming an act into a Mitzvah.

But this Biblical verse did more than help solve a number of important theological problems. It sanctioned and gave direction to the inner impulse in Judaism to transform all of life into a service to God. It said that the conscious intent which alone has the power to transform even a Biblically commanded act into a Mitzvah, also has the power to bestow the status of a Mitzvah upon any act which a human being performs if it is not an act specifically prohibited by the Torah and if it is performed in the spirit of "acknowledging Him"—of dedication to God.

The Talmud records the practice of Rabbi Zeira who, when he became weary studying, would say, "I shall go and sit at the entrance to the school of Rabbi Nathan bar Tovi so that when the Sages come out I shall rise before them and receive reward." The *Etz Yosef,*[43] commenting on this passage, points to the action of Rabbi Zeira as an illustration of the application by the pious of the injunction to "acknowledge God in all thy ways." "Thus," he says, "does the righteous man eat and drink to strengthen himself in the service of the Lord . . . and adds Mitzvot to the Mitzvot of the Lord, for with him even matters that are left entirely to his own discretion are thus included by him in the category of Mitzvot. Hence there is no number to the Mitzvot performed by the righteous for even the needs of their bodies are counted among the Mitzvot." Thus was the realm of the secular diminished and that of the holy enlarged.

Maimonides elaborates at considerable length all of the implications of the religious duty to sanctify all of our acts by dedicating them to the service of God. It is this idea which justifies the inclusion by him in his code of law of a whole section devoted to health laws as understood by the best medical authorities of his day.[44] He summarizes the teachings of Judaism on the subject thus: "He who conducts himself in accordance with the known laws of medicine, intending thereby merely that his body and limbs be healthy and that he have children who will do his work and be concerned with his welfare, is not acting properly. He should rather seek to have his body healthy and strong in order that his soul may be in condition to know the Lord. For it is impossible for one to pursue and understand wisdom when he is hungry or sick or in pain. He should hope that he have a son who will be wise and distinguished in Israel. One who conducts himself thus all his days serves the Lord continuously, even while he is conducting his business affairs or having sexual intercourse, because his intent in all things is to satisfy his needs in order that his body may be healthy to serve God. Hence even while he sleeps, if he sleeps to the end that his mind and body may rest so that he be not sick and thus unable to serve God, then his very sleep is a service to the Lord. And it is this that the Sages intended when they said 'Let all thy acts be for the sake of Heaven,' and what Solomon in his wisdom had in mind when he said 'Acknowledge Him in all thy ways and He will make straight thy paths.' "[45] Thus, then, did every normal human act become potentially a Mitzvah and thus was another great step taken towards the multiplication of the Mitzvot.

THE MITZVOT OF SELF-RESTRAINT

But the matter did not end there. The Rabbis recognized that life is sanctified as often by what men refrain from doing as by what they do. "Inaction" of the right kind is often the noblest of all action. The Rabbis found this moral truth also implied in the Pentateuch. Thus chapter 18 of Leviticus, which consists wholly of prohibitions, opens with the admonition (verse 5): "Ye shall keep therefore My statutes and Mine ordinances, which if a man *do,* he shall live by them." But this chapter is concerned exclusively with what should *not* be done. The Rabbis therefore conclude: "Thus to him that sits and commits no transgressions is given a reward as to one who performs a Mitzvah. Rabbi Simeon the son of Rabi taught: It says, 'Only be sure that thou eat not the blood, for the blood is the life' (Deuteronomy 12:23). If a man who does not eat blood—which man's soul abhors—receives a reward, how much more, if he does not commit robbery or incest—which man's soul delights in and covets—shall he gain merit for himself and his descendants and the descendants of his descendants unto the end of all generations" (Makkot 3:15).

What the Rabbis found implicit in the Pentateuch they found explicit in the Psalms (Yerushalmi Kiddushin 1:10). Rabbi Abun read the third verse of Psalm 119 to mean "Even those who merely do no unrighteousness walk in His ways." His son Jose reinforced his father's opinion by noting that the Psalmist does not say "Happy is the man who *walketh* in the counsel of the righteous" but "Happy is the man that *walketh not* in the counsel of the wicked" (Psalms 1:1). By merely refraining from walking in the counsel of the wicked he is accounted as one who walks in the counsel of the righteous.

THE EVIDENCE OF GOD'S LOVE AND LOVE OF GOD

Thus did the Rabbis "multiply the Mitzvot" so that their number became potentially infinite, including within their scope every normal human act and every noble human self-restraint if the act was performed and the restraint practiced as part of a pattern of life whose overarching objective was to glorify God by doing His will, as He gives us to understand His will.

The Rabbis see in this very multiplicity of the Mitzvot one of the greatest expressions of God's love for Man, for their very number makes it well-nigh impossible for one to live a life completely devoid of all virtue. If they were but few in number, then many people might not have found it possible to perform those few. The multiplicity of the Mitzvot enables us to judge every man except the willful, conscious and brazen villain "in the scale of merit," for the average individual believes in God and seeks to please Him. Nor is he so devoid of human virtue as to fail to perform a goodly number of the normal human acts which by being pleasing to God are among the Mitzvot. It is this which probably moved Resh Lakish to say that "even the empty in Israel are as full of Mitzvot as the pomegranate is full of seed" (Eruvin 19a, Hagigah 27a).

CONCLUSION

One of the explanations given for the popular conception that there were 613 Mitzvot is that the number represented a combination of the 248 different parts of the body and the 365 days of the solar year (Makkot 23b). Hence there is a Mitzvah for every part of the body and one for every day of the year. But one Mitzvah per day and one for each part of the body are not sufficient to bring the whole of life under the aegis of the Torah. Too much is left to the realm of the nonreligious. The Rabbis did not rest until they multiplied the Mitzvot to the point where their number was infinite so that every moment in life could be sanctified by a Mitzvah and every normal act of every part of the body could be a Mitzvah.

The impulse and tendency, so clearly present in the Pentateuch, to sanctify all of life was thus incessantly and powerfully at work in the life and thought of the Rabbis. They brought it to unprecedented heights of fulfillment. But the end is not yet, for such an impulse and tendency can never be completely and finally realized in the world as we now know it.[46] New situations constantly arise. New human activities constantly develop. The task of the religious leaders in Judaism remains the same: to multiply the Mitzvot—to see in the new situations of life and the new powers of man new opportunities to serve God and thus to sanctify life. The late, unforgettable Rabbi Abraham I. Kook formulated this idea in his memorable injunction to "renew the old and sanctify the new." But the religious leaders of our people must at the same time be sure that the new Mitzvah is in a legitimate and identifiable manner related to Scripture so that the fundamental unity of the Tradition be maintained both in the letter and in the spirit. "The words of the wise are as goads, and as nails well fastened are those that are composed in collections; they are given from one shepherd" (Ecclesiastes 12:11).

CHAPTER VII

Symbols and Symbolism[1]

(WITH PARTICULAR REFERENCE TO THE RELIGIOUS SYMBOL)

I

Any phenomenon, insofar as it rouses in consciousness an awareness of phenomena other than itself and/or stimulates in the observer a reaction appropriate to those phenomena, thereby functions as a symbol.[2]

Words spoken or written, are the most universal phenomena that serve primarily as symbols. Except for students of language, the sound represented by the letters *t a b l e* or the appearance of the written letters *per se,* interest very few people who speak, hear, write, or read the word. These letters or their sound ordinarily attract attention not to themselves but to a piece of furniture used for various well-known purposes.

But while words spoken or written are the most ubiquitous symbols, every other phenomenon may at times function as a symbol, whether it be a gesture, a building, a drawing, or a mood, for in the human consciousness no phenomenon is completely isolated from all other phenomena. Through the basic psychological process of association of ideas,[3] anything we think of can at once bring to mind something else to which it is in some manner related. Hence anything can be used as a symbol for any one of a vast number of other things with which it has been or can conceivably be related. The more obvious and widely recognized the association, the more likely that one will be used as symbol for the other. In more sophisticated circles, more subtle and esoteric associations will be recognized. The range of symbolism thus available to the poet, the artist, or the average citizen is infinite.

In the statement, "Man is a reed," the reed is symbolic of man, because both are related to the phenomenon of weakness and fragility. The Empire State Building is associated in our minds with America's tremendous industrial and engineering progress. Hence it can and undoubtedly has been used as a symbol for American civilization.[4] The number of illustrations readily available is infinite, for the association can be traceable either to correspondence between aspects of the form or quality of the symbol and its referent, or to some accidental, historical association or to a consciously planned association between the two, as the association between Paul Revere and community vigilance, the flag and the country, the red cross and emergency relief.

II

To the best of our knowledge, man is the only creature upon earth who has the power to symbolize.[5]

The power to symbolize is dependent upon the power to differentiate a quality from an object which concretizes it, and an object from the other objects with which it is associated when it impinges upon the senses. This power to differentiate is rooted basically in self-consciousness, which is in essence a differentiation by the self of itself from all else that transpires outside itself or within itself. To the best of our knowledge, man alone "knows that he knows," and can distinguish between himself as knower and the objects he knows, and hence also between one object of knowledge and another.

III

The power to symbolize makes human thought, as we know it, possible.

We probably could not think at all and we certainly cannot think on a level above the most elementary without first creating symbols for phenomena, whether those symbols be primarily aural,[6] visual, olfactory, or tactile in nature. There is good reason to believe that thought and symbols are inseparable and that what one does not have a "symbol" for, he cannot think about.[7]

IV

While significant distinctions can be made among symbols, depending upon the purposes they serve, all attempts to make significant distinctions between signs and symbols have, it seems to me, taught us a good deal about the nature of symbols but have beyond that been little more than interesting exercises in semantics.

The fact of the matter seems to be that we have thus far used both words interchangeably. The dictionary defines *symbol* as a "visible *sign* of something invisible," and *sign* as "a conventional *symbol* representing an idea," etc.

Some have attempted to restrict the use of "sign" to phenomena which represent a one-to-one relationship between the phenomenon used as a sign and the phenomenon which it is intended to suggest. Thus the + is a sign because it supposedly suggests only one thing, namely, that the phenomena on either side of it are to be added one to the other. But it has that limited meaning only when it appears in a mathematical equation. In different situations it can suggest other things. Teachers are in the habit of marking students as

B+ or A+. In such a setting the + no longer has a definite one-to-one relationship with any other phenomenon. In like manner the English word *road* when heard ordinarily, indicates or signifies a highway leading from one place to another. But the same word heard by an American in a foreign country may indicate or signify that someone who knows how to speak English is present. Under other circumstances it may symbolize the song, "The Road to Mandalay," and thus almost *ad infinitum*. The fact of the matter seems to be that man's mental capacities are so constituted that he cannot, except by conscious determination, limit the symbolic aspects of any phenomenon to only a one-to-one relationship. Through the inevitable process of association incessantly going on in the mind, the symbolic potentialities of every phenomenon are constantly being multiplied. All literary and artistic creativity is dependent upon it. It is undoubtedly true that the symbolic potentialities of some phenomena are more limited than those of other phenomena. But this limitation is as often due to the quality and range of the consciousness upon which the phenomenon impinges, as to the phenomenon itself.

Susanne K. Langer limits the use of "sign" to phenomena that produce a reaction to a referent without involving consciousness.[8] Thus defined, it would seem to me that *sign* is descriptive not of the phenomenon but of the subject upon whom the phenomenon impinges. Signs, thus defined, relate to the experiences of subhuman creatures or to man on the subconscious level. What appears to happen on that level is the identification of the sign with its referent. The dog hearing the bell acts as if the food were present. The bell is not known by the dog as an independent phenomenon. But on the human level every phenomenon is known in its own right, either before or after it is known as a sign or a symbol. Consciousness is never completely absent from the process which transforms a phenomenon into a symbol or sign. It may not always be present at the moment when a phenomenon is reacted to by the human being who encounters it. But at no time can a human being's reaction to a sign be equated with an animal's reaction to it, even though, technically speaking, we may say that the reaction in both instances did not involve consciousness. In the case of the human being such a reaction was on the subconscious level of habit which must have been preceded by a period of consciousness. However, in the animal's case the whole process occurred on the nonconscious level. The difference between the two is infinite.

Thus anyone can define sign or symbol as he prefers and use them in accordance with his definition. But there is little in the uses to which these words have thus far been put in ordinary English usage which justifies any very clear and consistent distinction between them. One can speak of a sign as belonging to the species "symbol" or *vice versa,* with equal validity.[9]

V

The symbolic aspect of a phenomenon is not inherent in it, and hence it is not self-evident. Before a phenomenon can take on the character of a symbol, a learning process must take place.

That is true even of the "natural" signs[10] such as clouds or thunder. A child who never saw snow fall will not associate clouds with snow the first time he finds himself in a temperate climate in the winter. He must see the phenomenon first. Nor do clouds always bring rain. Clouded heavens may have served as a sign that the Deity is displeased. Lightning is often seen without the accompaniment of claps of thunder. One must learn that the two are interrelated.

When we leave the area of "natural" symbols and enter the area of man-made symbols, the part that the learning process has in the creation of symbols becomes self-evident. There is nothing in the sound of the letters *t r e e* which when heard should rouse in consciousness the awareness of an object with roots, branches and leaves. There is nothing inherent in the stones of the Lincoln or the Washington Monuments, which makes their symbolic significance self-evident. *A phenomenon can, therefore, function as a symbol only in relation to phenomena which at one time or another are independently known by the observer, and then consciously or subconsciously related by him one to the other.*

The quality and the range of the symbolic aspects of any phenomenon depend, therefore, only secondarily upon the phenomenon itself, and primarily upon the quality and range of the learning process through which the observer of the phenomenon has passed.[11]

VI

In some areas of human activity, the efficacy of a phenomenon as a symbol depends upon the consciously defined limitations that are set by us to its symbolic aspects. This is particularly the case with the scientific symbol.

In mathematics, in all the sciences, in the military pursuits of man, the symbolic aspects of phenomena must be meticulously circumscribed, so that the symbolic aspect once having been consciously learned, may become almost as completely identified with the phenomenon itself as was the sound of the bell with the food in the case of Pavlov's dog. But there is never complete identification. Phenomena used in mathematics, science, and by the military as symbols, such as +, H_2O, or the officer's epaulet, remain phenomena in themselves, which when encountered in nonmathematical or nonscientific or nonmilitary circumstances, continue to be of some interest, even though they may have shed their dominantly symbolic aspects completely. But in these areas of human activity wisdom requires that the use of the symbols as symbols be strictly limited to the purposes for which they were originally created. Hence the laws forbidding civilians to wear military insignia or to use the flag indiscriminately.

VII

In some areas of human activity, the efficacy of a phenomenon as symbol depends upon the conscious and studied expansion of the range of phenomena which it summons into consciousness. This is particularly the case with group symbols.

The efficacy of a symbol as a unifying force in human society depends primarily upon the multiplicity of other phenomena which it is capable of mustering within the range of consciousness of its observers. It is this multiplicity of associations roused from the subconscious[12] by the symbol, which alone can achieve two results equally indispensable for the unification of large societies. On the one hand, the symbol binds the individual closer to itself by involving itself in the greatest possible number of his memories, emotions and capacities. On the other hand, it attaches the greatest possible number of individuals to itself, each one of whom may be personally involved in only one or two of its many symbolic aspects.

Hence each group in human society, whether it be a religious sect, a political party, a state, or a social club, strives incessantly, if it is wise, to associate its symbols with the greatest possible number of other phenomena. Hence our efforts consciously to multiply the symbolic aspect of the word *America,* as we did in the popular *Ballad for Americans* during the Second World War. Hence, also, our most staple theme for school children's essays, "What America Means to Me."

The demagogue's chief task is to make a symbol mean not "All things to every *man,*" but "*Something* to all men," *i.e.,* every man is to find in it the thing or things that he is seeking. Hence the demagogue is not concerned primarily that logical consistency characterize his program, but rather that it endow his emblem with maximum symbolic plenitude, so that each one may find in it what he seeks.

Most often, therefore, the demagogue will not create his own new symbol, as under the best of circumstances the association of meaning with a group symbol involves a long and difficult process. He will prefer to attach himself and his particular purposes to a symbol which already has vast and effective associations with the individuals of the group he seeks to dominate.[13] An American listening to a speaker whose stand is decorated with an American flag must make a conscious effort to dissociate what the speaker is saying from the emotionally laden phenomena which the flag *per se* recalls to his consciousness.

While, therefore, a phenomenon with a multiplicity of symbolic aspects, such as a flag, may be very effective as a force unifying different and often conflicting elements in a society, it is a most ineffective agent for exact communication. Two people can with equal vigor protest their loyalty to the flag of America, but can simultaneously associate it with altogether different phenomena. To the one, the American flag as symbol may call the far-visioned Marshall Plan into consciousness; to the other, the racially discriminatory McCarran immigration laws.

Hence the primary duty of the leaders of any group is not merely to multiply the symbolic aspects of the group's chief symbols, but to see to it that those aspects are not self-contradictory, that they are inherently consistent and make for a deepening and broadening of the group's highest moral and intellectual aspirations. That is the sacred and never ending obligation of the group's leader and teachers. *We cannot overemphasize the fact that the symbolic aspects of any phenomenon—whether flag or map, word or gesture—are learned, and that the learning process starts early and determines the meaning of the symbol.*[14] Waving the map of the United States will not bring the same reaction as waving the flag, not because the Stars and Stripes make a prettier picture than the map, but because a long learning process has taught us how to act when we see a piece of cloth colored in a given way waving from a pole, while a map recalls to consciousness either a teacher and a classroom or plans for a journey. There is no way other than that of the tireless, well-planned educational process whereby we may avoid the dangers inherent in the fact that the chief symbols of a group must have a multiplicity of symbolic aspects, if they are to serve as unifying factors in the group's life. Only thus can demagogues be prevented from corrupting the group's symbols into vehicles for their destructive, disruptive activities.

VIII

In some areas of human concern, the efficacy of a phenomenon as symbol depends neither upon the limitation nor the comprehensiveness of its symbolic impact, but rather upon the poignancy with which it involves human aspirations, moods, or emotions. Literary and artistic creations are such phenomena.[15]

Literature and art are not concerned merely with symbolizing phenomena other than themselves, but primarily with symbolizing them in such a manner as to involve the observer's emotional and esthetic capacities, his power to experience love and hate, pity and indignation, joy and sorrow, and his ability to sense the beautiful and the ugly, the attractive and repulsive. Art and literature are not concerned with depicting circumstances and disseminating information which involve merely the intellect. The truly great artist rouses hate in the observer for things that the intellect will adjudge as hateful and love for that which the intellect will adjudge as lovable, attachment to that which is beautiful and withdrawal from that which is ugly. But whether his success as an artist depends primarily upon his ability to direct the emotions properly, or rather merely upon his ability to stir them into being, is one of the perennially debated questions touching the nature of art. Dante's delight in the suffering of the sinner may be repugnant to our moral sense. Should we, therefore, deny him a place among the world's great poets, or adjudge the particular passage in which this unworthy rejoicing is expressed as "artistically inferior" to the rest of the poem?

Most of us fortunately resist all attempts to divorce our ethical from our esthetic sensitivities, so that we welcome all philosophical efforts to identify the beautiful with the good, or the good with the beautiful. But philosophical niceties notwithstanding, the experience of any normal individual involves him in situations in which he finds his ethical judgments and his esthetic sensitivities not so much in conflict with one another as apparently unrelated to one another. Obviously the greater the perfection of the artistic creation, *i.e.*, the greater its power to involve our esthetic sensitivities, the more difficult does it become to judge it on any basis other than the esthetic. A sufficiently effective esthetic appeal can and has overcome ethical considerations[16] in the judgment of works of literature or art. Only those who had an unwavering loyalty to a moral doctrine which for them is the final arbiter of their opinions and tastes, have had the courage or temerity—depending upon one's point of view—to place or to urge the placing of works of widely-acknowledged literary and artistic merit on a list of the condemned and forbidden.

As for the "liberals" who oppose Indexes and censorship, only a handful are willing to follow their position to its logical conclusion of opposing all and any censorship. Almost all would agree that the work which both lacks artistic merit and advocates or represents a morality obnoxious to our "normative insights" should be legally banned from circulation. The question then arises as to the point at which a work's artistic merit makes its moral quality irrelevant. No universally accepted measuring rod has as yet been found by anyone.

A somewhat larger number will argue that the artist need be as little concerned with the moral implications of his creations as is the scientists with the ethical import of his discoveries or creations. Beauty being as ultimate as truth, Beauty for Beauty's sake has as much validity as Truth for Truth's sake.

Most of us, however, who would argue against Indexes generally would most likely do so first for pragmatic reasons, namely, that in the long run the harm of censorship is greater than that of freedom. In addition, we would base our position on the belief that the mature individual can distinguish between the beautiful and the moral, and that he can enjoy the beautiful without injury to his moral personality. Finally we would most likely express our conviction, all experience notwithstanding, that all "significant form" inevitably embodies overtones of significant moral quality. Our esthetic sensitivities cannot be poignantly involved without at the same time beneficently involving our ethical sensitivities. That argument is more an expression of hope than a description of reality. It is, nevertheless, an irrepressible argument and as such may indicate that it represents reality at least in part.

Moreover, the literary and artistic symbol being concerned primarily with the involvement of mood, aspiration and emotion, its quality as a symbol may be judged either by the profundity of the emotion or mood, or by the multiplicity of emotions or moods which it involves. Each of the tragedies of Shakespeare involves one great human emotion. *Romeo and Juliet* involves the love of young lovers, *Othello* blind jealousy, *Macbeth* unbridled ambitions, *Hamlet* wavering resolution. None can doubt the emotion which dominates the action depicted in the play. *Othello* knows no mood of wavering resolution, nor *Hamlet* of jealousy, nor *Macbeth* of love. But just as often the great literary or artistic symbol is capable of symbolizing a vast variety of different and sometimes even conflicting moods and emotions. *Moby Dick, Ulysses, Peer Gynt* will continue to be subjects for wide differences of opinion among those who will seek to spell out their symbolism discursively, both in matters of detail and of basic meaning.[17]

IX

In some areas of human concern, the efficacy of a phenomenon as a symbol depends both upon the specificity of the phenomenon other than itself to which it refers and its capacity for bringing that phenomenon into consciousness in a manner that involves the aspirations, moods, emotions, and actions of the observer in a previously determined, desirable manner. Such in essence is the religious symbol.

The specific phenomenon to which all religious symbols refer *insofar as they are religious* is that which is considered as the fundamental, all-embracing, ultimate reality.[18] In the religious tradition of the West, the most common symbol for that ultimate reality is God. Hence the efficacy of the religious symbols in Western tradition is judged by their ability to involve man's emotional endowments and overt acts in a relationship of loyalty toward, dependence upon, hope in, obedience to, joy in, and love for, God. The symbol may, in addition, involve the emotional endowments of the observer with an almost infinite number of specific phenomena other than God. But if it stops short of involving him finally with God, it may be one of a number of other types of symbols—national, personal, esthetic, or scientific—but it is not a religious symbol.

Like all other symbols, the religious symbol also tends inevitably to gather around it an increasing number of secondary significances, which constantly threaten to overshadow or crowd out its primary significance.[19] Thus the Hebrew Scriptures designate a number of phenomena as *ot*, a "sign," and assign to each of them a specific referent. The Sabbath is to remind us of God the Creator of the Universe (Exodus 31:17). The fringes in the corners of the garment are to recall the commandments of the Lord which are to be obeyed (Numbers 15:37–41). Circumcision is the symbol recalling the covenant entered into between God and Abraham and his descendants (Genesis 17:11). Over a period of some three thousand years of history, however, each one of these symbols took on meanings and referents neither mentioned nor envisioned by Scripture.

In the life of observant Jews, the Sabbath rouses all the memories and emotions associated with family life, with mother kindling and blessing the Sabbath lights, with father pronouncing the *Kiddush,* with the father's blessing of the children, with the family in its best clothes gathering around the table for the festive meal of the week, and with any number of other deeply rooted emotional experiences. The Sabbath as a symbol has become a most effective instrument for galvanizing all the infinite strands of meaning and emotion associated with the intricate web of human relationships ever present in a normally functioning family. As such, the Sabbath has become for many for whom God no longer has any meaning, the symbol of Jewish family solidarity. Family solidarity undoubtedly is a most desirable virtue and activates a great number of desirable emotional experiences, such as love and loyalty. Scripture, however, declares the Sabbath to be the "sign between Me and the children of Israel forever that in six days the Lord made heaven and earth, and on the seventh day He rested." Hence, if the Sabbath as symbol is limited only to the involvements implied by family solidarity, important and significant as these undoubtedly are, it ceases to be a primarily religious symbol.

Scripture specifically designates the "commandments of the Lord" as the phenomenon which should be brought into the center of consciousness by the fringes in the corner of the outer garment. Note that it is to "the commandments of the Lord," that they are to direct attention and not simply to "commandments" issuing from folkways or group customs. Nor are they anywhere declared to be efficacious protectors against evil spirits or unfortunate mishaps. When viewed purely on the folkloristic or magical level, the fringes cease to be a religious symbol. They become instead either a charm or an anachronistic group custom.

Finally, circumcision is enjoined by Scripture as a sign of the covenant between God and Abraham and his descendants. As such, it is to be performed at a specified time and in a specified manner. Hence, if performed as a health measure even in the specified manner and time, it loses its character not merely as a religious symbol but as symbol *per se;* for that which is done because in itself it is good for one's physical health, has no symbolic import to the actor. To the observer it may be symbolic of the value that man places on health, in that he is willing to subject an infant to great pain merely in the hope that it will be good for his health even though an infinite number of males have lived long healthy lives without being circumcised. But surely circumcision used as symbol of man's concern with health has little or no symbolic meaning to anyone.

The religious symbols of Judaism, as of all religions, have constantly been exposed, therefore, to these three abuses: 1) Those charged with significant, desirable personal or group experience have been divorced from their religious moorings and associated with purely sociological and humanistic referents. 2) Many have been divorced from their symbolic character by being transformed into interesting folkways, important national bonds, or magically effective rites. 3) Some have lost their symbolic meaning by being emptied of all significance other than the desirable results inherently flowing from them to him who is immediately affected by them.

X

The Relationship of the Scientific Symbol to its Referent

Until comparatively recently it was universally accepted that the distinction of the scientific symbol consisted in this: that its referent was always in some manner directly or indirectly accessible to one or more of the five senses. Hence, the existence of the referent as independent from its symbol[20] was believed to be empirically demonstrable. Moreover, a scientific symbol whether it be a one-word concept like "the field," or a more elaborately formulated law like $E = mc^2$, was viewed as having a "one-to-one relationship" with its referent which could be demonstrated by ordering the referent in a pattern suggested by the scientific symbol and then actually observing that it behaved in the manner indicated by the symbol. Hence the validity of a scientific symbol depended upon its formal correspondence to a pattern formed by sensibly observable phenomena.

Scientists have been making great efforts to remain loyal to this conception of the scientific symbol. But they have repeatedly gone beyond the limits thus indicated, and used symbols whose referents were by no means empirically demonstrable. These deviations from the norm are most often due not to intellectual carelessness or willfulness but rather to intellectual necessity. Parts cannot be constructively studied without relating them to the whole, and the whole—which in this instance is the universe—can never be known directly through the senses. When, therefore, science creates for the whole a symbol which it validates to its own satisfaction on the basis of the evidence it gathers from the empirically accessible parts, it is no longer in the strictest sense "scientific."

Religion's profoundest differences with science occur in the area in which science employs such nonscientific symbols, as, for example, the "wound-up clock" as a "scientific" symbol for the universe. The wisest among the scientists always were conscious of the nonscientific character of these symbols, and distinguished between them and other scientific symbols by referring to them as tentative or working hypotheses. Nevertheless, they felt in duty bound vigorously to defend their scientific character since they appeared to be the "co-implicates"[21] indispensable to the rational organization of all the other empirically validated, scientific symbols. At this moment science seems to be in an era of uncertainty, precisely because the more recently empirically validated symbols of parts of the universe, such as the "nuclear particles" and the "quantum" do not as yet point to a "coimplicate," which would organize all the available scientific symbols into an acceptably rational system.

But these aspects of the problem take us beyond our immediate concern. The scientific symbol then has two basic characteristics: 1) It is a phenomenon that is consciously and carefully limited in its capacity to bring to the awareness of its observer phenomena other than itself. The ideal scientific symbol is one that has only a one-to-one relationship between itself and its referent. 2) The observer of the scientific symbol can verify empirically that the referent exists independent of its symbol and validate the "truth" of the symbol through empirically establishing the *formal* relationship between symbol and referent.

XI

The Relationship of the Literary and Artistic Symbol to its Referent

The literary and artistic symbol is not pointed primarily toward an empirically verifiable referent but toward stimulating the emotional and esthetic sensitivities of its human observer. These sensitivities are intertwined with the human instincts such as sex, hunger, fear, and play. The instincts are basically self-activating. But they can also be stimulated into action. On the exclusively animal level, they are to the best of our knowledge stimulated only by phenomena that impinge from without, directly upon the animal's senses. On the human level, they are stimulated both by phenomena that impinge directly on the senses and by phenomena that exist only in the human imagination. A human mind suffering from hallucinations induces emotional reactions in the body of its possessor that are completely unrelated to the phenomena immediately impinging upon the individual's senses. Imagination can often be more importunate than reality. Artistic and literary symbols feed the human imagination and stimulate our emotional sensitivities with a power at times surpassing the power of the stimulus occasioned by the referent itself. Since the literary and artistic symbol impinges upon the emotional sensitivities of the observer primarily through his imagination, its referent need not be a phenomenon whose being or existence could be empirically experienced. Hence the referents of literature and art need in no way be "scientific" facts. It is sufficient that they be "figments of the imagination" with which we can temporarily identify ourselves sympathetically. I stress the word "temporarily," because a more persistent self-identification with a figment of the imagination is among the most patent symptoms of a diseased human mind. Kafka's cockroach struggling to get out of bed was never seen by anyone. But the reader of that story can emotionally identify himself with that struggle. The emotional satisfaction produced by that story depends entirely upon its power to stimulate the emotions of the reader through leading him into a temporary self-identification with the cockroach. If even while reading the story the reader is not conscious of the fact that this is not the story of a cockroach that ever was, or that there is no real identification between himself and the cockroach, his emotional experience will be profounder. But it also may be very harmful to him, as was the identification of many a young reader with the inner struggles of Goethe's young Werther, leading in a number of instances to actual suicide.[22]

The literary and artistic symbol, insofar as its efficacy is concerned, belongs therefore to a category altogether different from that of the scientific symbol. The efficacy of the scientific symbol depends upon the observer's ability to observe and manipulate phenomena outside himself, in accordance with the pattern suggested by the symbol, and arrive at predictable results. The efficacy of literary and artistic symbols depends upon their ability to move an observer to experience emotional states appropriate to the phenomena, which *for the moment* dominate his imagination. The scientific symbol reflects objective truth and reality, insofar as it directs the senses to phenomena outside themselves. The literary and artistic symbol reflects objective truth and reality insofar as it directs the emotions to phenomena other than themselves which have power to affect them. "A figment of the imagination" may not be real scientifically, *i.e.,* it may not be validated by the senses, but it is very real esthetically, *i.e.,* it is validated by the emotions, and emotional validation is usually the more meaningful to the individual.

Whether on the highest level the esthetically real must also be at least the conceivably objectively real, depends upon one's opinion regarding the manner in which the artistic creation is to be approached by the observer. For those who would completely divorce the intellect from esthetic experience, there is no necessary, significant relationship whatsoever between the esthetically real and the objectively real. Like the religious mystics who claim that all attempts to "know God" through the intellect are not only futile but verge on the blasphemous, they too view the attempt to inject the intellect into the esthetic experience as a violation of the essence of that experience. But those who believe that music is not only to be listened to, paintings not only to be viewed, poetry not only to be experienced, *but also understood,* would maintain that on the highest level no artistic symbol has an intellectually inconceivable referent. One listening to a symphony does not necessarily have to put his mind and imagination to sleep, keeping only his emotions exposed to the sound emanating from the orchestra. On the contrary, his emotional response may be all the more profound precisely because his mind and imagination are involved on an equally high level—in translating what he hears into terms conceivably amenable to sight, smell, touch, or motion. Music does not make its impact upon us *only* through the ears,[23] any more than a painting impinges merely upon our sight. Through the imagination, what is heard by the ears is transformed into a phenomenon delightful to the eyes or the touch, and what is seen by the eyes the imagination transforms into phenomena delighting the ears or the nose. Hence literary or artistic symbols whose referents are intellectually inconceivable are either essentially religious symbols insofar as they incline man's mind to contemplation of the Ultimate or his emotions to involvement in some appropriate relationship to the Ultimate, or they are in essence "meaningless" in that they do not refer to anything beyond themselves and the immediate experience they occasioned in those upon whom they impinged. Man's greatest nonreligious artistic and literary symbols have, however, always had referents that may not have been objectively real, but were either believed to be real or were at least conceived as being possibly real. Otherwise they could not rouse a meaningful emotional reaction.

To be sure, there never was a Hamlet who actually spoke to the ghost of his foully-murdered father. But except for that one incident, which in Shakespeare's day was believed to be altogether objectively conceivable, there is nothing that Hamlet says or does which might not have been said or done by a "real" person. Had Shakespeare depicted in Hamlet an "unreal" person, Hamlet could never have become the great literary symbol that he is. But conceivable, objective reality alone would not be enough to make Hamlet a literary symbol. To those aspects of Hamlet which are conceivably empirically approachable, Shakespeare added aspects which while beyond the reach of the senses were completely within the grasp of the emotions—the Hamlet of deep mourning, of unfulfilled love, but, above and beyond all, the Hamlet of indecision, of resolution repeatedly thwarted by the "pale cast of thought." To establish the reality of this esthetically and emotionally real Hamlet, it is sufficient to have not an actual, historically real Hamlet but a conceivably real Hamlet.

The literary and artistic symbol, therefore, has the following characteristics: 1) Its referent need not be "objectively real" but should be "conceivably objectively real." 2) Its referent should be capable of sensitizing the emotional capacities of the observer—preferably without doing violence to his intellectual integrity, his ethical sensitivity, and his sense of reality.

XII

The Relationship of the Religious Symbol to its Referent

We said above that the fundamental characteristic of the religious symbol is that its ultimate referent is God. None of the Western religions have many symbols that refer exclusively to God. Judaism has none but the unpronounced and unpronounceable Tetragrammaton. All other symbols in Judaism refer to God only through the mediation of another phenomenon referred to by the symbol. It is in this other phenomenon that God's presence is involved. The Sabbath symbolizes first a created universe and only secondarily Him Who created it. The fringes directly symbolize the Commandments that are to be remembered and only secondarily Him Who is the Author of the Commandments. Circumcision symbolizes directly the covenant between God and Abraham and only indirectly the God with Whom the covenant is thus renewed in every generation.

The scientific aspects of the religious symbol

The religious symbol partakes of the nature of a scientific symbol in the fact that its referents are specific, *viz.,* the universe and God, the law and God, the covenant and God. But that is where the similitude between the two types of symbols ceases, and the conflict between them begins.

Insofar as the religious symbol refers exclusively to God or to those manifestations of God that have thus far remained completely beyond empirical verification, the religious symbols resemble the "pseudoscientific" symbols of science, such as the wound-up clock discussed above. The "created universe" symbolized by the Sabbath is as "scientific" as the universe symbolized by the machine or the clock. The differences between these "universal" symbols of religion and science derive in part from the differences in phenomena with which both are primarily concerned. For science derives its hypotheses or "necessary coimplicates" primarily from the phenomena which are made available to it by the five senses, namely, the physical universe, while religion derives its "necessary coimplicates" primarily from phenomena which are not subject to direct or conceivable empirical examination, namely, the moral and ethical conscience of man, his innate sense of responsibility and guilt, his sense of awe and wonder. In part these differences are due to the temperament of the individual investigator, for there were always many who after examining the same phenomena arrived at different conclusions regarding the nature of the "necessary coimplicates." It is on the level of the "necessary coimplicates" that the profoundest conflicts and attempted reconciliations between science and religion have repeatedly occurred from the days of Philo to our own.

But the conflicts between science and religion which take place on what we designated as the secondary level of reference of the religious symbol, are in many ways more damaging to religion and raise fundamental issues regarding the nature of the relationship between the religious symbol and its referent. Thus, for example, the relationship between the fringes and the Law which they symbolize is as clearly established as the relationship between the scientific symbol *E* and the actual physical energy which it symbolizes. The Law is there to be seen and read. Moreover, the fringes are, by Rabbinic legislation, so intertwined as to form a pattern corresponding to the number 613 which is the traditional number of commandments in the Torah. But these fringes are to remind us also of the divine origin of the Law, for the commandments are "the commandments of the Lord" (Numbers 15:39). In the passage discussing the fringes, nothing specific is said about the manner in which the Law was given to Israel. But it is described in Exodus 19. If then one is to recall when he looks upon the fringes the events described in that chapter, events which reportedly occurred in historic time and mundane space, is he called upon to apply to the fringes the same test that he applies to a scientific symbol, namely, to see if its referent is subject to or conceivably subject to independent empirical verification? Or is the religious symbol's validity to be compared rather to the validity of the literary and artistic symbol, namely, by its power to involve the emotions of the observer in an acceptable manner rather than by our ability to check its correspondence with its referent?

Since the days of Philo there have always been many who would validate the religious symbol by treating it as a "pseudoscientific" symbol on its primary level, namely, insofar as it refers directly to God, and as a literary or artistic symbol, or "myth," on its secondary level, namely, insofar as it refers directly to phenomena associated with time and space, and, therefore, actually or conceivably subject to independent verification by the senses. On this secondary level the validity of the religious symbol is vindicated by pointing to its power to involve the emotions and actions in an acceptable manner, rather than its reference to phenomena other than itself which were or are empirically verifiable. I doubt whether this method can successfully preserve the efficacy of the religious symbol to involve even the emotions, let alone the actions of their observers over an extended period of time. The referent of the religious symbol on this secondary level must have more than mere artistic or literary or "mythical" character if the symbol is to maintain its religious efficacy.

The present crisis in religion is due, it seems to me, not so much to the "pseudoscientific" aspects of our religious symbols as to those of their aspects which originated as "scientific" symbols and now can be accepted by many as little more than literary or artistic or mythical symbols. As such they can be, and in many instances are, accepted because they furnish pleasant *temporary* emotional involvements even as do literary and artistic symbols. But they do not have the power to sustain over extended periods of time those desirable actions which inferentially should follow upon the intellectual and emotional involvements stimulated by the effective religious symbol. Efforts to preserve the religious symbol by transforming it into a national, sociological, or artistic symbol have indeed helped to preserve it as a symbol, but have not been too helpful in preserving it as a religious symbol. Religious symbols must, therefore, on the primary level be "pseudoscientific" in the nonderogatory sense in which we use that term in this paper; and scientific on the secondary level, if they are to be both effective and religious. They cannot on either level be primarily literary or artistic.

But having said that, we hasten to add that, just as the great literary and artistic symbols are enhanced by their conformity or conceivable conformity to referents that have an existence independent of the symbols, so the great scientific or pseudoscientific religious symbols are enhanced when their expression involves great literary and artistic symbolism. The artistic, literary and sociological expressions that have become part of the Sabbath enhanced its efficacy as symbol of God the Creator. The efficacy of the Scroll of the Torah as symbol of God's self-revelation to man is enhanced by the manner in which it is written and chanted and by the artistic beauty of the Ark in which it is kept in the synagogue. The Jewish High Holidays—New Year's Day and the Day of Atonement—as symbols of man's responsibility toward his Creator, are the more effective because of the liturgy, the chants and the elaborate synagogue ritual enacted on those days. But if Judaism is to remain a religion, these artistic and literary addenda dare never replace the substance. Examples without number to illustrate this predicament can be readily adduced from the experiences of all Western religions. What is happening to Christmas in America, is probably the best illustration of the danger to religion when its symbols begin to have nonreligious referents which in number and immediate appeal overshadow its distinctly religious referents.

The case is somewhat different where the religious symbol is one like *Kol Nidre,* the legal formula for the annulment of vows, impressively chanted in all traditional synagogues immediately before the services on the eve of the Day of Atonement. The *Kol Nidre* has become for many the symbol of Jewish martyrdom for the faith, because of its association particularly with incidents that are believed to have occurred during the Spanish Inquisition and Expulsion. Assuming that the association of *Kol Nidre* with the Spanish Inquisition or any other particular historic event is not "scientific," the loyalty of many Jews to their faith under persecution *is* a scientifically established fact. Moreover, knowing as we do that the *Kol Nidre* when first composed had no relationship whatsoever to loyalty to one's faith under persecution, the gradual development of *Kol Nidre* as the symbol of this particular historic group experience, is nevertheless altogether valid. One can try to explain this development by examining the content or the melody of *Kol Nidre.* There undoubtedly must be something in both the words and the chant, as well as in the association of these words and chant with certain historic experiences of the group. But all of these may not be absolutely scientifically established. It is enough in this instance for *Kol Nidre* to serve as an *arbitrarily chosen artistic symbol of an actual historic experience.* Its efficacy as a religious symbol then depends completely upon its innate power to involve the emotions of the congregant in a manner that would incline him to be loyal to the faith. The validity of the scientifically established, larger experience of the group as a whole which *Kol Nidre* symbolizes is sufficient to validate the symbol, since the symbol itself is not dependent upon scientifically historic validation.

A group may thus arbitrarily bestow upon an actual phenomenon, in this instance the *Kol Nidre,* the status of a religious symbol, a status which is inherently valid because it is based on historic associations. But in such an instance it must be obvious that the association between the symbol and its referent is only a little more inherent than that between *table* and its referent. Such religious symbols retain their efficacy only if they possess inherent artistic or literary power to focus attention on the referent as long as the referent continues to be poignant and meaningful. If the referent remains significant while the symbol's artistic or literary expression loses its power to focus attention, the referent "will seek" another symbol. If the referent ceases to be significant while the symbol retains its artistic power, it "will seek" another referent. Should the "search" in either instance fail, the surviving member of this "phenomenon of pairing or coupling"[24] will also perish. For just as no "event" can become an experience without first acquiring unto itself a symbol, and just as no experience can continue to be significant when its symbol loses the power to attract attention to it, thus also can no symbol continue to hold interest if its referent ceases to be of significance. Referents may discard old symbols and take on new ones. Symbols may detach themselves from old referents and attach themselves to new ones. But neither can long maintain a solitary existence. Like a cut flower, either may live on for a while, but the end is inevitable.

In every generation there have been old referents looking for new symbols, old symbols looking for new referents, and new referents in search of appropriate symbols. This is particularly true of our generation for Jew and Christian alike. Rarely have so many treasured symbols ceased to be meaningfully associated by so many, with widely acknowledged significant referents, and so many significant referents been divorced from widely acceptable symbols. And rarely has a generation been so sterile in creating new effective symbols for either old or new significant referents. When this search of symbol for referent and referent for symbol goes unrewarded for too long a period of time, religions die and civilizations disintegrate.

CHAPTER VIII

One People[1]

Since the year of our Jubilee falls within the period set aside by our country to commemorate the hundredth anniversary of the War Between the States, and since more particularly it coincides with the hundredth anniversary of the promulgation of the Emancipation Proclamation and the Gettysburg Address, you will not, I hope, consider it inappropriate if I cast my remarks within a framework suggested by a passage in one of the historic addresses of the unforgettable Emancipator. I do so in sincere homage to his memory and to the memory of those whose tears and blood sealed the union of these American states.

Abraham Lincoln opened the address which he delivered in June of 1858 by saying: "If we could first know *where* we are, and *whither* we are tending, we could then better judge *what* to do, and *how* to do it."[2] By the "we" in the questions "where we are" and "whither we are tending" Lincoln referred to the whole American people. By the "we" in "we could then better judge what to do, and how to do it," he referred to the then newly-organized Republican Party. At this milestone in the history of our movement, our minds naturally ask the questions, "What should *we* as a *movement* do in the foreseeable future, and how should we do it?" And we too would be in a better position to answer these questions if we would first know *where we are as a people* and *whither we are tending as a people.*

Where are we today as a people? The answer to this question appears to me to be comparatively clear. We are today in the sixteenth year of an era inaugurated by the most revolutionary event that has occurred in Jewish history in the last 1,878 years. On the 5th of Iyar, 5708, in May of 1948, the State of Israel declared its independence. In the following year, it was accepted as a member of the United Nations.

Simultaneously with the events that culminated in the establishment of the State of Israel, other events were transpiring which culminated in two results whose impact upon the destiny of the Jewish people was of such magnitude as to justify their inclusion in the same category of historic significance as the establishment of the State. The one was the indescribably tragic destruction of the Jewish communities of Central and Eastern Europe, which had exercised spiritual and cultural hegemony in Jewish life for some three hundred years. The other was the magnificent rise of the American Jewish community to its present position of leadership of world Jewry, a leadership which it shares with the Jewish community in the State of Israel.

These three facts: the destruction of the great Jewish communities of Central and Eastern Europe, the rise of the American Jewish community and the establishment of the State of Israel indicate with what for me is unmistakable clarity *where we are as a people* at this juncture in our history.

I find no equally clear indication pointing to the answer to the question *"Whither are we tending as a people?"* The voices that rise from our hectically busy Jewish communities sound as indecisive as those which Moses heard when he descended from Mount Sinai. "It is not the sound of the tune of triumph, Or the sound of the tune of defeat" (Exodus

32:18). One who looks at Jewish life in America and in Israel today will, unless he is an irredeemable pessimist, find much in it that is, thank God, healthy and creative, and holds great promise for the future. But unless he is an irredeemable Pollyanna, he will also, without great effort, discern not only symptoms of future dangers, but substantial evidence of present and overt danger toward which we are tending. The present and overt danger which looms most ominously upon our horizon is the increasingly disastrous speed with which we are tending toward an irreconcilable spiritual and cultural fragmentation as a people. I believe that if this tendency is not vigorously and wisely counteracted, it will lead to consequences as serious as those which occurred when the Ten Tribes turned their backs on the House of David, and when implacably warring sects multiplied during the centuries immediately preceding and following the rise of Christianity, and when in the eighth century the Karaites and Rabbanites faced one another as strangers.

This tendency toward fragmentation is glaringly evidenced in at least four areas: (1) the increasingly acrimonious debate between the secularly oriented and the religiously oriented Jew; (2) the sharpening of the differences between the religious groups; (3) the spiritual, cultural and social gap that is developing between us in America and the Jewish community in Israel, and (4) the inability of the American Jewish community to establish something resembling a national Jewish body that would be truly representative of the highest interest of the largest number of American Jews.

The tendency toward fragmentation is present in every society. It is inherent in the healthy mind's insistence upon deciding for itself what is right and what is wrong. Differences of opinion within a society are therefore unavoidable. Healthy societies encourage their expression. However, a society remains healthy only as long as the differences of opinion and of mores which prevail within it are contained within a large and firm framework of commonly held opinions and mores. Otherwise they eventually prove to be the undoing even of peoples that are held together by a common government, a common language and a commonly occupied territory. These are extremely important subsidiary bonds of union. They function effectively only in a society whose members share in common a large body of significant ideas and ideals. Lord Balfour is reported to have said of the English: "Our whole political machinery presupposes a people so fundamentally at one that they can afford to bicker."

Now throughout most of our long history, we too were a people so fundamentally at one that we could safely afford to bicker. I do not accept the widespread cliché that wherever there are three Jews, there are four opinions. Indeed, I believe that considering the difficult circumstances we had to face during most of our 3,500 years, we displayed extraordinary powers of cooperation and cohesion. At this period in our history, however, new factors have appeared in the life of our people which I believe tend to weaken the cohesive forces and to reinforce the divisive forces constantly vying for supremacy in every normal social organism. We are today confronted by that universally experienced paradox, that the seeds of our disaster are often sown by our blessings. The two greatest blessings which we as a people enjoy today are the freedom which, as citizens of the United States, is ours as individuals, and the status which is ours as a people by virtue of the existence of the State of Israel. Both of these blessings, however, contain within them the seeds of spiritual fragmentation.

The secularist-religionist controversy, the most serious spiritual threat to our future, is not of recent origin, nor is it limited to the confines of the Jewish people. Today all religions are faced with the secularist challenge. However, the establishment of the State of Israel has accelerated the tempo of this debate amongst us. It has immeasurably increased its heat and passion, and has effected a very significant shift in the alignment of the opposing forces.

The State of Israel has, by its very existence, bestowed unprecedented Jewish status upon the secularist Jew, so much so that a recent column by an American-born Israeli journalist lists among the freedoms enjoyed by a Jew in the State of Israel "the freedom to be a religious renegade." Since the establishment of the State of Israel, I have heard repeated *ad nauseam* the canard that Jews in the State of Israel do not need the Synagogue to identify them as Jews, while Jews in the Diaspora, and especially in America, need it and use it primarily as a sort of identification label. The grain of truth which this sociological observation contains fades into insignificance in comparison with the perilous distortion of Jewish life and history which it encourages.

The very name the "State of Israel" tends to confuse the general and Jewish public mind. For the terms *Children of Israel, Israelite* and *Jew* have been used interchangeably in common parlance. Now a new term has been introduced, *Israeli,* so that there are today *Christian-Israelis, Moslem-Israelis,* and every other kind of Israeli. Heretofore it was well-nigh universally accepted that the terms *Christian-Jew* or *Moslem-Jew* designated individuals who had to all intents and purposes read themselves out of the Jewish people. To an increasing number of secularist Jews today, the distinction between *Christian-Israeli* and *Christian-Jew* is beginning to appear less and less warranted. Heretofore, those who advocated the legitimization within the Jewish people of the concept *Christian-Jew* were either born Christians or were Jewish converts to Christianity who sought to persuade Jews that in accepting Christianity one was not a renegade to the Jewish people. Today, however, the legitimization of the concepts *Christian-Jew* or *Moslem-Jew* is being advocated by Jews who have no concern either for the Jewish religion or for Christianity or for any other religion. They are advocating it because the Jewish legitimization of the concept *Christian-Jew* is philosophically indispensable for the ultimate vindication of the secularist Jewish position. The political framework supplied by the State of Israel appears to the secularist Jewish nationalist to make such legitimization not only possible, but necessary.[3]

Moreover, the State of Israel provides both an international platform upon which to carry on this secularist-religionist debate, as well as the human situations in which the issues at stake are vividly concretized. The drama enacted on that exposed, avidly watched stage has wide repercussions in every Jewish community. The heat and confusion engendered by the verbal exchanges are reinforced by the living reality of the so-called normal secular-nationalist Jew who is appearing in increasing number in the State of Israel and in the Diaspora. As a result there is today greater uncertainty than ever in Jewish history regarding the answer to the question of what it means to be a Jew, and what component of one's Jewishness constitutes its ultimate, Jewishly determinative essence.

In addition, the existence within the State of Israel of a legally constituted, governmentally supported religious establishment has unquestionably not only intensified the conflict between secularists and religionists within the State; it has also contributed considerably toward the hardening of the lines among the religious groups within American Jewry. It is not my purpose at this time to pass judgment upon the wisdom or the rightness of the relations between State and Religion in Israel. I want now only to point out that the existence of a governmentally supported religious establishment in the State of Israel has led to an intensification of the differences among the Jewish religious groups in America, because the governmentally supported religious group in Israel and its allies in the Diaspora are taking the course natural to any group exercising power, namely, they are seeking to establish their *organizational* and not merely their *theological* hegemony over the whole of the Jewish people everywhere. This course of action goads the other religious groups to greater self-assertion than they might ordinarily have sought, and it leads to a widening of the spiritual chasm between the religious groupings.

The alienation between the Jewish community of the United States and that of the State of Israel which many foresee with justifiable foreboding, is but an aspect of the alienation between the secularist and the religionist Jew on the one hand, and the alienation between the Israeli government supported religious groups and the other Jewish religious groups on the other. The experience of the other ethnic groups in the United States as well as our own experience indicates that with the passing of another generation, and with the stabilization of the world situation generally and of Jewish affairs in particular, the average American secularly oriented Jew, who will have no Jewish religious nostalgic hangovers, will feel no greater attachment to the State of Israel nor concern for its welfare than the average American feels toward the country of his ancestors' origin. On the other hand, many American religiously oriented Jews will feel progressively alienated from the State of Israel if its Jewish citizens will remain divided as they are now between two camps, one consisting of secular nationalists and the other of religionists whose spokesmen will be a governmentally supported religious establishment which will be allied with one of the religious groupings in the Diaspora, and in opposition to all other religiously oriented Jewish groups.

The manner in which American democracy is contributing toward the fragmentation of our people is obvious. While each one of us as an *individual* enjoys to the full all the rights of American citizenship, *as a group* we have no legal status whatsoever. Never before in Jewish history has the Jewish community been so completely voluntaristic in its structure. We always had some minimal legal status as a group, and membership in the Jewish community, therefore, had some minimum political sanction to fortify it. In the United States we have absolutely no legally sanctioned way of knowing who is a Jew. The law never requires one to identify his religious affiliation, and we would not want it otherwise. Hence, while heretofore a Jew had to take some positive action to *dissociate* himself from the community, in the United States he must take some positive step to *associate* himself with the community. To develop a sense of Jewish community and community solidarity and discipline under such circumstances requires a consciously espoused conviction which is sustained and implemented by great financial generosity and voluntary physical exertion. These are virtues which are not found in overabundance among any people. This, then, is where we are tending as a people.

I turn now to the questions "What shall we do as a movement and how shall we do it?" I shall discuss both questions together for they are inextricably intertwined. The "what" directs our attention to the theoretical aspects of our movement, the "how" to the practical programmatic aspects. Both aspects must be pursued simultaneously, for theory must be constantly subjected to practice and practice must be directed by theory.

As a movement, therefore, we must on the one hand labor ceaselessly in the never-ending intellectual endeavor to formulate, reformulate, clarify and refine the principles which should guide our activities as a movement, and on the other hand we must diligently strive to create the institutions through which these principles will find expression in the daily personal lives of our people and in the activities of our communities. It is in this spirit that I present for your consideration those principles which I believe to be of paramount importance and to indicate the means for their implementation. What I shall say will in large measure be but a reformulation and a further extension of principles that we have consciously or intuitively followed and of things that we have done during these fifty years. Their restatement seems to me to be appropriate on this occasion.

1. *The meaningful existence and the creative unity of the Jewish people depend upon the extent to which all Jews,*

regardless of where they live, share commonly treasured historic memories, spiritual values and patterns of behavior. As a people we have lived for two thousand years, and hope in the future to live, on all known continents and among every civilized people. That necessarily implies that our unity cannot depend upon any external factors such as a common spoken language, a common political government, nor upon any kind of a contrived international organization. *Nor do we want or expect our unity to depend upon a common enemy.* I consider the oft-repeated statement that anti-Semitism has kept the Jewish people alive not only to be factually false, but also to be the greatest insult to us as a people and to our martyrs, saints and sages. Our existence and our unity as a people have in the past been rooted in, and dependent upon, commonly shared historic memories, spiritual values and patterns of behavior. If we are to continue to live meaningfully as a united people, the same will have to be true of our children.

But if this is to be true for our children we must provide for them an adequate supply of properly trained intellectual, spiritual and educational leadership. *The most serious bottleneck in Jewish life today is the dearth of Jewish scholars, rabbis and educators.* That is why our movement started in this country with the founding of a school of higher Jewish learning, the Jewish Theological Seminary of America. That is why, some seventeen years ago, when we turned our attention to the new great Jewish community developing on the Pacific coast, the first thing we did was to found a school of higher Jewish learning, the University of Judaism in Los Angeles. That is why we must, as congregations and as individuals, give highest priority in terms of thought, effort, affection, and generosity to the educational enterprise in all of its manifold expressions. Our congregational schools must be immeasurably strengthened. Our congregations must co-operate in the establishment of day schools, of high schools and of Ramah camps. What we do within this area within the next decade or two will determine our place in Jewish history.

2. *A Jew who is alienated from the Jewish religion is a Jew who is himself, and has set his children, on the highway leading away from the Jewish people.* We must ask ourselves, and we must incessantly ask our fellow Jews, to face up squarely to the full implications of the incontrovertible fact that the last link between a Jew and his people is his eligibility for membership in the Synagogue, *i.e.*, his eligibility to be counted as one of a *minyan* for public Jewish worship. When that link is broken, the individual has read himself out, and is read out, of membership in the Jewish people. Note that the criterion is eligibility for membership in *the* Synagogue, and not *actual* membership in *a* synagogue. *As long as there are ten Jews eligible for being included in a* minyan, *there is a Jewish people; without them, there is no Jewish people.*

That means that the fundamental social unit constituting the Jewish people is the *minyan,* the congregation, and that the one basic indispensable institution for Jewish community life is the Synagogue. That means that the establishment of congregations must become a matter of far greater concern for us as a movement than it has thus far been. The difficulties to be overcome in this area are tremendous, but wrestling with those difficulties must be ever on our agenda. Literally tens of thousands are being lost to us in the small and large centers of Jewish life, here and abroad, because local groups are too small or lack the religious and economic resources to organize themselves into congregations.

3. *We must maintain within our ranks a profound concern for the advancement of the highest interests of the Jewish community in* Eretz Yisrael *and an increasing involvement in all that makes for that advancement.* We were, as a movement, more completely identified with Zionism than any other Jewish religious group. Our concern for the advancement of Jewish life in *Eretz Yisrael* has in no way diminished, but we have not as yet found the appropriate channel

through which to express it. We should not be satisfied with merely doing what others ask us to do. We did, on our own initiative, build the synagogue structure now occupied by the Yeshurun congregation in Jerusalem. The Seminary does have a beautiful Student Center and the Schocken Institute in Jerusalem. Our Israel Ramah Camp and our United Synagogue Youth with its "Building Spiritual Bridges" projects and its pilgrimages to Israel are splendid achievements. But this is not enough. We should be more than loyal fellow travelers. We should, on our own as well as in cooperation with others, initiate activities that would contribute directly and substantially to the solution of the many educational, social, religious, and economic problems facing our people there today.

Integral to our concern for the advancement of Jewish life in *Eretz Yisrael* is our concern for the advancement of modern Hebrew literature in America. We want not only to preserve Hebrew in the liturgy of the Synagogue. We want to see it as a medium of literary expression not only in Israel but also in the Diaspora.

4. *We must engage in an unceasing, tireless effort to implement the whole of Torah, its moral and ethical injunctions governing our relations to our fellow men, as well as those of its injunctions whose aim it is to make us ever conscious of God's presence so that we may live lives of holiness in our homes and in our businesses and in our community relations.*

The establishment of alert social action groups in every synagogue may introduce some controversial matters into the congregation's life but it will be a "controversy for the sake of Heaven" which will bear rewarding fruit. Synagogue social action groups should be concerned not only with civil liberties but with every form of disability—political, social, economic, and educational—to which large sections of our population are still subjected. Such significant involvement will make us ever so much more vital and relevant as a movement. Only as we become thus involved shall we make Judaism an integral part *of,* and a vital force *in,* the spiritual life of America.

We must at the same time bear in mind that in the final analysis Judaism can be no greater force in the spiritual life of America than it is in our own lives. Our personal lives, our homes, our communities must reflect Judaism's call to righteousness, to lives striving to fulfill the injunction to love our neighbor as ourselves, and Judaism's injunction "Be ye holy, for I the Lord your God am holy" (Leviticus 19:2). We must strengthen and encourage one another in the pursuit of these aims. We can do this best in attending our synagogues and in joining with our friends and fellow congregants in the weekend Torah sessions where we can study, pray and observe the Sabbath authentically and return home invigorated spiritually. If we would turn our attention to the implementation of the great teachings of Judaism about whose relevancy and beauty all of us agree, the differences among us on some minor matters of ritual observance would assume their proper proportions and find their equitable solutions.

5. *We must try to implement the admonition addressed by Dr. Schechter to the graduates of the Seminary. "You must avoid," he said, "every action of a sectarian or of a schismatic nature, calculated to loosen the ties between you and your brethren scattered over our globe."*[4] *He wanted us to be a force for reconciliation in Jewish life.*

Of all the tasks Dr. Schechter set before us this is the most difficult. He knew that the Seminary and its graduates would be subjected to attacks from both the so-called "right" and "left." He knew that the request he made of the graduates ran counter to every natural human instinct of self-assertion and self-aggrandizement. But it is not an impossible task.

Our primary task as a movement is not to attack others or to answer their attacks upon us. It is rather to cultivate within our ranks every positive Jewish value which is treasured by any group in Jewish life. Our task is *not* to remake the whole Jewish people in our image; it is rather to transform ourselves so that in and through us, differing and even conflicting elements within our people should discover and experience their common spiritual kinship. We should be so ardently concerned with the nurturing of Hebrew, with the practice of piety, with the pursuit of the esthetic and the rational, with the exposition of the contemporaneously relevant in Judaism, and with the welfare of the Jewish community in *Eretz Yisrael,* that the secular Zionist who loves *Eretz Yisrael* more than he hates religion, the Orthodox religionist whose love of Jews is greater than his hate of those who deviate from his religious practice, and the religious reformer who loves those who seek justice and knowledge more than he hates those who wear *kippot* and eat kosher, and our secular culturalist who is more concerned with the development of the cultural heritage of our people than he is with destroying our religious heritage—that all of these should of necessity have to acknowledge their kinship with us, and through us with the whole Jewish people. That does not mean that we want or can be everything to everyone. It does mean that we want every Jew who sincerely loves anything which is authentically Jewish more than he hates anything which is authentically Jewish to find friendship, understanding and encouragement within our ranks.

6. *We should explore constantly and indefatigably every avenue which may lead to the creation of a national and ultimately even an international body that would be truly representative of the overwhelming majority of American and world Jewry.*

To be sure, Jewish unity depends essentially upon our sharing a common body of memories, ideals and patterns of life. But that does not mean that external organizational structure is of no importance. It is important, and those concerned with the future of the Jewish people should not weary in their efforts to create such an appropriate organizational structure.

Fortunately we do not have to start from scratch. We have, as a people, considerable experience in national and international cooperation. But each one of our rather numerous national or international bodies involves only a small fraction of the total people. And when an effort enlisted the support of representatives of substantially the whole people as in the case of the Jewish delegation at Versailles after the First World War, or of the American Jewish Conference 1943–1947, it had to be previously agreed that its aim was to be limited in scope, and its organizational structure was to be loose and temporary.

Because of the constant anti-Semitic accusation that there exists an international Jewish conspiracy, there is widespread and understandable hesitancy among many about setting up any permanent national or international organizational structure. But since the accusation has continued to flourish though it has no iota of truth, whether we do or do not create an effective publicly functioning international body for Jewish affairs will have little influence upon the thinking or the activities of our enemies. On the contrary it may be that since it would carry on all of its activities in the open, it would help dissipate the doubts that may be in the minds of even well-disposed men.

The Conservative Movement generally, and the United Synagogue in particular, are today among the largest and most effective bodies functioning on the national scene in the United States. Its international activities, through the World Council of Synagogues and other branches of the movement, are also steadily expanding. It should therefore be increasingly in a position to make its voice heard and its leadership felt in the difficult and complicated matter of setting up an effective, acceptable, permanent organizational structure for Jewish national and international cooperation in all matters affecting the welfare of the Jewish people and the role of the Jewish people in advancing the welfare of all mankind. This is obviously a goal that cannot and will not be easily achieved, but it is a goal that should always remain high on the agenda of our movement.

Every section of the Bible in one way or another sets before us the goal that must be ours as individuals and as a people. The United Synagogue has for some time now held its biennial conventions during the week when we read the Biblical portion containing the most dramatic and memorable symbol of that goal. It is the symbol of the lonely, frightened, fleeing Jacob dreaming of a ladder whose head reached unto Heaven, while his own head was resting on a rock. For 2,000 years the lonely, frightened, fleeing Jacob was the perfect symbol of his descendants who continued to dream his dream while they had naught but stones for pillows. The lot of Jacob's descendants in this land has undergone, thank God, a radical change for the better. Fifty years ago, Dr. Schechter expressed his faith that "In this great, glorious and free country we Jews need not sacrifice a single iota of our Torah; and, in the enjoyment of absolute equality with our fellow citizens we can live to carry out those ideals for which our ancestors so often had to die."[5]

In that faith he came to these shores to lead the Seminary. In that faith he founded the United Synagogue. Thank God, we have not entirely failed him. Looking back over these fifty years we too can say, as Lincoln said as he closed the address I referred to at the opening of my remarks:

> Of *strange, discordant,* and even *hostile* elements, we gathered from the four winds, and *formed* and fought the battle through, under the constant hot fire of a disciplined, proud, and pampered enemy. Did we brave all *then,* to *falter* now? . . . The result is not doubtful. . . . *Wise councils* may *accelerate* or *mistakes delay* it, but, sooner or later, the victory is *sure* to come.[6]

CHAPTER IX

The Concept of K'lal Yisrael[1]

Concepts are either denominative or valuational.[2] Denominative concepts have no overtones of judgment. They merely designate or name. Hence, their chief characteristic is that they can be defined absolutely or with a very high degree of exactitude. The concepts of mathematics and the natural sciences are denominative. The concepts of art, morals and religion are primarily valuational. They are not amenable to exact definition. They imply an attitude of approbation or of disapprobation. Concepts such as Beauty, Ugliness, Heroism, Cowardice, *Kiddush Ha-Shem* and *Hillul Ha-Shem* are valuational concepts. Insofar as they indicate approval or disapproval, they also simultaneously serve as stimuli, consciously or subconsciously motivating us to perform acts which they approve and to avoid acts which they disapprove. Some nouns start out as being primarily denominative in character, but for various reasons become more and more valuational in character. The word "nobleman" is such a noun. It was used at first primarily to designate individuals who by reason of birth or special royal favor had certain well-defined privileges. Today it is most frequently used in passing favorable judgment upon one who is deemed to have certain highly esteemed qualities of character. The Hebrew phrase *K'lal*

Yisrael represents such a compound noun. Its use even as a denominative concept was not very widespread before modern times. Today it is one of the valuational concepts most frequently found in articles and books dealing with problems of contemporary Jewish life. It is of some importance therefore that we know something about the history of this concept and the circumstances that brought it into such comparative prominence in our day.

Let us start by noting that the compound noun *K'lal Yisrael* is very rarely found in our classical or medieval literature. So rare is it and so unimportant that no dictionary of the Hebrew language, no anthology of Jewish thought or literature, deems it sufficiently significant to be listed as a separate item or even to include it under the rubric *K'lal* or *Yisrael*. Wherever it is found in these early sources its exact meaning is rather difficult to establish.

The concepts *K'lal* and *Yisrael* were, to be sure, widely used separately as denominative concepts. *Yisrael* is used to designate both an individual Israelite and the people as a whole. Thus in the expression *Yisrael Mumar* (Eruvin 69b, Kiddushin 18a) —"an apostate or a non-observant Israelite"— the term *Yisrael* obviously designates an individual Israelite. Far more often, however, the term *Yisrael* designates the whole people, as in the well-known prayer *Shomer Yisrael,* "Guardian of Israel."[3] As a designation for an individual Israelite, *Yisrael* is a denominative concept whose definition until very recently was both exact and universally accepted. An Israelite was anyone who was born of a Jewish mother or who by his own free action was converted to Judaism in a clearly specified and universally accepted manner. When used to designate the whole people, *Yisrael* refers to that group of individuals each one of whom may himself be designated as an Israelite. In modern times there is wide disagreement regarding procedures of conversion. Since the number of conversions is not inconsiderable and since there are those who accept as Israelites children of Jewish fathers and non-Jewish mothers even though neither the mother nor the children went through a universally acceptable ritual of conversion, the concept *Yisrael* as applied to an individual is today no longer a denominative concept whose definition has universal acceptance. Its usefulness as a denominative concept designating either the individual Israelite or the group as a whole has been considerably impaired.

The problem of whether one who is born of a Jewish mother may ever be deprived of the privilege of being denominated as *Yisrael,* or can voluntarily emancipate himself from the obligations inherent in being thus denominated, is one which occupied not only Rabbinic authorities for the last 2,000 years, but also many religiously neutral but ethnically proud Jews. Should one born a Jew who converted to another religion continue to be included within the concept of *Yisrael*? Should his name be listed in a volume devoted to biographies of Jews? We know that Rabbinic law continues, for certain purposes, to consider him an Israelite. We know also that in some respects it deprives him of privileges accorded even to one who is not born a Jew. But that problem does not here concern us.[3a] Our concern is to examine briefly the manner in which the terms *K'lal* and *Yisrael* were used in the past either singly or in combination and how they are used today.

The concept *K'lal* had and has a great variety of uses. One of its uses is to designate a group of any size, particularly as over against an individual. Thus, in discussing the procedure for reciting the Grace after Meals in company, the question is raised whether, when there are more than three participants, the leader should say *"barekhu"*—"Bless ye the Lord" or *"nevaraykh"*—"Let us bless the Lord." Samuel is of the opinion that he should say *"nevaraykh"* because *"le-olam al yotzi adam et atzmo min ha-k'lal"*—"one should never exclude himself from the group" (Berakhot 49b). Obviously, *K'lal* here refers to the group with which one happens at the moment to be associated. Samuel's statement is reminiscent of Hillel's admonition *"al tifrosh min ha-tzibbur"* (Avot 2:5)—"Do not separate yourself from the community," or the congregation, or the group. To be part of the *K'lal* or the *tzibbur* is generally deemed to be the ethically right thing to do, and to separate yourself from the *K'lal* is the wrong thing to do.

The term *K'lal* is also used as the equivalent of "category." Thus the statement *"yatza mi-k'lal kuti ve-likhlal Yisrael lo ba"* (Sanhedrin 58b) may be translated "he no longer belongs to the group or category known as *kuti* but cannot as yet be considered a member of the group or category known as *Yisrael.*"

The meaning of the expression *hotzi et atzmo min ha-k'lal*—"he has taken himself out of the *K'lal,*" found in the Mekhilta passage which is quoted in the Pesah Haggadah has given the commentators all through the ages a great deal of trouble. The text states that because the wicked son asked, "What does this ritual mean *to you*?", he "removed himself from the *K'lal.*" Does it mean that he ceased being an Israelite? Obviously not. And what is the *ikkar,* "the basic principle" which he has denied in asking his question? One of the widely-held opinions of the medieval commentators identifies the sin of the wicked son as consisting not so much in his separating himself from the community, but rather in denying that God had commanded the Israelites to perform the Passover rituals.[4] The use of the expression to designate apostasy is apparently first found in the *Shevet Yehudah,* a work of the sixteenth century.[5]

From other passages in Rabbinic literature it seems reasonable to conclude that the terms *ha-k'lal*—"the community" and *K'lal Yisrael*—"the community of Israel" came to be used interchangeably,[6] but always in their denominative connotation. Obviously for one to be identified with the community of Israel was always deemed a virtue, while separation from it was always deemed a grievous vice.

This brief excursion into the history of the term of *K'lal Yisrael* is, we believe, sufficient to indicate that it was heretofore a rather infrequently used denominative concept. Let us turn now to a brief inquiry into its use in our own day.

The frequency with which this concept is used nowadays was strikingly illustrated by the ease with which the examples herein to be cited were gathered. These passages were found, not as a result of diligent research, but in the course of casual reading while this paper was being prepared.

Thus, a well-known educator, in discussing a program for secondary Jewish education in the United States writes that "A sound program of secondary Jewish education requires an articulated philosophy which would provide for the needs of the individual student as well as those of the specific ideological group with which he is affiliated, the American Jewish Community and *Klal Yisrael, the community of the Jewish people the world-over*"[7] (italics mine, S.G.). *K'lal Yisrael* is here obviously used merely as a denominative concept, as the Hebrew equivalent of the English phrase "the community of the Jewish people the world over." As such its role in Jewish education is important and rather easily delineated. Jewish educators are in duty bound to make their pupils aware of "the community of the Jewish people the world-over," to help them identify themselves with that community and to rouse in them the desire to help meet the needs of that community.

A learned and thoughtful rabbi, writing in his synagogue bulletin, urges his congregants to accept the Sefardic pronunciation of Hebrew because "that will bind us more closely to *K'lal Yisrael*."[8] To whom does *K'lal Yisrael* as used here refer? Does the rabbi have the Jews of Soviet Russia in mind? Will the use of the Sefardic pronunciation bind us more closely to them or to the overwhelming majority of the Jews of America, who know nothing about either the Sefardic or the Ashkenazic pronunciation? Or is he subconsciously identifying the Jewish community in the State of Israel as *K'lal*

Yisrael? But even in the State of Israel not all Jews use the Sefardic pronunciation. How, then, does its use bind us more closely to *K'lal Yisrael*? And yet that rabbi's statement has meaning and many of us would intuitively react positively to it. What he consciously or subconsciously had in mind when he expressed this opinion was probably the concept of *K'lal* as constituting the totality of Israel's historic experience as a people. But he did not deem it necessary to go into such detail. It was enough for him to associate the Sefardic accent with the concept *K'lal Yisrael* to give it ultimate sanction, even as we do when we describe an act to be "truly American."

A rabbi in another bulletin urges his colleagues "to assert their collective authority and to provide directional signals for *K'lal Yisrael*."[9] It is quite apparent that the rabbi in this particular instance does not have the world Jewish community in mind but the American Jewish community. He uses *K'lal Yisrael,* therefore, not as an exact denominative concept, but as a valuational concept to designate an activity reaching out beyond what he considers to be parochial limits. In the same issue of the magazine, another rabbi hails the appearance of a publication and points to what he calls its "ecumenical or K'lal Yisraeldig staff," since its editors represent all three Jewish religious groupings. In this instance *K'lal Yisrael* is used to designate the *transdenominational* as opposed to the *denominational,* the all-inclusive rather than the particular.

One can, without much trouble, multiply passages from modern and particularly current literature in which the concept *K'lal Yisrael* is used primarily as an evaluational concept for commending activities and attitudes which are deemed to be transdenominational.[10] We certainly do not want directly or indirectly to underrate the significance of activities and attitudes which reach out beyond the organizational or ideological interests of any group within the Jewish people. However, in order to evaluate the full import of this emphasis upon transdenominationalism or transparty lines, we should recall the historic circumstances that brought *K'lal Yisrael* as a valuational concept into such prominence in our day.

The chain of historic circumstances which culminated in our present situation originated with the appearance of the modern Westernized Jew who rejected the Jewish religious heritage, but who did not want to sever his association with the physical reality known as the Jewish people. In order to maintain his intellectual integrity he had need of a concept that would enable him to subsume himself under the category *Yisrael* without violating his convictions and without being burdened with a sense of guilt. This new type of Jew is an intellectual problem not only to himself but also to the modern, religiously identified, democratically oriented Jew. The latter's religious convictions do not require him to deny his secular fellow Jew the right to identify himself as a Jew, and his attachment to the democratic principle of tolerance of differences requires him to refrain from passing judgment upon the quality of the Jewishness of his secular fellow Jew. How can he maintain his own religious convictions and his own spiritual and intellectual integrity and at the same time believe that his secular fellow Jew is as good a Jew as he is?

The second circumstance which contributed to the rise of the concept of *K'lal Yisrael* into prominence was the division of the religiously oriented Jews into different identifiable parties, which may become ultimately irreconcilable groups. This has happened before in Jewish history. If this real danger is to be avoided, there must be introduced into the innermost fabric of Jewish thought a concept which would enable the members of these groups to continue to maintain a sense of real historic and spiritual kinship among them.

The third historic circumstance that necessitated the creation of a new concept was the wide dispersal of the Jewish people in modern times, associated with the phenomenal advances made in means of transportation and communication. To be sure the concept of *haverim kol Yisrael*[11] ("all Jews are related to one another") and the dictum *kol Yisrael arevim zeh ba-zeh*[12] ("all Jews are responsible one for the other") are very old. However, heretofore, the chances that a Jewish community other than the one within which the individual happened to live would ever become real to him were very slight. The individual Jew was rarely called upon to exercise towards Jews in a geographically distant land, other than *Eretz Yisrael,* the responsibilities implied in either of the two dicta. However, beginning with the second half of the nineteenth century, the Jews of the West, because of their favored economic and political position, started to assume responsibility for the welfare of their fellow Jews, first in the Near East and Northern Africa and then in Eastern Europe. This, followed by the large-scale Jewish immigration from Central and Eastern Europe to the West, and by the tragedies that swept over the Jews of Central and Eastern Europe and other lands during the twentieth century, created the irrepressible intellectual need for a concept that would stress the essential kinship of Jews regardless of the physical distances and the ideological differences that separated them.

To meet this threefold need a number of concepts, Hebrew and non-Hebrew, were mustered into service with varying degrees of success. The Hebrew concept which for a long time won widest approval was the concept of *Am Yisrael,* with the term *Am* used as the closest equivalent of the term "Nation." This concept was widely favored, particularly by the religiously unidentified, politically disfranchised East European Jew. Obviously reflecting the mood of nineteenth century Nationalism, which envisioned nations as units harboring within their ranks and with equal ardor the religious as well as the non- or even anti-religious, the concept *Am,* when associated with *Yisrael,* specifically and pointedly subsumed the non- and anti-religious Jew under the concept of *Yisrael.*

While the concept *Am Yisrael,* thus interpreted, emancipated the individual Israelite from what were deemed to be purely religious obligations, it did place upon him at least two obligations which were inherent in the denominative concept "Nation" as used by Nationalists of the nineteenth century. These were the obligation to cultivate a national language, and the obligation to establish an identifiable political order within which this *Am Yisrael* would live as a politically, or at least a culturally autonomous unit, either upon the soil of its ancient homeland *Eretz Yisrael,* or as a politically recognized minority elsewhere in the world. Insofar, then, as the concept *Am Yisrael* implied obligations, it was more than merely a denominative concept. It had very clear valuational overtones. It implied that while one who did not cultivate the language or advance the political autonomy of *Am Yisrael* could not be read out of membership in *Am Yisrael,* he could and should be adjudged as either a wayward or a recalcitrant or even a traitorous member of the *Am,* the degree of censure being directly related to the degree of the indifference or the conscious opposition of the individual to obligations inherent in the concept *Am.* We need but recall the acrimonious debates between Zionists, non-Zionists and anti-Zionists that have been going on within the Jewish community since the rise of the *Hovevei Zion* groups. The concept *Am Yisrael* is, therefore, in its own way a very rigorous, evaluational concept, having within it a force making for divisiveness which at times appears to be as great as its power to unify. While it does not disown those who disown it, it nevertheless passes severe judgment upon them, designating them as erring or rebellious children.

There can be no doubt that the concept *Am Yisrael* was the indispensable intellectual tool of the Zionist Movement. It made the renascence of the Hebrew language and the establishment of the State of Israel at least implicitly obligatory. Without it the movement could not have attracted the religiously unaffiliated *halutzim,* nor could it have made itself intelligible to the statesmen of the world.

It is one of the ironies of our day that the historically unparalleled triumph of the concept *Am Yisrael* as concretized in the renascence of Hebrew and the establishment of the State of Israel is the cause of its present eclipse, particularly in the United States. Insofar as the concept *Am Yisrael* has come to be equated with Nation and to be identified primarily with its twofold concretization of State and language, the average American Jew, whether he is religiously oriented or not, shies away from it.

This change from "nation" to "people" is dramatically evidenced in the writings of Professor Mordecai M. Kaplan. In his history-making volume *Judaism as a Civilization,* published in 1934, the concept "peoplehood" does not even appear and the Index has only one reference to the concept "people." Under the concepts of "nation," "Nationhood" and "Jewish Nationhood," however, the Index has two full columns of references. On the other hand in his *New Zionism* published in 1955, Dr. Kaplan seems pointedly to reject the concept of Jewish nationhood. In a chapter entitled "The Reaffirmation of Jewish Peoplehood," he writes: "Not nationhood but peoplehood, would be the objective of the New Zionism, since it would have to embrace the entire House, or community of Israel."[13]

But even before the rise of the State of Israel there was a significant sector of the American Jewish community, both among the religiously oriented as well as among the secularly oriented, who did not want to be subsumed under the concept of *Am Yisrael*—Jewish nation—and yet wanted to be identified with the effort to revive the Hebrew language and to build the Jewish community in *Eretz Yisrael.* They rationalized their interest in a variety of ways such as nostalgic historic memory, or creating a new social order, or aid to the needy and the persecuted. Among them there were many who while they refused to think of themselves as members of the Jewish nation, readily and proudly acknowledged themselves as members of the Jewish *people.* Their greatest spokesman in America was Louis Marshall. He was undoubtedly one of the very few truly intellectually and spiritually distinguished lay leaders who have thus far appeared on the American Jewish scene, and he has not as yet been given his proper due. The two volumes of his letters and addresses reveal a mind and heart of majestic stature. The concept of "people" which Louis Marshall used in his correspondence regarding the Balfour Declaration[14] has now become the concept most widely used when referring to the totality of individuals known as Jews. The concept *K'lal Yisrael,* whose rising popularity is evidenced on all sides, is in essence its Hebrew counterpart.

There is nothing sacrosanct about the concept of "nation" or "nationhood" which makes it incumbent upon us to continue to prefer it to the concepts of "people" or "peoplehood," but we should not deceive ourselves as to the reason why we prefer the one to the other. The concept "people" is to be sure more "embracing" but that is due to the fact that its definition is far more vague. The concept of "nation" calls to mind a "race or people characterized by common descent, language, or history usually organized as a separate political state and occupying a definite territory" (*Shorter Oxford English Dictionary*). To be sure, the concept "people" is often used as a synonym of nation, but since its use is being advocated amongst us to distinguish us as a people rather than as a nation, we have in mind its vaguer, ambiguous connotations "designating persons belonging to a place, constituting a particular concourse, congregation, company or class" (*ibid.*). When we designate a group as a "people," we say nothing more specific than that there is something about the group thus designated which differentiates it from other groups thus designated. But it gives us no clue to what that something may be.

Since the concept of "people" or "peoplehood" as such gives us no significant clue regarding the qualities or characteristics of the group thus identified, it takes on significance only when an adjective is associated with it such as the American, or Jewish, or English people. It derives its significance from the adjective. As a denominative concept it is, therefore, quite useless. Does it have any significance as a valuational concept? It does, if one attaches significance to the mere fact of being a people, that is, to being in some way identifiable as a group different from other groups. If some precious "good" inheres in the *very existence of a people,* then anything which helps insure the existence of that people of necessity partakes of that "good." Hence, to say of something—whether it be an act or an object—that it contributes towards the preservation of the "people," at once bestows value upon that act or object. Moreover, if the preservation of the "people" is adjudged to be the highest value of the people then whatever helps to preserve it takes on the quality of the highest value.

This emphasis upon peoplehood and its preservation has, like everything else, its positive as well as its negative aspects. Its negative aspect is that it tends to "sanctify" equally, as it were, everything that sustains the people's self-awareness whether it be lox and bagels on Sunday morning, or gefilte fish on Friday night, or maintaining a membership in a synagogue or in a Jewish country club. Its positive aspect is that it affords an additional, powerful natural sanction to the maintenance of the group's more precious spiritual heritage of religious observance and social mores, so that Jews are urged to observe the Sabbath in order to preserve the Jewish people. But this more positive aspect is associated with the adjective which modifies the noun, that is, with the adjective "Jewish" rather than with the noun "people."[15] The ongoing discussion or controversy between the secularists and the religionists amongst us, or between the maximalists and the minimalists, thus concerns the comparative roles of the words "Jewish" and "people" in the valuational concept "Jewish people." Which of the two is the valuationally determinative one? Is everything that preserves us as a people good, or is only that which preserves us as a *Jewish* people good? Are those things which preserve us as a people as good as those things which preserve us as a *Jewish* people?

This controversy as to which of the two terms in the concept "Jewish people" is to be valuationally determinative will, inevitably, continue for there is nothing inherent within the concept "Jewish people" that indicates which one of its two terms is or should be determinative.

The concept *K'lal Yisrael,* which is the Hebrew counterpart of "Jewish people," also suffers from the ambiguity inherent in a two-word concept, but not to the same extent as does the term "Jewish people." *Yisrael* is infinitely more significant and meaningful a concept than *K'lal*. Moreover, *K'lal* itself has no independent meaning equivalent to the concept "people." No matter how broadly one may define the term *K'lal* in this context, it cannot possibly go beyond the boundaries to which *Yisrael* limits it. The English equivalent of *K'lal Yisrael* would be "Israel in its most inclusive connotations." The emphasis remains upon Israel. As a valuational concept, *K'lal Yisrael* therefore adjudges as good any act or attitude which concretizes the broadest possible implications and meanings of the term *Yisrael*.

There can be no doubt that the leading spokesmen for the Conservative Movement in Judaism have always advocated an attitude which is best described by the concept *K'lal Yisrael*. Solomon Schechter, of blessed memory, popularized the concept of "Catholic Israel."[16] He hoped thereby to indicate that Israel cannot be identified with any one era in the history of Judaism, nor with any one historic community, or ideology or theology. This eternal reaching out beyond narrow historic, intellectual, social, or religious horizons requires a concept whereby it can be identified. In our day it is the concept of *K'lal Yisrael*. As such it is an indispensable intellectual tool for us. However, like every tool of the hand or the intellect, it can be used properly or improperly. The concept *K'lal Yisrael* is no exception to this rule. Let us note some of its misuses.

The basic misuse results from the tendency inherent in all broad definitions of valuational concepts, namely, that of attenuating their meaning almost to the vanishing point. This attenuation of meaning in turn is used as the most powerful battering ram to break down standards, to level down values and undermine all criteria of judgment. In our day the concept *K'lal Yisrael* is all too often used to derogate directly or indirectly any activity which does not have the support of the overwhelming majority of contemporary Jewry and hence deemed to be divisive. The lowest common denominator uniting all Jews is probably fear of, and opposition to, anti-Semitism. No activity has more universal, more generous support than that of fighting anti-Semitism. There is nothing wrong and much that is right in fighting anti-Semitism. But the fact that it is a *K'lal Yisrael* activity does not make it more important than such so-called denominational activities as intensive Hebrew education, Sabbath observance and participation in the religious life of the Synagogue. Next to anti-Semitism or perhaps equally universal in its appeal to the vast majority of Jews is the establishment and maintenance of institutions for medical care and for care of the aged. Again, no one can gainsay the importance of these institutions nor the fact that they have wide community support and are therefore significant concretizations of the concept of *K'lal Yisrael*. But if *K'lal Yisrael* is to be treated as a valuational concept of the highest order and then to be applied only to activities which appeal to the lowest common denominator among Jews, it will become the concept which will give sanction to all those tendencies in Jewish community life which empty it of all of its rich cultural and religious content. Indeed, that has in large measure already happened. Unfortunately, this is precisely the chief use to which the concept *K'lal Yisrael* is put in our day.

Our generation of Jews probably has the greatest percentage of believers in the anonymous, obviously hyperbolic Rabbinic statement: "*Hamurah avodat elilim she-kol ha-*

kofayr bah, ke-ilu modeh be-khol ha-Torah kulah"—"The sin of idolatry is so great that the mere negation of idolatry is to be accounted as if it implied the acceptance of the whole Torah" (Kiddushin 40a). As long as a Jew has not been actually converted to another faith, even though his wife and children may belong to another faith, he is not merely accepted within the Jewish fellowship, but is also readily accepted as a Jewish community leader and the quality of his Jewishness dare not be questioned. As long as he is willing to identify himself with the Jewish people, as long as he can be included under the concept *K'lal Yisrael,* his Jewishness is accepted as being as good as anyone else's.

It is true that Judaism recognizes the principle of *"yaysh koneh olamo be-sha'ah ahat"* (Avodah Zarah 10b), that one great deed may outweigh in significance a long life of mediocre routine acts. But no society can construct standards of conduct on the basis of that principle, and most people as well as most societies must look to more prosaic means whereby to attain their portion in the world to come. We have taught ourselves to say rather glibly that one Jew is as good as another and to condemn anyone who as much as implies in word or act that one Jew may be a better Jew than another.

Moreover, the term *K'lal Yisrael* is all too often used to condemn or at least to minimize the significance of any activity which does not conform to the lowest possible denominator of the term Jew. Since not all Jews want to study Hebrew, emphasis upon Hebrew in the Jewish school curriculum is considered inimical to *K'lal Yisrael,* divisive and therefore bad. Since the Synagogue stresses the religious aspects of Judaism and not all Jews accept it, the Synagogue is an anti-*K'lal Yisrael* institution and therefore suspect. The Jewish Community Center, meanwhile, is upheld as the finest concretization of the concept *K'lal Yisrael* because its program of recreation serves the whole Jewish community. Not only does the concept *K'lal Yisrael,* when thus applied, reduce the contents of the term to a pale, meaningless shadow of a rich and vibrant substance, but it also condemns all efforts to create standards in Jewish life. It inhibits the indispensable need that each one of us has to evaluate phenomena by some measuring rod whereby one line of action is declared and believed to be better than another. If through the magic of the concept *K'lal Yisrael* the Jew who does not observe *mitzvot,* does not give his children a Jewish education, does not believe Hebrew should be taught, is explicitly or implicitly declared to be as good a Jew as one who does, then we can surely say of this concept that *yatza sekharo behefsaydo*[17]—whatever good it does is counterbalanced by the evil.

This problem of reconciling convictions and standards with the broadest possible human sympathy and sincere broadmindedness is one which is not peculiarly Jewish. It is the basic spiritual and intellectual problem of all societies that are open and democratic rather than closed and totalitarian. It is the problem involved in the nature of "tolerance." Is a person truly tolerant who, while giving the other man the right to think as he does, nevertheless considers his own way of acting and thinking to be superior to that which he is tolerating in the other man? Is it enough to say, "I thoroughly disagree with you and I believe your opinion to be wrong and harmful, yet I will fight for your right to uphold it"? Or must the man of true tolerance say, "I shall fight for your right to uphold your opinion even though I disagree with you, because I believe that your opinion is as good as mine"?[18]

I am strongly inclined to the opinion that the concept of *K'lal Yisrael* as used valuationally today tends to derogate anyone who says, "I utterly and unalterably oppose what you say," even though he goes on to say, "but I shall fight for your right to say it." It is used all too often as the ethical sanction for the attitude that all Jews are equally good Jews and hence as the tool for the breakdown of convictions and standards.

What then must we do in order to preserve the immense

blessings for good inherent in the concept *K'lal Yisrael* and reduce to a minimum its potential for harm?

If the concept *K'lal Yisrael* is to serve us best, it must, in the first place, be integrally associated with two other concepts, namely *Posh'ay Yisrael*—"the sinners in Israel," and *Ahavat Yisrael*—"love for the people of Israel." By associating it with the concept *Posh'ay Yisrael,* we prevent it from breaking down standards in Jewish life. There are people who belong to *K'lal Yisrael* but they are *Posh'ay Yisrael,* they do things that are contrary to or inimical to the highest welfare of *Yisrael.* By associating the concept *Ahavat Yisrael* with *Posh'ay Yisrael* we are reminded of our obligations to treat everyone who is part of *K'lal Yisrael* with affection and to exclude no one who does not exclude himself.

Jewish educators therefore have the very difficult task to teach that there *are* standards of conduct in Jewish life and some ways of living as a Jew are to be preferred to other ways, even though these ways may in some manner divide us off or separate us from large sections of the Jewish people. At the same time we must seek to nurture a sense of special kinship and identification with, and a sincere love for, all who may properly be included under the concept Israel. We must resist the imputation that because we have standards we are violating the concept *K'lal Yisrael.* However, we must do that not only in words but also in deeds. If we want the concept *K'lal Yisrael* to serve us best, we should seek every opportunity to maintain frequent physical contact and all possible organizational ties with Jews who do not think and act as we do. At the same time we must be ready to define *K'lal Yisrael* not in terms of its minimum, lowest common denominator, but in terms of its richest possible content. *K'lal Yisrael* includes the pious, the saintly, the secularist, the Hebraist, the Yiddishist, the Sefardi, the Ashkenazi, the Yemenite. All of us should strive to be Jews who appreciate and embody whatever is Jewishly positive in any Jew. Thereby anyone, insofar as he is a Jew, should be able to establish a meaningful contact with us on the basis of whatever is our common Jewish concern. Our education program must be based upon the proposition that for us Jewish unity does not mean advocating that everyone should be like we are, but rather the determination to train Jews of such broad Jewish knowledge, skill and sympathy that every Jew who is devoted to any significant positive value associated with Jewish life and history will find a brother in them. The concept *K'lal Yisrael* should imply the injunction that we be Jews with the widest possible sympathies for every positive expression of Judaism, basing ourselves upon the proposition that the wider a Jew's intellectual and spiritual appreciation of all things Jewish, the better a Jew he is; the narrower they are, the worse a Jew he is. And as Jews of broad intellectual and spiritual appreciation of all things Jewish, we do not hesitate to pass judgment; for our judgment does not mitigate our love for any Jew even as our judgment of our fellow man, Jew or non-Jew, should not negate our concern for him, nor our respect for his humanity.

We are, fortunately, not living in an age when religious controversy is a popular pastime. I fear, however, that the American Jewish community may well be entering upon such an era. There are warning signals that seem to be presaging another period when those to the far left and those to the far right will be withdrawing from the main body of *K'lal Yisrael*. In this era the Conservative Movement in Judaism, through its schools and educators, has an historic function of the first order to fulfill. We are the group that has very much in common both with those to the right and those to the left of us. We share with the former, allegiance to the central place of the Law, of the *mitzvot ma'asiyot*—the ritual and ethical commandments in Jewish life—and with the latter, the faith that Judaism has naught to fear from contact with the best in modern scientific and philosophic thought. With our secular nationalist brethren we share a fervent attachment to the Hebrew language and to the land of Israel. We must therefore stress the inescapable religious and moral obligation that the concept *K'lal Yisrael* places upon us—the obligation to nurture the bonds of fellowship between us and all Jews—while at the same time maintaining our own conception of what constitutes the noblest expression of the Jewish ideal of human conduct.

And in so acting, our problem is, in essence, no different from that of educators in any democratic society. Every American must strive to serve the interests of all America and identify himself with all Americans. He must, however, at the same time have some standards by which he evaluates the behavior of Americans and have the courage to say that Robert E. Lee, splendid a man as he was, was not as good an American as Lincoln, that Calhoun was not as good an American as Webster, though both men were fine gentlemen and considered themselves to be loyal Americans.

It has been said that the anti-Semite hates *K'lal Yisrael* but on occasion likes *Reb Yisrael,* while the average Jew likes *K'lal Yisrael* but all too often hates *Reb Yisrael.* Our duty is to be Jews who love both *K'lal Yisrael* and *Reb Yisrael.* This love should not, however, be *ahavah ha-mekalkelet et ha-shurah,* a love that cannot distinguish between the authentic and the non-authentic in Judaism, but rather the love with which the prophets loved Israel, or with which Rabbi Akiba or Rabbi Kook loved them. It is a love that embraces everyone not because one is as good as the other, for love does not require a sacrifice of standards and of judgment, nor because the beloved agrees with the lover in thought and action. Love does not imply such agreement. It is rather to be a love rooted in the divine injunction to love our fellow man as ourselves and in our duty to imitate God, Who loves Israel with *ahavah rabah* and *ahavat olam*—with great and everlasting love.

CHAPTER X

The Role of Higher Jewish Learning—An Evaluation of The Jewish Theological Seminary of America[1]

Public self-appraisal taxes equally the integrity of the saint and of the sinner. The saint labors under the admonition "Let the stranger praise you, and not your own mouth" (Proverbs 27:2). His self-appraisal will therefore be weighted towards self-disparagement. The sinner will take refuge in the principle "Man is not permitted to incriminate himself" (Yevamot 25b). No one can be asked or expected to incriminate or even disparage himself publicly. Need I add that I am not worried about succumbing to the weaknesses of the saint.

To the best of my knowledge, this is the first time that such a comprehensive self-appraisal has been attempted within the ranks of the Conservative Movement. It seems to be particularly timely because the last fifteen years have witnessed the very remarkable and encouraging physical growth of the Rabbinical Assembly and the United Synagogue as well as the extraordinary expansion of the scope of the Seminary.

In preparation for the writing of this paper I reread many

of the basic documents in which the founders of the Seminary recorded their reasons for establishing it and the end results they hoped to achieve. And even though we may imagine, as I had, that we are thoroughly acquainted with the thought and writings of these men, I believe that we owe it to ourselves as well as to them, to recall the goals they had formulated for the School they founded with such sacrifice and devotion. For while one may disagree with the aims that an institution has set for itself, it is to be judged not in relation to what we think it should have done, but rather in relation to the goals it set out to attain.

THE AIMS AND PURPOSES OF THE SEMINARY

1. The first clearly formulated aim of the founders of the Seminary was the determination to stem the tide of ruthless surgery then being performed on the body of the doctrine and practice of Judaism by the leaders of the Reform Movement in the United States.

It is of the utmost importance for us to remember that the men who founded the Seminary or were its spiritual forerunners were in many instances active in the founding of the Hebrew Union College. None had their hearts more firmly set than they upon the hope of creating one great institution of higher Jewish learning that would train spiritual leaders for all American Jewry. They had hoped that the Hebrew Union College might become that institution. Hence, Sabato Morais, the founder of the Seminary, for a time acted as one of its examiners. At one time he even exhorted his congregation, Mikveh Israel of Philadelphia, to join the Union of American Hebrew Congregations. In 1878 he "journeyed to Cincinnati and delivered the address at the closing exercises of the Hebrew Union College." He felt impelled to sever his relations with Hebrew Union College only when, in 1885, the Faculty and the then graduates of Hebrew Union College adopted the Pittsburgh platform and identified the College with it.[2]

The founders of the Reform Movement gloried in being religious innovators, in declaring that they were the fashioners of an American Judaism which was to differentiate itself from the Judaism of the past by rejecting the authority of both Rabbinic and Biblical law, by dissociating itself from all hopes and prayers centered upon Zion, by reducing the place of Hebrew in Jewish life to a mere symbol of the past, and by adopting a series of theological principles or dogmas at basic variance in many essentials with traditional or historical Judaism.[3] The men who gathered around Morais to found the Seminary were bent upon "maintaining the thesis that the Biblical and Rabbinical Law as handed down and interpreted by the Rabbis and sages of Israel, was binding on the Jewish people, and that Judaism was an historical growth and not a mushroom sect whose character was to be changed from time to time by platforms or resolutions."[4]

Dr. Schechter never tired in stressing that "There is no other Jewish religion but that taught by the Torah and confirmed by history and tradition, and sunk into the conscience of Catholic Israel."[5] "Judaism," Schechter maintained, "insists upon the observance both of the spirit and of the letter . . . (it) is absolutely incompatible with the abandonment of the Torah."[6] Hence "Those who are entrusted with carrying out the purpose of this institution . . . both pupils and masters, must faithfully and manfully maintain their loyalty to the Torah."[7]

Loyalty to the Torah, then, was the primary motivation that led both to the organization of the Seminary in 1886 and to its reorganization in 1901.

2. The second aim envisaged by its founders and most forcefully and clearly enunciated by its reorganizers was to root loyalty to the Torah in, and associate it with, the most comprehensive knowledge possible of all aspects of the Torah.

That included not only the Bible, the Talmud, the Midrashim and their ancient and modern commentators, but also Jewish history, Jewish medieval literature, its poetry and philosophy and the great codes of Jewish law. "We cannot," Dr. Schechter said, "hope to carry the student through all these vast fields of learning. . . . But this fact must not prevent us from making the attempt to bring the students on terms of acquaintance at least with all those manifestations of Jewish life and thought."[8] Hence the bewildering array of subjects in the Seminary curriculum. In addition, the Seminary graduate was to be one who was deeply rooted in all aspects of the best in the thought and achievements of human civilization. Loyalty to the Torah was not to be equated either with an obscurantist fundamentalism or with what Schechter called an "artificial ignorance" maintained by isolating Judaism, its rabbis and its teachers from the main stream of human, philosophic and scientific achievement. Hence the requirement for a college degree before entrance into the Rabbinical School, a rather novel requirement at the time. The Seminary founders built upon the conviction that the future of Judaism depended not so much upon a reformation of it as upon a knowledge of it and of its place in the totality of human thought.

3. Thirdly, the Seminary was to be a center for original scholarly research, carried on in an atmosphere of maximum academic freedom and maximum opportunity for each man to develop his own intellectual endowments and spiritual inclinations.

The Seminary's emphasis upon loyalty to the Torah was not to be interpreted as a desire to create a community of uniformity in thought and conformity in action. "You must not think," Dr. Schechter told the audience that came to celebrate Seminary Charter Day in 1902, "that our intention is to convert this school of learning into a certain groove of thinking, or, rather, not thinking."[9] "I would consider my work . . . a complete failure if this institution would not in the future produce such extremes as on the one side a raving mystic who would denounce me as a sober Philistine; on the other side, an advanced critic, who would rail at me as a narrow-minded fanatic, while a third devotee of strict orthodoxy would raise protest against any critical views I may entertain."[10]

Since "the crown and climax of all learning is research"[11] the Seminary's Faculty was to be made up of men who in addition to being men of piety and knowledge would also be creative scholars whose works would be distinguished from "the mere erudition of olden times" in that they would conform to the principles of all modern, scientific research.[12] Such modern, scientific scholarship would not only add new and vital data to the total sum of our knowledge of the past, but would inevitably also focus greater and more penetrating light upon our problems of the present and our responsibilities to the future.

All of this could and was to be achieved under the canopy and within the framework of the Torah, for as Schechter repeatedly reminded his generation, "The Torah gave spiritual accommodation for thousands of years to all sorts and conditions of men, sages, philosophers, scholars, mystics, casuists, school men, and skeptics; and it should also prove broad enough to harbor the different minds of the present century."[13]

4. Fourthly, the Seminary was to strive ceaselessly to be a force for the "Reconciliation of Israel."

Dr. Schechter's address to the first graduating class was devoted to this theme. It constantly recurs in the writings of the Seminary's founders. They were profoundly aware of the danger that threatened Judaism in the widening breach between the militant Reform and the militant Neo-Orthodox parties. "I in no way wish you," Dr. Schechter said to those first graduates, "to constitute yourselves into a sort of *Synagoga Militans,* and to widen the gap which is already deep enough to divide Israel into regular sects. . . .[14] "It is only by proceeding on the lines mapped out for us by Zunz, Krochmal, Rappaport, Frankel, and others, that traditional Judaism, built up on the broad basis of science and history, can ever hope to become a force and to bring about that reconciliation among the parties to which every well-wisher of Israel is looking forward."[15]

The founders of the Seminary were, of course, fully conscious of the fact that they were acting "in the midst of many movements"[16] and that the Seminary occupied a "conservative position."[17] Schechter refers to "the spirit of conservative Judaism"[18] with a small "c" and called the United Synagogue into being in order to nurture that spirit within the community. But he and all other leaders of the Seminary were ever hopeful that the small "c" would never be transformed into a capital "C" and that the spirit of conservative Judaism would be most fully reflected not in those aspects of it which make it conservative, but rather in those which make it Judaism.

5. The fifth goal which motivated the founders of the Seminary was the hope that, through it, Judaism would become again an accepted, recognized, respected and effective participant in the advancement of human thought generally. Dr. Schechter wanted the Seminary to make its contribution towards what he termed the "Emancipation of Jewish Science," for he believed with Zunz that "The emancipation of the Jews will never be complete until Jewish science is emancipated. That is to say, till Jewish learning and Jewish scholarship and the knowledge of its literature have become recognized factors in the march of human intellect: till Jewish science should occupy a position among other sciences worthy of its long history and its influence upon mankind."[19]

Louis Marshall, undoubtedly one of the greatest lay leaders of our people in this country, and one who perhaps better than any other lay leader understood and articulated the purposes of the Seminary, in writing to S. W. Strauss in October 1924, summarized the goals of the Seminary as being "The perpetuation of Judaism as a living religion and as a great influence upon civilization."[20]

Because of the modesty of its beginnings as compared with the enormity of the task envisaged by this hope, this aspect of the Seminary's goals received but little attention during the first four decades following its reorganization. But those decades prepared the soil in which the seminal idea could take root and laid the groundwork for the developments to follow.

6. Finally, in the spirit of *sof ma'aseh be-mahshavah tehilah* (last in deed but first in thought), "The Seminary as an institution of Jewish learning was designed for the purpose of creating an educated Jewish Rabbinate in the U.S."[21]

The Seminary founders obviously had a very clear idea of what they had in mind when they spoke of "an educated Jewish Rabbinate in the U.S.," but it is equally obvious that in the early years of this century no one, including the founders of the Seminary, had a very clear idea of the role that the rabbis, particularly those who were to be the bearers of the Conservative Movement, were to play in the life of the American Jewish community. Dr. Schechter, of course, recognized that education, knowledge alone, does not yet make a rabbi. His commencement addresses therefore "contain admonitions with regard to the special virtues expected from the spiritual leaders in Israel, such as humility, meekness, peacefulness and considerateness," though he readily acknowledged that "there is nothing new in these admonitions."[22] Moreover, though Dr. Schechter takes justifiable pride in the fact that the Seminary was "among the first public bodies which tried to grapple" with the problem of the religious education of the young, a long time passed before it recognized that the rabbi had a special part to play in this area and that the Seminary has a responsibility to prepare him for it properly.

Nor was there clarity on the nature of the Rabbinic ordination bestowed by the Seminary upon its graduates. One thing was obvious from the beginning, namely that the title of "Rabbi, Teacher and Preacher" was not the equivalent of the traditional *Semikhah,* for the attainment of which a special course of studies had been outlined. This lack of precision in the thinking of the founders of the Seminary in regard to the functions and the authority of the rabbis the Seminary was to train is but a reflection of their intellectual honesty and integrity. They did not know how the American Jewish community was to develop, nor could they foresee the variety of roles the American rabbi would be called upon to assume. All they knew clearly was that the new situation could not be met by men trained in the methods of the East European *Yeshivot,* nor by men ignorant of the sources of Judaism and lacking reverence for its traditions. Hence Dr. Adler spoke for all of them when with his characteristic simplicity, honesty and clarity, he said that the Seminary "aims to carry the student back to the sources of Jewish law, history, liturgy, philosophy, theology and practice, believing that men so grounded in the knowledge and essentials of the great historic structure which we call Judaism, will preach it and practice it."[23] Beyond that, they were not ready to define their conception of the Seminary's role as a training school for rabbis.

DID THE SEMINARY FULFILL ITS AIMS?

One may legitimately question whether any one of the enumerated aims is in itself significant and whether as a whole they constitute an adequate program. I believe that we of the Rabbinical Assembly would by and large agree that each one of the aims separately is of the utmost significance and that together they constitute an impressive program to meet many of the urgent needs of our people. The question we shall now try to answer is whether the Seminary has succeeded in reasonable measure to attain them.

No one can gainsay the statement that the Seminary through its Faculty and its graduates was among the chief forces that stemmed the tidal wave of radical religious reform and radical secularism that threatened to overwhelm American Judaism in the first quarter of the twentieth century. It played a decisive role of undisputed primacy in transforming the atmosphere of Jewish life in America from one in which the Jewish religious tradition was the target of constant abuse and ridicule in all the so-called modern synagogue pulpits of the country and in a major portion of the Yiddish and American Anglo-Jewish press, to one of general regard and reverence for the basic teachings and institutions of that tradition. A detailed historical account of what happened in cities like Philadelphia with the coming of men like Harry Davidowitz, Abraham A. Neuman, Max D. Klein and Samuel Fredman before the first World War, or in Chicago with the coming of Solomon Goldman in the early twenties, or Los Angeles with the founding of the University of Judaism, and in scores upon scores of smaller communities throughout the land, and a study of the impact of Schechter, Ginzberg, Friedlaender, Marx, Davidson and Adler—to speak only of those members of the Faculty who are no longer with us—would validate this statement.

Nor need one addressing any audience that has any knowledge of the world of learning, belabor the undisputed assertion that the Seminary's contribution to what Zunz called the "emancipation of Judaism" was surpassed by no institution anywhere in the world and equalled by none on this continent. Signal recognition of the Seminary's role in restoring Jewish learning and Jewish scholarship to a place of honor and equality among "the factors in the march of human intellect" was given by Harvard University when, in celebrating its Tercentenary, it included Professor Louis Ginzberg among the sixty-two world leaders of thought and scholarship whom it chose to honor on that occasion. And having made a contribution of the highest order towards the "emancipation of Judaism," the Seminary was in a position to take significant steps towards fulfilling another of its cherished goals, namely that of redirecting Judaism upon the highest possible level into the main currents of contemporary human thought, thus subjecting it to the ultimate test of the free play of the human intellect, while giving it the opportunity to make its contribution to the molding of the new human civilization that will and must arise out of the physical and spiritual unrest of our day. This it was enabled to do through the inspired, self-sacrificial leadership of Dr. Louis Finkelstein, through whose initiative the Institute for Religious and Social Studies and the Conference on Science, Philosophy and Religion were originally conceived and sustained all these years.

The fond hope of creating an institution which in all of its practices would be unswervingly loyal to the Torah, and at the same time be the center of free inquiry, enabling and even encouraging everyone to seek the truth and to express it fearlessly as he sees it, has, I believe, also been fulfilled in larger measure at the Seminary than at any other institution in Jewish history. Of all of the Seminary's achievements, I would account this to be its most unique and historically its most significant one, for without it all of its other achievements would have been impossible. No one has thus far made a thorough study of the crises through which the Seminary has passed in order to maintain this position, nor analyzed the day-to-day decisions that have enabled it to function with extraordinary smoothness, in the face of the problems that are constantly confronted by those who strive to keep tradition and freedom in a harmonious, cooperative and fruitful partnership. All that I can do on this occasion is to draw attention to a few of these matters. No evaluation of the Seminary is possible without some reference to them.

The first principle that was early established is that the academic and religious policies of the Seminary are absolutely independent of its lay Board. This policy is symbolized by the fact that ordination is given only by the President of the Faculty or by one designated by him, and by no one else; that all appointments to the Faculty originate with recommendations by the President of the Faculty and by no one else; and that the Seminary buildings, its kitchen and dining room are conducted insofar as Jewish law impinges upon their conduct, in accordance with the instructions of the President of the Faculty and no one else.

Secondly, the Seminary as an institution was, on the one hand, not to become involved in issues in which as an institution it had no special competency, and on the other hand it would not restrain members either of its Faculties or of its Boards from expressing opinions or participating in activities which may or may not be generally popular in the community at large, but which in themselves do not relate directly to the specific aims and purposes of the Seminary. The only thing the Seminary ever required of the members of its Faculties is that they be competent in the areas which they have been assigned to teach, and live personal lives in accordance with the teachings of the Torah as traditionally understood. With this given, every Faculty member enjoys absolute academic freedom, as well as absolute freedom of action and expression outside the walls of the Seminary. The only thing it ever required of members of its Boards in addition to being devoted to the welfare of the Seminary is that they be men and women of unimpeachable personal integrity, living their own lives and raising their children within the fellowship of Judaism, and devoted to the advancement of the Seminary as an effective institution of teaching and research.

The attitude of some of the lay members of the Seminary's Boards was strikingly summarized in a story told by Mr. Alan Stroock, the present chairman of the Board of Directors. He himself is by choice and conviction a member of a synagogue affiliated with the United Synagogue. He was asked one day by a rabbinical student in a group that he was addressing why men who are not members of Conservative congregations should have chosen to serve as members of the Board of the Seminary. In response he told a story of volunteers for the paratroops. Each volunteer was asked why he joined, and invariably each in his turn answered, "Because I like to jump." The officer, tiring of receiving the same answer, turned to the next volunteer and said, "I suppose you also joined because you like to jump." Much to his surprise the answer was, "No, I do not like to jump." "Why then did you join?" the officer asked. To which the soldier replied, "Because I like to be with fellows who like to jump." Thus there are many who, though they may not in their own lives identify themselves with the goals of the Seminary, do have a high appreciation of them and want to be associated with those who teach them and try to live by them.

The distinction between a man's activities as a member of the Seminary Board and his other activities was drawn from the very beginning by the fact that many, perhaps most, of the members of the group that brought the reorganized Seminary into being were themselves prominently associated with the Reform Movement. Many there were and are who may consider this to have been unfortunate. I do not think so. It was and is indicative of the transparty role of the Seminary in Jewish life, a role it will, I hope, never willingly abandon, and about which I hope to have something more to say later in this paper.

The importance of the fact that the Seminary was founded by men free of that frame of mind which approaches every man with the alternative of "you are either all for me or all against me," is highlighted by the simple fact that while Louis Marshall was never made to feel uncomfortable as a member of the Seminary Board because he was also president of a Reform temple, he did feel constrained to resign from membership in the Isaac M. Wise Memorial Fund National Committee because of criticism levelled against him because he was a member of the Seminary Board.[24]

The first real test of the atmosphere of general freedom

that was to characterize the Seminary came in 1906, when Dr. Schechter issued his "Statement on Zionism." It is the only paper included in his volume of Seminary addresses which contains what might be called a policy statement equal in importance to those which he made during the course of his official Seminary addresses. In the introduction to the volume, Schechter took great pains to point out, however, that in this instance he was not speaking in behalf of the Seminary. "I should like it to be distinctly understood," he wrote, "that this allegiance [to Zionism] can not be predicated of the Institution over which I have the honor to preside, and which has never committed itself to the Movement, leaving this to the individual inclination of the students and Faculty, composed of Zionists, anti-Zionists and indifferentists."[25]

At that time the leading men of the Seminary's Board were, to put it mildly, not sympathetic to Zionism. Yet, let it be recorded to their everlasting credit, that none of them, to the best of my knowledge, withdrew support from the Seminary because of Schechter's statement or because of the activities of other members of the Faculty in the Zionist Movement, or because the Rabbinical Assembly and the United Synagogue were from their very inception overwhelmingly identified with the Zionist Movement. While the question did not raise serious differences between the Seminary lay Board and its Faculty, it was the first area in which considerable tension developed between the Seminary Faculty and Administration, on the one hand, and the student body, the Rabbinical Assembly and the United Synagogue on the other. The refusal of the Seminary to display the Zionist flag or to have *"Hatikvah"* sung—even as it does not display the American flag nor sing "The Star-Spangled Banner"—as a regular feature at all its functions, particularly at Commencement exercises, occasioned minor unpleasant scenes from time to time and called forth impassioned words in private and public debate. Fortunately, almost everyone concerned had the good sense to keep these tensions and differences within manageable bounds, concentrating on the vast areas of agreement and not permitting the area of disagreement, significant and emotion-laden though it was, to envelop and overwhelm the whole. The fact that the Seminary did not succumb to the pressures of its closest affiliates, the Rabbinical Assembly and the United Synagogue, even though its Faculty was overwhelmingly committed to Zionism, and that on the other hand, the pressures upon the Seminary of the Rabbinical Assembly and the United Synagogue were within manageable bounds, was due, I believe, to the clarity with which the Seminary had stated its goals and purposes and to the widespread recognition within the Movement of the overriding primacy of those purposes.

The Seminary's adherence to the principle of maximum possible academic freedom, of freedom for its Faculty members to express and to follow outside its walls as well as within them whatever truths they believed to be compatible with historical Judaism, was put to its greatest and most glorious test some thirty-five years ago when the controversy between Professor Mordecai M. Kaplan and the Jewish Center, which he had founded, reached its climax. Dr. Kaplan's theological views, which differed radically from those of the leaders of the congregation, resulted ultimately in his resignation as its rabbi. A goodly portion of the Seminary's financial support at that time came from the leading members of that congregation. The Seminary knew that that support would be withdrawn if it retained Dr. Kaplan. Moreover, Dr. Kaplan's theological views were also vigorously opposed by many of the Faculty and the lay leaders of the Seminary. Nevertheless, not only was Dr. Kaplan's resignation not asked for, but on the contrary, both Faculty and Administration went out of their way to assure him that he would continue to be free to teach his convictions.

The fact that during its almost seventy-five years of existence no member of the Seminary Faculty was either asked to leave or made so uncomfortable as to be forced to resign—

as was the case in other institutions—because of his theological, political or economic views, constitutes a singularly precious heritage not only for itself, or for the Conservative Movement, but for our whole people, a heritage which must be preserved. That, however, will require unflagging and intelligent vigilance.

This atmosphere of spiritual integrity and intellectual freedom within the framework of loyalty to the Torah, the Seminary strives to nurture within the student body. The Seminary is under constant attack on the one hand from those who believe that it is too lax in the demands that it makes upon its students in regard to Jewish observances, and on the other hand from those who believe that there is too much pressure exerted for conformity in thought and act. There is nothing new in these attacks from the so-called left and right wings. They merely bear out the consistency with which the Seminary has over the years striven to follow its purpose of combining loyalty to the Tradition with scientific truth and intellectual integrity, and how accurate Schechter was in his prognosis that this would subject the Seminary to attacks from its own rightist and leftist alumni.

What does the Seminary expect of its students when they enter, and what does it claim to offer them?

The Seminary does not expect its students upon entering to be "finished and finite clods, untroubled by a spark." It does not expect them to have all the answers to all spiritual and philosophic problems whether those answers conform to the answers given in the past or are radically opposed to them. It expects of the applicant, in addition to certain academic requirements, an attitude of great concern with theological and ethical problems, a love for, and an ability to discuss and comprehend ideas, a passion to know the Tradition and to experience it in daily action, a desire to teach the Torah, to serve the Jewish people and above all to fathom the meaning of the Torah's injunction of *"kedoshim tiheyu"* —"Be ye holy."

A student who comes to the Seminary with the hope of having his thinking done for him by some member of the Faculty, will be disappointed. Most students come to us because they know that the Seminary does not presume to indoctrinate them with either the latest edition of the *Shulhan Arukh* or the latest revision of a theological catechism of creeds or deeds, or with a party platform.

Most of the students who apply to the Seminary know that the Seminary strives to offer them primarily three things. (1) The opportunity to mature spiritually, intellectually and religiously under the guidance and in the company of teachers of the highest integrity and of sincere personal piety rooted in loyalty to the *mitzvot* of the Torah. (2) An environment in which one can live a life of personal piety and experience traditional Judaism to the full, not merely as a doctrine but as a way of daily life. (3) Instruction in the theory and practice of those skills needed by a rabbi who is to lead a traditionally-oriented American congregation, most of whose members are secularly well-educated but Jewishly illiterate.

The student, upon entrance, knows that during his years at the Seminary he will be living in an environment radically different from that of the world from which he came and to which as a practicing rabbi he will return. Within the Seminary walls he is exposed to a world of simplicity and comparative austerity in personal living, of scholarship and piety, of excitement about ideas and of intensity of feeling about nuances of thought and behavior which he will most likely not experience beyond the Seminary's walls. He knows he is expected to identify himself to the limit of his intellectual and spiritual ability with that world. He knows also that the extent of his identification with it will, in the last analysis, depend upon his inner convictions. No one peeps through the keyhole of his room to see whether he does or does not put on his *talit* and *tefilin* every morning. His teachers assume that there are days when he is wracked by profound doubts and hesitations. His years at the Seminary are years when, within the atmosphere of the Seminary, he is expected to think through, on his own, his understanding of the Tradition he is to live and to teach the rest of his life.

This very often involves many a student in untold inner turmoil and suffering. There are those who find their personal answers by identification with one or another of their teachers. The very variety of personalities available is in itself a boon to the student. But the extent to which each Seminary student thinks through his position for himself is reflected in the fact that there is a great variety of practice and opinion among the graduates of the Seminary. I consider that a great compliment to the Seminary and a great source of strength to the Conservative Movement.

I know no other institution which itself is so staunch in its loyalty to a tradition and at the same time gives greater latitude to its students to examine and question it. I know of no other institution which is itself as fully committed to a tradition as is the Seminary, which has greater sympathy with or understanding for the doubts and hesitations of its students and its graduates. To a degree never heretofore achieved in Jewish history, and rarely achieved in any society, the Seminary has succeeded in maintaining an atmosphere of free inquiry, and of intellectual and spiritual integrity within the framework of loyalty to the letter and the spirit of a tradition. This is an achievement of the highest and noblest order and one which we should treasure and protect with every fibre of our being.

THE SEMINARY AS A "FORCE FOR RECONCILIATION IN ISRAEL"

Among the aims that Schechter and his colleagues had set for the Seminary, none was more fervently espoused than that of being a force for reconciliation in Israel. "The ultimate goal at which we are aiming," said Schechter, "is union and peace in American Israel."[26]

Viewed superficially, the Seminary seems to have met with least success in its efforts to achieve this one of its goals. It has not succeeded in eliminating parties or sects from Jewish life. On the contrary, it seems merely to have added another party or movement to the number already in existence when it appeared on the scene. This, however, is but a superficial evaluation of what the Seminary has achieved, and one which is based upon a superficial understanding of what it means to be a force for reconciliation within the life of any historic group.

A force for reconciliation within the body of a people is not one that eliminates all parties or all differences. It is rather that force whose kinship the various parties cannot deny and through which all parties feel an unseverable kinship to one another. Schechter knew too much about Jewish life in the past and he was too wise a man to expect the elimination of all parties in Jewish life or even to desire such monolithic uniformity and conformity. He knew it was rarely, if ever, the case in the past, and that within modern democratic society such uniformity becomes practically impossible even if it were desirable. Hence he did not admonish the Seminary graduates to *eliminate* the gap which divides Israel into competing groups. He asked them merely not "*to widen*" it[27] (italics mine, S.G.). In the light of what has occurred in the past six decades, I believe I would not be violating the principles of extrapolation or *derash* if I say that what Schechter and his colleagues had in mind was not so much the complete elimination of the gap as the bridging of it, and the gradual reduction of its width and depth so that those walking the bridge may not lose their balance when contemplating the abyss below them.

This bridging of the gap and the reduction of its width and depth has taken place in American Jewish life during the past sixty years. Many external factors undoubtedly contributed towards this end. But to the extent that this was achieved through the conscious effort of Jewish leadership and to the extent that this reconciliation is reflected not merely in external, organizational procedures but in the spirit, in the heart and the mind of Jews, I believe it can be fairly said that the Seminary has played a role of primary importance in the achievement.

Sixty years ago there was real danger that the Jews of America would be divided into two or perhaps three irreconcilable groups: radical religious reformers, secularist-nationalists, and isolationist orthodox. If this did not happen, it was not due merely to accident, or to external pressures. It was due in large measure to the fact that at the Seminary an attitude of mind, an outlook, a way of life and of thought was being nurtured which embodied lovingly the sturdiest strands from each of the conflicting patterns and wove them into a new pattern which none of the others could completely reject because they saw themselves represented in it, sympathetically and at their best. The Reform emphasis upon facing up to the modern world and its scientific and philosophic thought was there. The Orthodox emphasis upon observance of the *mitzvot* was there. The secularist emphasis upon the cultural heritage of the Jewish people and upon concern for the security and the dignity of the life of this people, was there. These were all embodied not merely in words but in living personalities whose authenticity as Jews and as citizens of the modern world could not be gainsaid.

The Seminary proved to be a force for the reconciliation of Israel because within its walls the noblest representatives of all parties in Israel could and did feel at home. The most constructive element in the philosophies or attitudes of the other groups is not merely *also* present, but is profoundly respected within the Seminary. Hence no one of them can completely deny the Seminary without denying a vital element within its own thinking.

This inability on the part of the best in all groups to deny the Seminary, explains in part the bitterness of the hostility towards us of those whose intellectual and spiritual horizons do not reach beyond narrow party lines. They are angry at us because they claim that we confuse their followers. Would-be members of the Reform Movement are, we are told, misled by our modernism to believe that we are reformers when in reality we are not. Orthodox Jews are, we are told, misled by our concern for the *mitzvot ma'asiyot* to believe that we are Orthodox when, according to their thinking, we are not. But the truth of the matter is that we mislead no one. There simply happens to be a growing number of men and women who have eyes of their own and refuse to wear the party blinders. These instinctively seek to identify themselves with the main body of the Jewish tradition and the Jewish people rather than with any rigidly-defined conception of Judaism or segment of Jewry. They sense in what others term our "confusion," a blessed, disciplined breadth of sympathy and understanding, a generosity of spirit whose scope of concern, though rooted in an unswerving loyalty to the historic tradition, is broader than any party platform. They intuitively recognize in it our people's surest safeguard against disintegration into irreconcilably hostile camps, each camp rigidly loyal to one aspect of our spiritual heritage and seeking to present it as the total heritage. The American Council for Judaism on the one hand, and the American counterparts of the *Neturay Karta* on the other hand, are indicative of what might have been, had the Seminary not planted the seed of "constructive confusion" in the American Jewish soil at the beginning of this century and had it not nurtured it as effectively as it did all these years.

There is nothing more detrimental to the spiritual life of a people than a crystal-clear philosophy or theology that has all final answers, whether negative or positive, and nothing more dangerous to its unity than the effort to impose such a crystallized, finalized system of thought upon the entire group. The living, creative unity of a people is preserved by those among it who, having firm hold upon the basic factors that brought the people into being and preserved it in meaningful existence, provide for these factors the greatest possible realm for intellectual maneuverability and, for the people, the greatest number of opportunities for vital contact with these creative, life-giving and life-preserving factors.

This, I believe, is what Schechter had in mind when he wrote that the "union and peace in American Israel" at which the Seminary was aiming was not "a union of mere organization." The union he had in mind, he said, was "one of principle and the recognition of vital facts, decisive in our past and indispensable for our safety in the future. . . . Such a recognition, however, can only be brought about by a thorough knowledge of our great literature . . . joined to broad sympathy and loving understanding for all the aspirations and cravings and longings and hopes recorded in this very literature."[28]

This is the mission that all the great academies of Jewish learning in the past have consciously or subconsciously fulfilled. It is the mission which the Seminary has consciously set for itself. Given the historic conditions under which it has functioned these sixty years, it is, I believe, fair to say that the Seminary has in great measure fulfilled that mission. This it has done not by cleverly contriving an eclectic philosophy or theology which it asks all of its Faculty, students and alumni to accept, but by embracing with affection the totality of the Jewish heritage and exposing it fearlessly to the full impact of the totality of human thought.

THE AREAS OF CREATIVE TENSION WITHIN THE SEMINARY TODAY

There are two main areas of creative tension within the Seminary today. The first involves the dual role of the Seminary as a center of scholarly research and as a training school for rabbis who are to serve congregations. This area of tension is at least as old as the reorganized Seminary. This tension is reflected specifically in the curriculum and less specifically but no less tangibly in the widespread feeling among alumni and students that their professors have, or had, little respect for the American rabbinate as a profession or the American rabbi as a Jewish spiritual leader.

That feeling, as far as I can recall the attitude of the Seminary Faculty towards the rabbinate in my student days (1922–25), was well-grounded. One rarely heard kind things said about the rabbinate by Faculty members, but one did hear many directly and indirectly derogatory remarks. For myself, I always felt that those remarks belonged to the category of jokes told about the institution of the family by the most domesticated of men, or those told by a former generation about its rabbis. I sometimes think that the deep hurt many of us felt at those friendly jibes was, and to this day largely is, but a reflection of our own insecurity, of our own doubts regarding the significance of our work and of our own recognition that there is unfortunately much too much still present within the ranks of the American rabbinate that furnishes justifiable targets for the scorn or the laughter of the learned, the serious and the pious. It is also true that many of the painful darts were shot because of a lack of sufficient appreciation of the gigantic obstacles the rabbi had and has to face in the average American Jewish community: the abysmal ignorance, the spiritual callousness, the moral crassness that so often surround him.

But I believe that the era of lighthearted derogation of the rabbi and the rabbinate by the Seminary Faculty has long ended. That role has now been taken over by students and alumni. It would be a sad day indeed when we lose the ability to laugh at ourselves, at the peculiar foibles and infirmities to which we as rabbis fall prey. The Faculty has, I believe without exception, come to realize how thin-skinned we really are. It understands the reasons for our supersensitivity and refrains from testing too often the weak spots in our mental armor.

Would that the problem inherent in the curriculum could

be as easily disposed of. Unfortunately, however, no one has ever created a curriculum for any school, from the kindergarten to the Graduate School, that has had universal approval of the students, the faculty or educators generally. The best thing that can be said about any specific curriculum is that it is not as bad as another. In preparing a curriculum for the Rabbinical School there is such a vast area of content matter to choose from that there is always the insoluble problem of what to include. Moreover, having decided upon the subjects to be included, there is always the problem of the amount of time to be devoted to each of them. Thus, though Talmud is assigned more hours per week than any other single subject, to the Talmudist even that is hopelessly inadequate. The same is true for any of the other subjects. No professor, regardless of what subject he teaches, ever admits that enough time is given to it in the curriculum, just as no general ever readily admits that his army is large enough or sufficiently well supplied.

In addition, there are special skills one must master if he is to be an effective American rabbi. The problem of what to teach in order to prepare the student specifically for his career as an American rabbi is as complicated as the problem of what Jewish content courses are to be included in the curriculum and how much time is to be assigned to each one of them, if he is to be an adequately learned rabbi.

I had the rare privilege in March of 1947 of spending three days on the train with Professor Kaplan, returning with him from our month's mission in Los Angeles to set up the organizational structure for the University of Judaism. I recall that we spent most of those three days in an effort to construct a more acceptable curriculum for our Rabbinical School. While I am sure that Dr. Kaplan made many valuable suggestions, the main impression that was left with me of that effort is a sense of its well-nigh insurmountable difficulties. We ended with having more courses in our curriculum than in the present one, but with the same five school days in the week. The only solution was to add a year or two to the basic four-year course, a suggestion whose popularity we both questioned.

In the image of the rabbi that the founders of the Seminary had before them, scholarship was a dominant, perhaps *the* dominant characteristic. Whatever other endowments of heart and mind the rabbi required, he was a rabbi in the great Jewish tradition only if he was completely at home in the highways and byways of the cultural heritage of our people, and only if he possessed an unquenchable thirst for ever greater knowledge of the Torah. Those who are not ready to reject this image of the rabbi, even for the American rabbinate, find it difficult to point out what can be eliminated from the present curriculum. On the contrary, they feel much more should be added.

On the other hand, no one denies the need to introduce into the curriculum additional opportunities for the student to be equipped with the special skills and knowledge indispensable to an *American* rabbi of the twentieth century. Though we can never arrive at the perfect curriculum, we all agree, and none more completely than the Faculty itself, that we can do better than we are doing now.

While no radical reconstruction of the Rabbinical School curriculum has been made during these sixty years, it has undergone considerable significant change. Courses in education, in modern Hebrew literature, and in practical problems of the ministry were added after 1925. More recently, courses in the philosophies of religion and in the area of mental health have been added.

The boldest experiments with the Rabbinical School curriculum, however, were inaugurated some ten years ago, when a small group of specially qualified students were offered the opportunity for concentrated study of theology under the guidance of Professors Leo Strauss and Richard McKeon, who came to the Seminary from Chicago once a week or twice a month. The experiment lasted for about two years. It made permanent and significant impressions upon a number of promising young Jewish scholars. I believe every one in that original group is today making a significant contribution to Jewish thought and scholarly research.

After some two years the experiment, for various reasons, had to be terminated. Some three years ago it was resumed. Though the presently designated areas of concentration are Talmud and Bible, the area that has been most substantially encouraged is that of Talmud. The reason for it should be obvious. It is the area of Jewish studies that has been most catastrophically hurt by the destruction of the great *Yeshivot* of Eastern Europe. Moreover, traditional, or historical Judaism, the Judaism the Seminary is pledged to teach, is the Judaism of the great Talmudic and Rabbinic tradition. Unfortunately, there are no schools today where that tradition is being nurtured in the spirit in which we want to see it nurtured, namely with a great reverence and personal identification, but also with scientific accuracy and philosophic grasp. If we do not produce the great Talmudic scholars of tomorrow, we will have failed to provide for ourselves that scholarly leadership without which we cannot maintain ourselves as a significant development of historic Judaism. Moreover, if such scholars are eventually to appear from amongst us or even if they are to be welcomed in our midst in the future, our Movement must always contain a substantial number of members who are themselves sufficiently steeped in Talmudic learning to be able to appreciate Rabbinic scholarship at its highest and noblest and to understand its indispensability to us as a people. Hence the Seminary must place paramount emphasis upon Talmudic studies.

All of this, however, does not mean that we are or should be satisfied with the present limitations of opportunities for concentrated study only to the fields of Talmud and Bible. There are many who feel equally strongly that the areas of theology and the history and psychology of religion, need far greater emphasis at the Seminary than they have ever been given heretofore, both within the regular curriculum and as areas of special study.[29]

The problem of the Rabbinical School curriculum will never have a final and a satisfactory answer. No one of us would want our Seminary to be only a professional training school for rabbis, and no one would want to convert it into an exclusively research center. Our ideal for the Seminary graduate must remain the image of the scholarly rabbi or the Rabbinic-minded scholar. The Seminary Faculty must continue to be the greatest possible center of scholarly research and yet have among its members men who are as thoroughly acquainted with the daily problems of the American rabbinate as the scholars are with the area of research. A tug of war of greater or lesser intensity between these two groups for the mind and heart of the student is not only inevitable, it is indispensable if there is to be at the Seminary an atmosphere of creative tension. The price in terms of personal suffering is often high, but unfortunately unavoidable.

The second area of creative tension involves the question of whether the Seminary should be the fountainhead of a movement in Judaism or the embodiment and prime model, as it were, of that movement.

The founders and reorganizers of the Seminary set a task for it, the core of which consists of two apparently contradictory goals. On the one hand, the Seminary was to dissociate itself from the religious anarchism of the left and the "artificial ignorance" of the right and aim to produce a new spiritual and intellectual atmosphere in American Jewry. On the other hand, it was to strive ceaselessly to stand above the battle and to avoid total identification with any movement or party. Though its activities would by their very nature create a body of followers who would look to it as their spiritual and cultural fountainhead, the Seminary was to be ever on guard against the temptation to identify itself completely with them, so that it become little more than a reflection of its spiritual offspring. The Seminary was never to lose sight of its original purpose, namely that of expounding traditional, historical Judaism and to identify itself only with that which it believed to be authentic in Judaism. The authentic serves no one group or party. It serves everyone, and with equal concern.

This twofold role has also exposed the Seminary to attacks from both those near to, and those far from, it. The Seminary's children—the Rabbinical Assembly and the United Synagogue—tend to demand complete identification of the Seminary with them. The others interpret the Seminary's protestations of concern for all that is authentic in Judaism, regardless of party, as but a façade to capture the unwary.

There is not much that we can do in response to the accusations of those who view the Seminary's totality of concern as a mere façade, except to follow Schechter's advice to "do your duty, state your principles clearly, and for the rest, remember the Talmudical saying, 'Silence of a Babylonian testifies to his noble descent.' "[30] I think that by and large we have followed that principle. But there is much more that we can and must do in regard to the relationship between the Seminary and the Rabbinical Assembly and the United Synagogue.

Historic circumstances abetted the principle enunciated by Schechter when he said, "Any attempt to place the centre of gravity [of Judaism] outside of the Torah must end in disaster."[31] A movement which places the center of gravity of Judaism in the Torah must have at its own center an institution in which Torah is lived and expounded. The historic circumstances which made the Seminary the "centre of gravity" of the Conservative Movement are readily identified. The Seminary was the first of the three coordinate branches of the Conservative Movement to take on effective reality. Its graduates organized the Rabbinical Assembly and the President of the Seminary organized the United Synagogue. For many years the President of the Seminary was also the President of the United Synagogue.

Nevertheless, the Seminary never sought to impose its authority upon its spiritual offsprings, the Rabbinical Assembly and the United Synagogue. That broad intellectual and spiritual freedom which the Seminary granted its Faculty and student body, it extended to its alumni and affiliated congregations from the very beginning. It never sought to fashion either of them in precisely its own image. Other institutions prescribed within rather narrow limits the kind of pulpit their graduates might occupy. There was a time when tempting financial offers were made to the Seminary if it would repudiate those of its graduates who served non-Orthodox congregations. The Seminary refused to do it.

Dr. Schechter set the order of the service for the synagogue of the Seminary, but he did not insist that it necessarily become the model to be followed by all synagogues to be served by Seminary graduates. In the preamble to the constitution of the United Synagogue, he clearly indicated that within the framework of the United Synagogue there would be opportunity for experimentation and individuation, consistent with the fundamental teachings and practices of traditional Judaism.

Thus, also, when the Rabbinical Assembly first came into being it was natural for its young members to turn to their teachers whenever questions of law or ritual arose. But the Seminary Faculty never declared itself to be the final court of authority in matters of Jewish law. There was thus early sympathetic understanding on the part of the Seminary that life beyond its walls can not be compelled to conform to life within its walls, and that the differences between the two, as long as each remained loyal to basic common aims and practices, did not and should not constitute an unfavorable judgment of one upon the other.

The tension that we often experience today in the relationship of the Seminary to its closest sister organizations, the Rabbinical Assembly and the United Synagogue, is due not so much to the Seminary's effort to impose its image upon them but rather to the effort of some of them to impose their own image upon it. Though this tension appears in a number of areas, we shall for purposes of illustration discuss only one such area, namely that of the Seminary synagogue's services, at which men and women do not sit together, though they both sit on the same floor level, and at which the Rabbinical Assembly–United Synagogue Sabbath and Festival Prayer Book is not used.

Various reasons are advanced for the dissatisfaction with the Seminary's services. One of them is rooted in theological or ideological convictions. Graduates of the Seminary do not want their alma mater to be "behind the times." They do not want their teachers to pray for the restoration of the sacrifices, nor do they want them to treat the women at the services in a manner that to them, *i.e.,* to these graduates, sets the Jewish woman apart as inferior to the man in the Synagogue.

This attitude, worthy as it is in essence, at the same time reflects a self-assurance that is not altogether worthy. I think that we who know our teachers should know that they are as capable of passing judgment on what is morally and religiously right as we are. They surely are ethically as sensitive as we are and if they find religious satisfaction in praying as they do, without pressing their convictions upon us, the least we can do is try to emulate their breadth of understanding and honor their convictions at least as generously and sincerely as they honor ours. The Seminary never expressed its dissatisfaction with the Rabbinical Assembly–United Synagogue Prayer Book. It is an area in which we have a mutual, unspoken agreement to give one another the utmost freedom possible, within the framework of tradition.

Members of the Faculty participate in the services of congregations affiliated with the United Synagogue, even though their order of the service may in many aspects differ from that of the services at the Seminary. They recognize that services must be related to the intellectual and spiritual capacities of the congregants. Synagogue services in America are largely in the category of instruction, and in that category much may and must be done which need not be done at a service in which instruction is not at all required. Above all, however, they recognize that within the Tradition there has always been considerable room for differences in this area and that the compulsive need for complete uniformity that some experience is not necessarily the highest expression of the religious or the Jewish group aspiration.

The reason most often advanced, however, for the efforts of some of our alumni and United Synagogue leaders to remodel the Seminary service in the image of the services in their own congregations, is one based on practical and organizational considerations. We are told that our laity are confused when they come to the Seminary service. How can they decide who is right, the Seminary or their own rabbi? Since the congregations are not prepared to model their services after that of the Seminary, the easiest way to eliminate the "confusion" from the mind of the laymen is to have the Seminary change its services. The Seminary, it is argued, is only one synagogue, as over against the hundreds of synagogues in the United Synagogue. Moreover, the Seminary should be ready to make concessions for the unity of the Movement.

This argument in behalf of the "unity of the Movement" is usually advanced by men who in other areas do not identify uniformity with unity, and who see in plurality under the Constitution one of the greatest virtues of American civilization. We should hesitate to advance the attainment of unity within our ranks at the risk of transforming ourselves into a sect, and severing vital links between us and other large segments of our people. The Seminary is the most vital link between us and the vast mass of traditionally minded Jews outside the ranks of the Conservative Movement. To snap that link would be too great a price to pay for the questionable good of group uniformity.

We must rather pursue the more difficult, but ultimately

the more rewarding, path of educating our laymen that within the limits of traditional Judaism there is more than one way of conducting synagogue services. The synagogue ritual is not a magic formula whose effectiveness depends upon the recitation of certain specified words in a given, fixed order. The Seminary recognizes the authority of the *mara de-atra,* of each rabbi in his community, to determine the order of the service in his synagogue. Every Rabbinical Assembly member ought to teach his congregants to have the same regard for the authority of the Chancellor of the Seminary to fix the order of the Seminary's services.

No analogy is perfect, but I have been helped in my thinking about the relationship between the Seminary and the Rabbinical Assembly and the United Synagogue if I think of the Seminary as the fountainhead or the headwaters of a river and the Rabbinical Assembly and the United Synagogue as its channels. The headwaters of a river pour into the river's channels a steady stream of refreshing waters. These constitute the main body of the river. But the headwaters do not and cannot by themselves determine the depth and shape of the river's channel. The force of the current they generate plays a part in carving out the shape of the channel, but so do the rocks and hills, the valleys and tributary streams that the headwaters meet on their way to the sea. The conditions under which the average American congregation lives and functions are so different from those under which the Seminary synagogue functions that the one cannot possibly be in all things the exact model for the other. The best that we have a right to hope for is that there always be a strong and obvious affinity between them. The Seminary has faith in the Rabbinical Assembly and the United Synagogue. It probably indulges from time to time in the human weakness of wanting the offspring to be like the parent. But it has thus far curbed this weakness to a very extraordinary degree. It might be well for the offspring also not to be too zealous in "Bringing Up Father."

THE PRIMARY TASK OF THE LEADERSHIP OF THE CONSERVATIVE MOVEMENT

The three national bodies that constitute the Conservative Movement in Judaism, namely the Jewish Theological Seminary of America, the Rabbinical Assembly and the United Synagogue of America are in theory absolutely autonomous. Their interrelationship is not governed by a constitution or bylaws. They cooperate because they share common goals and common or overlapping leadership. There is a gentleman's agreement among them that no one of the three is to do anything that would embarrass either of the other two, and make it impossible to continue the present cooperative effort. This fruitful cooperation can be continued only if (a) all of us together tirelessly and sincerely nurture among us the spirit of mutual regard; (b) no one of the three makes ostensibly unreasonable demands upon the other, demands which any one of the three may consider as impinging upon its essential character; (c) no one of the three in any of its acts strains beyond reason the implications of the concept of traditional or historical Judaism.

No one can define now and for all time what would constitute an "unreasonable demand" or what would "strain beyond reason the implications of the concept of traditional or historical Judaism." Statesmanship within our Movement will be reflected in our ability to maintain the cooperative effort of the three organizations with a minimum of friction, a maximum of freedom for each one of the three, and an ever-increasing number of common enterprises. The leaders of each one of the three groups will have to prove equal to this delicate task.

That we are capable of producing such leadership in all branches of our Movement has thus far been successfully demonstrated. But no one of us is naive enough to believe that it is the organizational structure which enables us to function, important as that unquestionably is. We all recognize that it is the spirit behind the organizational structure, the conviction that in maintaining this threefold partnership, we are making our most significant contribution to Judaism, the Jewish people and to human civilization. Sectarianism, justifying itself by appeals to logical consistency, is nothing new in human history. Hostile groups cooperating with one another because they have a common enemy is also nothing new. What is new is the sincere cooperation of honest men of conviction with equally honest men of differing conviction, the recognition that, important as it is for an individual to be logically consistent in his life and to be true to his convictions, it is even more important for him to be convinced that when a conviction makes it impossible for him to cooperate with one with whom he shares many other very precious common goals and purposes, he should carefully reexamine that conviction before he permits it to endanger the total relationship.

In evaluating the sixty years of Seminary leadership, I believe we can truthfully say that it set an extraordinary example for all of us of conviction plus understanding, of unwavering loyalty to personal ideologies plus sincere and sympathetic cooperation with those differing from them. This is the most difficult of all human achievements. It is this which exposes an individual to charges of weakness and hypocrisy, and a movement to charges of intellectual confusion. But it is this which makes a human being civilized, which saves a man of faith from becoming a fanatic and redeems a movement from the deadening hand of sterile uniformity. It is this which endows the Conservative Movement in Judaism with creative tension, keeping it ever spiritually adventuresome and intellectually exciting.

CHAPTER XI

Building Spiritual Bridges[1]

Among man's many endowments, none gives him a greater sense of fulfillment than does his power to communicate with his fellow man. It transforms an animal herd into a human society and bestows upon human kinship its unique capacity to emancipate itself from bondage to blood and physical proximity. But it is this very power that all too often transforms individuals bound to one another by ties of heredity, history, geography, and destiny, into implacable enemies. For men can communicate not only their agreements but their differences as well. America's great folk philosopher Will Rogers once remarked that international conferences, convened with the hope of arriving at some common points of agreement, usually end with a greater clarification of the irreconcilable differences among the participants.

Because of this power of communication and our pride in our own opinions, the threat of inner dissension hovers ominously over every people. Fourscore and seven years of common, glorious, historic experience, a common government and language, could not avert the tragedy of the American Civil War. Lincoln's hope that ". . . the mystic cords of memory stretching from every battlefield and patriot grave . . . will yet swell the chorus of the Union when again touched . . . by the better angels of our nature,"[2] was not realized. For four blood-drenched years the existence of the nation hung precariously in the balance.

The constant nurturing of "the mystic chords of memory," those intangible spiritual bonds which bind one section of a nation to another, is of primary importance even to a people that lives upon a contiguous territory and under a common political government. How can we possibly overestimate its importance to the Jewish people, whose dispersed segments live under such vastly varying political, economic and social conditions?

If I believed, as some do, that Jewish existence and unity depended upon anti-Semitism in the past and will continue to be dependent upon it in the future, I would have little respect for our past and even less interest in our future. It is my firm faith that we have succeeded, not merely in surviving, but in maintaining a considerable degree of unity amongst ourselves, despite the many obstacles that faced us, because each Jewish community, wittingly or unwittingly, was constantly building spiritual bridges between itself and all other Jewish communities.

What is a spiritual bridge? It is that which links two human beings in devotion to one another because they share a loyalty to something which they acknowledge to be greater and more precious than either of them, something which each one can claim wholly as his own without feeling that his ownership infringes upon the ownership of the other. A spiritual bridge is one on which human souls, venturing forth in search of understanding, love and purpose, meet one another, recognize one another and forever after remain loyal companions. A spiritual bridge is that over which we travel without leaving our physical habitats.

The task of building such bridges was never an easy one, nor was it always performed with complete success. The sad truth that we dare never forget is that the fathers of the Jewish people repeatedly failed, and that we have paid dearly for their failure. The United Kingdom which David established 3,000 years ago was hopelessly divided less than one hundred years after its establishment. Shortly after the triumphant reestablishment of the Jewish state by the Maccabees, sectarian movements developed within the Jewish community, dividing the people into irreconcilably hostile camps. The Karaite movement in the eighth century split our people into two vindictively antagonistic groups that never found the way back to mutual understanding.

The failures of our forefathers would have been far greater and more serious than they were during the centuries following the destruction of the Temple by the Romans had they not possessed one great advantage. There was widespread agreement among them regarding the nature of the spiritual bridge that they were called upon to erect and regarding the pillars upon which that bridge was to rest. For let us bear this truth ever in mind: while spiritual bridges are in essence intangible, they require tangible moorings. During the seventeen centuries that elapsed between the destruction of the Temple and the opening of the modern era in Jewish history, it was universally acknowledged that the tangible moorings of the spiritual bridges that united the scattered Jewish communities were the synagogues. Each community planted such a mooring firmly in its midst. The tenuous but powerful overarching spiritual structure connecting the widely scattered communities was thus provided with tangible piers to which it could attach itself. The Synagogue was a living organism which spun out the fine threads of faith, emotion, aspiration, and memory, forming the substance of the spiritual bridge between Jew and Jew.

The opening of the modern era in Jewish history removed none of the old threats to the existence and the unity of the Jewish people. It added new ones. The blessings of political freedom, which enabled Jewish communities to integrate themselves more fully than ever into the larger cultural environment of which they were a part, tended to diminish the specifically Jewish element in their lives and to envelop that element with many and substantial cultural layers that were not the common property of all other Jewish communities. These outer cultural layers had to be penetrated before Jew could reach out to Jew. We in America discovered how great an impediment they are to Jewish mutual understanding—even when geographic distances are removed—when German Jew met Polish or Russian Jew on American soil. We are discovering it anew in the State of Israel where Jews coming from a vast variety of non-Jewish cultural backgrounds are seeking to rediscover the eternal bonds that unite them. Moreover, the revolutionary changes in the political, economic, social, and intellectual life that swept over the Jewish communities of Europe during the past two centuries, violently shook and undermined the Synagogue, threatening with utter collapse the spiritual bridge which rested upon it. For a while it appeared as if the spiritual fabric of Jewish life would disintegrate, never to be rewoven.

Fortunately, long before the cataclysmic debacles that befell our people between 1914 and 1945, its most loyal and sensitive sons and daughters became aware of the danger. They heard the ominous echoes of the crumbling bridges. They saw the deep breeches in the old supporting towers. Some set themselves to the task of mending the towers of the bridges. Others abandoned them and determined to build new spiritual bridges, resting upon new supports. But of what were these to be made? Many answers were offered. The one that concerns us now consisted of two words—"territory" and "language." There were those who said "Any territory." There were others who said, "A modern European language." But the most creative and determined among them said, "The land of Israel and the Hebrew language." It was they who, in the last quarter of the nineteenth century, initiated the chain of events that led to a Jewish community in Palestine capable of proclaiming itself a politically independent state.

This community differs from all contemporary Jewish communities in two basic aspects: (1) It exercises political sovereignty over a geographic area within whose boundaries it constitutes the majority population, and (2) the Hebrew language is the official language of its state, the vernacular of its citizens and the vehicle through which the dynamic culture being fashioned by it finds literary expression.

While the Jewish community of the State of Israel was coming into being, the American Jewish community was also taking shape. It, too, is unique in the annals of our history. Never before was there a Jewish community in the Diaspora numerically so large, politically so free and economically so soundly established. It is now self-evident to even the most casual observer that, insofar as it is given man to determine his future, the future of the Jewish people and the destiny of the State of Israel depend upon close and faithful cooperation between the Jewish community in Israel and the American Jewish community. Hence, every thoughtful observer of the Jewish scene should be profoundly disturbed by even the slightest indication that a chasm of misunderstanding or estrangement may be developing between them. Only the willfully blind will deny the evidence pointing to the possibility of such a development and even to its existence. No matter, therefore, how urgent any political or economic task may be, there can be no doubt that, from the long-range point of view, no task is more important than that of building spiritual bridges between these two communities. How shall this be done? Let us start by defining our task negatively, by pointing to a number of things that we should not do, or which we at least should transfer from the center to the distant periphery of our thought and action.

Chief among the things to be avoided is the passionate elaboration of the differences between us. We dwell upon them with a well-nigh pathological compulsion, broadening and deepening them in the process. Thus, for example, there is legitimate room for differences of opinion on the future role of the Diaspora in Jewish history. But nothing significantly new has been said in this discussion for many a decade. The only thing added has been heat, without light. If we must continue this fruitless debate let us at least speak with the utmost possible awareness of the ultimate meaning of what we say. Let us not speak as if we actually hoped for the rapid liquidation of the American Jewish community or as if we believed that Jewish emigration from America to Israel is an act of treason either to America or to the American Jewish community. The truth of the matter is that no one of us—either in Israel or America—wants to see the American Jewish community disappear, either through inner disintegration or persecution. Nor does any one really believe that all or even half of the Jews of America can or will emigrate to the State of Israel within the next twenty-five years. No one is more outspoken than Premier David Ben-Gurion in this insistence upon the duty of every Jew who would describe himself as a Zionist to settle or to plan to settle in the State of Israel. Yet even he does not expect, and certainly does not hope for, the early or even the eventual dissolution of the Jewish Diaspora, least of all, of the Jewish community in America. Speaking in Jerusalem at the historic occasion in May 1952 when Dr. Louis Finkelstein, in behalf of the Jewish Theological Seminary, bestowed upon him the honorary degree of Doctor of Hebrew Letters, Mr. Ben-Gurion said: "The State of Israel is not intended merely for its residents, but for the whole of the Jewish people, even for those who do not intend to settle within its borders." Hence, regardless of how anxious we may be for American Jewish immigration to the State of Israel, or how sincerely concerned some may be about the future of the Jew in America, let us agree that no debate is more barren of good than the one which is based on the assumption that American Jewry is doomed to a rapid disintegration.

On the other hand, no matter how sanguine we may be about the future of Judaism and the Jews in America, let us not talk as if we believed that the Jewish community in

America can contribute as much to the development of a distinctly Hebraic civilization in the world as can the Jews in the State of Israel. On the occasion previously referred to, Dr. Finkelstein said, "It is our view that Judaism does not have two centers in the world, but only one, and that is the place in which the Lord delighted to dwell. . . . It is our fervent desire to be your partners in the common enterprise whose center is located here in Jerusalem, and whose interests encompass the world."

Nor does it help to create a true sense of brotherhood and equality if we think of the State of Israel as a place chiefly for the persecuted who have no other place to go, and of ourselves as their benefactors. No one likes to be cast in the role of either the poor, inept relative or the spiritually insensitive, materialistic, rich uncle.

There can be no real spiritual bridges erected between communities whose best sons and daughters do not honestly and deeply respect one another's integrity, and who do not view one another as equally worthy members of the people whose spiritual treasures are their common possession and to which both of them can make unique and indispensable contributions.

These "Thou Shalt Nots" are important, yet they are but the clearing of the approaches to the spiritual bridge and the preparation of the ground upon which its pillars are to be erected. The bridge itself will not rise unless we focus our attention upon the great need we have for it and unless we muster our resources for a long and incessant effort to build it.

I have pointed out that spiritual bridges, though tenuous and intangible, must rest upon substantial and tangible pillars. How are we to identify and define these pillars? I have frequently heard the opinion that personal involvement of American Jews in the economic life of the State of Israel should become the significant pillar upon which to erect the bridge between them. Every American Jew who has the means, should—to be sure—own State of Israel bonds and should invest in some specific economic enterprise in Israel. But, in my opinion, looking to stocks and bonds as the chief building-blocks for the bridge between American and Israeli Jewry borders upon the sacrilegious. It will be a sad day when American Jewry's concern for the welfare of the State of Israel will be motivated primarily by concern for the capital it has invested in Israel's economy.

The pillars upon which the spiritual bridge between us and the Jewish community is to rest must in their essence be independent of time and space. They must be transferable, as it were, from one era into another and from one country into another. And they must, in the second place, embody the innermost spiritual essence that animates the life of both the American and the Israeli Jewish community. It is only as each of these communities plants firmly within its midst such visible pillars that we can hope for the rise of spiritual bridges that will bind us to one another with bonds that are lighter than air but stronger than steel.

What is the most tangible evidence of the unique quality of the spiritual life of our brethren in Israel and is at the same time independent of the peculiarities of time and space? The political institutions of the State of Israel—its *Knesset,* its courts and its political party structure—are tangible embodiments of spiritual qualities, but we can neither transplant nor effectively imitate them, for they derive from the privileges and powers inherent in political sovereignty.

The economic institutions and patterns of a society also embody spiritual qualities, but it seems obvious that the American Jewish community will not look to Israel for models for its own economic life. The *kibbutz* is the most inspiring economic expression of the spiritual ideals animating a very large segment of the Israeli Jewish community. However, it is far from being universally representative of it, and infinitely farther from being a possible form of expression for the economic life of any substantial portion of American Jewry.

There is only one factor in the life of the Israeli Jewish community which embodies its innermost spiritual quality and which can be appropriated by the Jews of America: the Hebrew language. The revival of Hebrew in Israel concretizes more dramatically than any other single phenomenon the spiritual vitality that was at the core of the Zionist movement and epitomizes in unmistakable terms the essential quality of this vitality.

Language is always more than a means for intelligent communication. In the case of the Jewish people, during the last century, the renaissance of Hebrew symbolized the final and irrefutable vindication of the proposition that Judaism is as broad as the life of the mind and the soul and that it welcomes all truth, all beauty and all goodness. In Israel, the language of Scripture has become the language of the marketplace as well, exemplifying the essential unity of the two which it was intended should prevail between them.

But while the Hebrew language is the key that opens the door to the innermost soul of the Jewish community being fashioned in the State of Israel and is at the center of cultural and spiritual life there, it belongs to United States Jewry as much as it belongs to the Israelis. We have an inescapable duty to claim it and to make it a most treasured possession. For Hebrew is one of the pillars upon which any spiritual bridge to be built between us and our Israeli brethren must firmly rest. It is a tower which the Israel community has lovingly and self-sacrificingly erected. If we fail to erect a sturdy tower of living Hebrew in our midst, then the spiritual bridge which our Israeli brethren project towards us will never be completed, for there will be no tower amongst us to which it might be moored. It will remain suspended in midair.

Obviously, Hebrew cannot play the same all-pervasive role in the life of the American Jew that it plays in the life of the Israeli Jew. But our community life can be so structured, our educational system can be so directed, and our personal lives can be so fashioned that the place of high priority which Hebrew occupies within them would be easily recognizable. The Hebrew spice must be readily distinguishable by any one who tastes any aspect of Jewish life in America, so that an Israeli Jew may at once sense a spiritual kinship between himself and his American Jewish brother. Every American Jew should know Hebrew well enough to feel at home amidst the Hebrew signs and sounds of the streets of Tel Aviv and Jerusalem, even though he may never be in a position to visit them. Some amongst us justify their indifference to Hebrew by maintaining that the Hebrew language's only natural and possible habitat is the State of Israel. If this should become the dominant attitude in American Jewish life, we would abdicate our rights to the heritage which is equally the possession of Jews everywhere, namely the vast spiritual treasures of Hebrew literature from the days of the Bible to our own day. We would thus reject the conception of Judaism as an all-embodying intellectual and spiritual experience. To our brethren in Israel, this will mean more than merely the rejection of a language. They will intuitively and correctly sense in it the rejection of themselves as well.

It is no simple or easy matter to give to Hebrew a central place in our lives in this country. It will require of us a quality of devotion and of spiritual, if not physical, heroism bordering on the devotion and heroism of the men and women who revived the Hebrew language, who built the *Emek,* and who are now pouring their heart's substance into the *Negev.* This effort will identify us more intimately with the travail of the hundreds of thousands who, in Israel today, are struggling to acquire a mastery of Hebrew. Let us not imagine that the acquisition of Hebrew by the new immigrants in Israel is a simple process. We know the difficulties of our own fathers and mothers in their struggles with the English language. We are living in the generation of the great Return. Not all of us can return physically to the land of Israel. But we can all return to the language of Israel. Not all of us can be *halutzim* working the fields in Sdeh Boker. But we can all be *halutzim* studying the Hebrew language in an *ulpan*. It will be striking evidence of our determination to maintain a rich Jewish life here and of our willingness to give not only of our funds, but of ourselves, even as they do, for our common spiritual heritage.

If we mean to give to Hebrew a high place of priority on the American Jewish scene, we will have to reverse the current trend in Jewish elementary and secondary education, and increase rather than diminish the amount of time we expect our children to devote to their Hebrew studies. This will require an intensification of our efforts to introduce Hebrew as the second language in the Jewish home, and of the establishment of Hebrew Foundation Schools and elementary and secondary all-day schools, in which Hebrew has a fair opportunity to be studied under favorable conditions. With the renewed interest in language studies in our high schools and universities, we should do far more than what has been done to encourage the introduction of courses in Hebrew in the high schools and universities and to persuade our children to attend these courses.

Nor should any effort be spared to enable boys and girls of high school and college age to spend a year of study in the schools of the State of Israel so that they may acquire a basic knowledge of the language in its most natural setting. Above all, we must increase the number of Hebrew summer camps such as Massad and Ramah. There should be a hundred such camps in the United States and Canada. Such summer camps crystallize the Hebrew educational program of our congregational and communal schools. They will prepare the student for our institutions of higher Jewish learning. These camps furnish the most natural setting for the introduction into American Jewish life of the literature, the dance, the drama, the music, and the arts and crafts being developed in Israel, upon the folk level as well as on a more sophisticated level. Through the camps, these creative forces can reach into hundreds of Jewish communities and into the personal lives of hundreds of thousands of Jews. Only thus can we give a final answer to the question of whether or not Jewish life on this continent has the possibility of acquiring a significant Hebrew coloration. Only thus can we erect in our midst that pillar which embodies the innermost spiritual essence of the new Jewish life arising in the State of Israel.

Is there anything in the life of the American Jewish community which parallels the role of Hebrew in the life of Israeli Jewry? I believe there is. I believe that in America the Synagogue is the chief tangible vehicle of the uniquely Jewish and the essentially spiritual component of the life of the Jewish community. The conditions of political freedom, legal equality and economic opportunity under which we in America live have inevitably and benignly resulted in our integration into American life. Our non-Jewish fellow citizens think of us as a community founded upon a religious principle and associate all of us with the Synagogue, whether we are individually affiliated with it or not. An increasing number amongst us are affiliated with the Synagogue and identify it with the principle that gives meaning and significance to our Jewish identity. Hence even as our Israeli brethren project their spiritual life towards us via the Hebrew language, we project our spiritual life towards them via the Synagogue.

If our brethren in Israel, therefore, are to contribute towards the maintenance of the spiritual bridges between us, they must keep in good repair the pillar of the Synagogue at their terminal of the bridge. Israeli Jews should not speak of the Synagogue in terms that are carbon copies of the opinions expressed by many American Jews about the Hebrew language. Israeli Jews in all stations of life have told me repeatedly that while we in America need the Synagogue to identify ourselves as Jews, they in Israel do not require such self-identification. Hence they do not need the Synagogue.

The role of the Synagogue, thus interpreted, declares it to

be essentially a Diaspora institution, and as such it carries a stigma for many an Israeli. However, though the Synagogue may have had its origin among the exiles in Babylon, it developed its full stature in the land of Israel during the Second Commonwealth when the Jews there enjoyed either political independence or at least spiritual autonomy. Even as the Hebrew language is more than a means of communication, so the Synagogue is more than a means of group identification. If the Hebrew language in Israel today symbolizes Judaism's universality of cultural interest, the Synagogue symbolizes Judaism's message to mankind, its rootedness in a world outlook associated with a conception of God unique in the annals of human history, and its message of hope and faith, of courage and purpose to the individual human soul. The Synagogue is no more the exclusive possession of Diaspora Jewry than Hebrew is of Israeli Jewry. Hence it is to be regretted beyond words that the renascent Hebrew civilization in the State of Israel, so creative in many aspects of Jewish life, has thus far been virtually barren in the realm of the Synagogue and all that it represents in the history and the aspirations of our people.

It would serve little purpose to apportion blame for this situation or to justify it. But it should be a matter of great concern to all of us that the Synagogue, which to the American Jew is the chief institution for Jewish self-expression, is presented to him in Israel as an item on a tourist's itinerary to which he pays a hurried visit in order to observe what to him may appear as bizarre customs brought from distant lands. The Synagogue in the State of Israel—the institution through which the American Jew visiting Israel should make contacts with his Israeli brethren on the deepest spiritual levels and in a manner that would most effectively carry over into his life as a Jew when he returns to the States—is simply not as yet equipped to fulfill its most significant function.

The Synagogue, despite its obvious and well-advertised shortcomings, continues to embody the spiritual essence of the *raison d'être* of Jewish communities throughout the world. No Jewish community has ever succeeded in creating a long-term meaningful existence for itself centered in an institution other than the Synagogue. The most heralded large-scale attempt to organize such a Jewish community has been made in our time in Soviet Russia. The failure, and the causes and the consequences of that failure, constitute a chapter in Jewish history second only to the one written by the Nazis, in the scope and depth of its tragedy. Despite four decades of barbarous and unrelenting persecution of the Synagogue, the only evidences of Jewish group life still found among the Jews of Soviet Russia are associated with it. It is the only place where a visitor in Russia can find some semblance of a living Jewish community. It was therefore tragic indeed to read the report of the experiences of young Israelis who on their recent visit to Russia could not make full use of the one opportunity they had to reach out to their Jewish brethren there, because these youth were strangers to the one institution in which the Russian Jews could as a community receive them—namely, the Synagogue. The inside of a synagogue and its ritual were as strange to those Israelis as the inside of a Hebrew book is to most American Jewish youths.

The failure of the Synagogue and what it represents to find its proper place in the education of the entire Jewish youth of Israel is, I believe, largely responsible for the widespread phenomenon which is disturbing Israeli educators so deeply —the fact that so many of the best Israeli youth do not identify themselves with the totality of the Jewish people of the past and of the present. The geographical and chronological parochialism which is all too prevalent among them, was poignantly summarized by the Yiddish poet and essayist H. Leivick in a report of his conversation with a young *sabra* who had participated in the Sinai campaign. With deep emotion, the young man poured forth his innermost convictions: "The members of the old generation (of Israelis), though they are citizens of Israel, belong emotionally with you. Like you, they are history-conscious or religion-conscious Jews. Like you, they are still either *Kiddush Ha-Shem*[3] or *Kiddush Ha-am*[4] Jews. But I, and those like me, are simply Jews and nothing more. We, who were born here, pride ourselves in the one great merit which we possess; we were born here. It is a merit bestowed upon us by nature. We require no other. Because of it, I participated in the Sinai campaign and if necessary I will be ready to participate in other campaigns to defend and save my homeland. For it I am ready to give my life. For it and not for anything else. . . . I know you will accuse me of trying to identify myself with the pre-Israelite Canaanites. But I tell you it is not so. I am not, nor do I want to be, a Canaanite. I need neither idols nor gods. I need not exist by virtue of my pedigree. My own personal reputation is enough for me. I need not skip generations nor leap into the bosom of any previous generation, be it that of Isaiah or Joshua. What I am is enough for me. Let all the gods leave us alone."

Israeli educators propose to correct this unfortunate development by introducing into the curriculum an area of studies to be known as "Jewish consciousness" or "Jewish self-identification." It would include courses in the history and the institutions of the Diaspora, in which a course on the customs of the Synagogue would be included. All of this should undoubtedly be most helpful. But the classroom itself cannot achieve the hoped-for transformation. There must be an institution with which an individual can be identified all his life, one which would concretize and embody within itself this sense of unity in space and time, not only with the Jewish people but with the highest ideals of all mankind. The Synagogue is the only institution that can fulfill this function, for at its core is a message of eternal and universal import, responding to the needs of the individual human soul.

The Synagogue in Israel is far from fulfilling the purposes we envision for it. Our brethren there will have to exercise at least as much courage and creativity in restoring the Synagogue to a place of centrality in their spiritual life as they exercised when they transformed Hebrew into their language of daily discourse, and as we will have to exercise if we are to Hebraize our own lives. In this task we may perhaps be more helpful to them than we were in their herculean efforts to revive Hebrew. But it is a task which will have to be done by them primarily, even as the Hebraization of American Jewish life is a task that will have to be done by us primarily.

If these gigantic tasks are to be pursued with any hope of success and with any degree of intelligence, there must be constant and intensive contacts between those in both communities who are most aware of the need and who mean to devote themselves most persistently to the meeting of that need. It is with that in mind that the Jewish Theological Seminary, the United Synagogue, and the Rabbinical Assembly decided to erect in Jerusalem a center that would vividly testify to the spiritual ties that exist between the land of Israel and the entire people of Israel. We hope that every one preparing himself for the American rabbinate or for leadership in American Jewish education will live at least for one year at this center and attend either the Hebrew University or other schools of higher Jewish learning in Jerusalem. It is our hope that students from Israel or from other Jewish communities, who are also preparing for educational or religious leadership, would share quarters with our students in our center. The future leaders of the Jewish people throughout the world should be given the opportunity to live together during their formative years in the shadow of the prophets and the sages of old, so that in friendship and in an atmosphere of utter honesty and devotion they may probe one another's deepest levels and together forge the bonds of spiritual understanding and conviction.[5]

I do not delude myself into believing that there is anything which can guarantee any people absolute protection against disintegration from within. Every people faces that danger constantly, the Jewish people perhaps more so than others.

Nor do I imagine that if all Jews spoke Hebrew and all Jews were loyal members of the Synagogue, peace, tranquility and idyllic mutual understanding would follow. I can easily envision most acrimonious controversy carried on in perfect Hebrew by Jews adorned with *talit* and *tefilin*. But, to return to the metaphor which is the title of this chapter—spiritual bridges, moored to Hebrew and the Synagogue, can, I believe, stand up under the most violent storms of controversy. Nor do I believe that any other moorings can replace these. If these moorings should disappear, the bridge would collapse completely and the winds of controversy would cease blowing, for there would be nothing to stir them into motion; the silence of death would descend upon the scene.

It is that silence which, above everything else, our people has dreaded and has successfully held at bay for thousands of years. More than two millenia ago they sang—"We shall not die but live and proclaim God's glory."[6] To proclaim a message to mankind requires a language; to proclaim God's glory implies that we make Him a sanctuary.[7] Hebrew is the language of our proclamation. God is the theme. The Synagogue is the sanctuary. Wherever and whenever Jews in their sanctuaries proclaim God's message in Hebrew, they not only bring benediction to man, but they simultaneously build for themselves spiritual bridges which storms cannot destroy nor time corrode.

CHAPTER XII

Auto-Emancipation and Zionism[1]

In September of 1882 Leon Pinsker published his history-making pamphlet *Auto-Emancipation,* thereby injecting into the superficially placid realm of Jewish thought a revolutionary concept. It set before the mighty spiritual and intellectual forces seething in the depths of the Jewish ocean of life a new and challenging task. Since then that concept has been among the most powerful forces consciously and subconsciously energizing the hearts, minds and hands of the most devoted and most creative members of our people.

Auto-emancipation—free yourself—take your destiny into your own hands! Pinsker's call to his people partook, as it were, of one of the dominant characteristics of prophecy in that it had infinite potentialities for growth in meaning and significance. Though the prophet speaks to his own generation, though his mind is directed exclusively to the problems of the present that press for a solution, yet the course of action which he suggests for his own contemporaries has greater import than even he himself recognizes, so that as the generations that follow explore it in depth they find it applicable to problems of their own day. This quality inheres in large measure in Pinsker's call to his contemporaries to emancipate themselves.

The call was intended as an answer to the problem occupying the center of attention of his generation. It was a generation that above everything else sought emancipation from the political and economic discriminations and handicaps that hung like a weight around its neck. The "enlightened" Jewish leaders of Pinsker's generation, those that had gone out beyond the ghetto walls and had succeeded in acquiring a general secular education, saw the process of emancipation for East European Jewry as part of the process that would bring political freedom to all the people of the Russian empire. In this process the Jews, too, would be politically emancipated, not as a people but as individuals. More than that they neither sought nor hoped for.

After the pogroms of 1881, Pinsker concluded that it was an illusion to believe that the nations of Eastern Europe would include the Jews in their programs of liberalism and democratic equality. But even of greater significance was his conclusion that it was an illusion to believe that the individual Jew would be a really free man, feel himself and be considered by others to be the equal of his fellow non-Jews, as long as the Jewish people *as a people* did not occupy a position of recognized equality with the other peoples of the world. But except for Moses Hess in his *Rome and Jerusalem,* which was unknown among the Jews of Eastern Europe, no one had previously even ventured to suggest that the political emancipation of the Jews as a people is a humanly attainable goal at all, and certainly not through their own efforts. The idea appeared too quixotic to be taken seriously by any reasonable individual. The Jews were too weak, too disorganized, too hemmed in by relentlessly hostile forces.

It was this mood of pessimism that Pinsker hoped to dispel. It was a mood unworthy of the Jewish people. Let them but depend upon their own spiritual and economic resources and upon their righteous cause and they will prevail.

How was auto-emancipation to be achieved? Some suggested mass migration to new territories where they could form their own communities primarily as agriculturalists subsisting on the land. Baron de Hirsch was the outstanding exponent of that view. Others suggested the revival on a modern basis of the medieval *kahal,* of Jewish cultural and religious self-government in the countries where they lived. The historian Simon Dubnow was the chief exponent of that point of view. More gradually than many believe, there crystallized the view which finally became predominant—that the path of auto-emancipation for the Jewish people is the path that leads to Zion, to a self-governing Jewish community in *Eretz Yisrael.* That definition of auto-emancipation seemed to include all essentials. It included mass emigration from the lands of oppression. It included a return to the soil, that so many held indispensable for true national emancipation. It included, above all, the cultural factor and especially the Hebraic character of that culture which to so many was not merely the *sine qua non* but the ultimate *summum bonum* to be achieved by auto-emancipation.

The Zionist interpretation and application of Pinsker's call for auto-emancipation proved to be the most vital and realistic and has made by far the greatest contribution towards the fulfillment of the vision of a free Jewish people. Time has vindicated, in some cases even more completely than Zionists themselves could have hoped, the truth of some of the fundamental premises upon which they had based their program.

Zionism said that any program of action which aims to achieve the full emancipation of the Jew within the sphere of the Diaspora only, is doomed to failure. Zionists did not fear to assert that anti-Semitism is a permanent and ineradicable factor in the attitude of the world towards the Jew. They said this at a time when to make such an assertion branded one as a short-sighted, narrow, bigoted, and hypersensitive creature. How could one who kept pace with the tremendous advances in the physical sciences—the one great pursuit of the human mind which is supposedly uncontaminated by any prejudice, hate or discrimination—how could one who saw the remarkable progress of literacy and of higher education, be so pessimistic as to believe that anti-Semitism will not be overcome in civilized Europe! Yet how tragically have events corroborated this Zionist position. The last half century has witnessed the cold-blooded, scientifically calculated murder of more Jews than any other era in Jewish history and a more ruthless persistent and uncompromising effort to destroy Judaism and Jewish culture than was ever made before by Church or State. All of this took and is taking place in countries that are among the scientifically and "culturally" most advanced in the world. There was a time when Zionists hesitated to give anti-Semitism—active, vicious anti-Semitism—as a reason for the need of a Jewish state. Today no Zionist need hesitate to list that as one of his arguments. There is more virulent religious, racial and nationalistic hatred abroad in the world today than probably at any other period in recorded history.

Zionism further based itself on the contention that *Eretz Yisrael* has the agricultural, commercial and industrial possibilities to furnish a modest but satisfying livelihood not merely for a handful, but for hundreds of thousands, yea, for some few millions of Jews. What supercilious mockery was poured upon our faith in the economic resources of *Eretz Yisrael*! How often were we reminded that it was small, swampy, stony, dry, and sandy, without any natural riches in the form of coal, iron, or oil! We proved the truth of the Rabbinic comment that the size of *Eretz Yisrael* is a relative matter. *Eretz Yisrael,* when Jews do not dwell within her, is small. It seems to shrivel up. But when Jews do dwell within her, the land unfolds itself, so to speak, and expands.[2] We found natural resources in the Dead Sea. We found the power to give light and to turn the wheels of industry, and the water to fructify the desert. The orange, the grapefruit, the grapevine, the banana plant and a host of other new plants and improved methods made it possible for ten to live in comparative comfort where previously one subsisted with the greatest of hardship. The industrial potentialities of a population of skilled and trained laborers, managers and entrepreneurs has as yet only been lightly tapped. The Rabbis frequently speak of the unique rapport that they believe exists between the people and the land of Israel. In that spirit they interpret the curse pronounced upon the land because of Israel's sins, "I will make the land desolate so that your enemies who settle in it shall be appalled by it" (Leviticus 26:32) to mean that after the Exile, the land will not respond to the strangers who will try to till it.[3]

One must be made of exceptionally hard, rationalistic stuff who, knowing of the wonders wrought before our very eyes by the meeting of the long-neglected, barren land of Israel and the people of Israel, yet remains completely impervious to the mystic lure of this Rabbinic reflection.

We might with profit also dwell at some length upon the other basic contentions of Zionism whose truth has been amply testified to by the events of the last half century. I stress the problems of the permanency of anti-Semitism and the resources of the land because these seemed to be the most vulnerable spots in the structure of Zionist theory. Is there anyone who still doubts the soundness of the other basic Zionist contentions—namely that only in *Eretz Yisrael* can a free Hebrew culture be developed? Or that only *Eretz Yisrael* can serve as the focal point towards which there will converge the myriad mystic threads of national loyalty and solidarity radiating from the hearts of Jews scattered all over this globe,[4] and that in *Eretz Yisrael* these separately frail threads will weave themselves into a new pattern of strength and beauty? Or is there still serious doubt left concerning the regenerative influence exerted by the State of Israel upon the character of the individual Jew, wherever he dwells, whether it be in Israel or in the Diaspora? The revival of the Hebrew language, the creation of a school system ranging from the Kindergarten to the University, the extraordinary activity of the Hebrew press and publishing houses of *Eretz Yisrael* as contrasted with the blight that has fallen upon Hebraic cultural work in the Diaspora, the establishment of the State of Israel, the absorption within its boundaries of over a million mostly impoverished immigrants within a period of less than twenty years and the signal military victories it thrice achieved against overwhelming odds all eloquently bear testimony to the truth of the major Zionist contentions.

Yet despite all of its victories, Zionism today is facing a crisis in the United States the gravity of which can hardly be overstated. That crisis is reflected in the demoralization we witness in the ranks of the American Zionist organizations when judged by the number of individuals actively affiliated as members, or by the achievements in the political, economic or cultural realm that may be credited directly to them. One wonders why this should be so? Why should a movement be apparently weakening at a time when events proved so conclusively every claim made in its behalf? One could understand why non-Zionist individuals and organizations should have taken over the task of raising the funds required for implementing the economic programs in Israel. Fund raising is not necessarily the forte of ideologically properly oriented individuals. One can understand also why the activities on the political front should have largely passed from the hands of the organized Zionists after the establishment of the State of Israel. There is a very large number of influential organizations and individuals who are vitally concerned with the political welfare of the State of Israel without at the same time being ideological Zionists. There is above all the State of Israel itself with its well-organized and effective diplomatic representatives to attend to its political problems. What disturbs one most therefore is that the Zionist Movement ceased being a vital force even in the *cultural* and *spiritual* life of the Jews of the United States. How did this happen? I believe that this happened because

American Zionists wittingly or unwittingly accepted as the complete definition of the concept of auto-emancipation the opening paragraph of the Basle program which states the aim of Zionism to be the establishment of "a publicly recognized and legally assured home for the Jewish people in Palestine."

For the purpose of concentrating attention upon a limited and clearly defined task, this narrowing of the concept of auto-emancipation served admirably. But a very high price was paid for this advantage. The concept of auto-emancipation, which should have served as a challenge to every American Jew as *an individual,* was transformed into a challenge to the impersonal entity called the Jewish people. The Jewish people was to emancipate itself. And since there were and still are millions of Jews suffering palpable physical and spiritual persecution, Zionism as a movement of Jewish auto-emancipation was most easily and readily understood, especially by the Jews in the United States, as a movement that would bring freedom and opportunity to their disadvantaged brethren. Hence Zionism for American Jews was in essence a philanthropic movement. A Zionist became one who helped establish a Jewish State in order to provide a home for those Jews who had no country in which they could live with dignity.

American Jews never explored in depth the concept of auto-emancipation *per se.* But auto-emancipation is a concept which should challenge each individual Jew in his own life as a Jew no matter where he lives. In the case of lands of oppression, auto-emancipation calls for heroic political action not only by those who are being directly oppressed but by their fellow Jews throughout the world. In the lands of freedom, the call of auto-emancipation is equally urgent and challenging. We dare never forget that the existence of the Jewish people is and has always been in jeopardy not only because of physical persecutions but also because of the enticements and the blandishments of the cultures in whose midst we live as a politically free and economically secure community. The doctrine of auto-emancipation is applicable not only to the political life of our people. It is equally and more obviously applicable to our spiritual and cultural life. Nobody can emancipate us from our cultural and spiritual subservience to the culture of the dominant majority except we ourselves.

Auto-emancipation, properly defined, implies that there rests upon every Jew no matter where he lives the moral responsibility as a free human being to do all within his power to create for his personal and family life—as well as for the life of the Jewish community of which he is a part—the framework within which he could live as rich and meaningful a Jewish life as his talents, his resources and his environment make possible. In the State of Israel that framework is there, and the average Jew in the country cannot step outside of it unless he makes a very great and determined effort. That framework consists primarily of language and holidays, and internal political and social organization. But for the millions of Jews who are destined to remain living in the Diaspora, for us who will continue to live here, such a framework for our lives must be consciously created and maintained by us. The establishment of the State of Israel undoubtedly can help us create that Jewish framework for our lives in the Diaspora. But we now know beyond a shadow of a doubt that it will not do so, in and by itself, without a conscious, well-directed and self-sacrificing effort on our part.

Such a stubbornly sustained, generously supported, spiritually auto-emancipatory effort must be made not only by those who believe that the Diaspora should and can be preserved, but even by those Zionists who believe that the dissolution of the Diaspora is inevitable and that the Zionist goal should be that of salvaging for Israel as many Jews as possible from the West, particularly from the United States, as rapidly as possible. Nobody is quite that pessimistic as to believe that American Jewry is going to disappear within the next decade or two. Though I know how urgent is Israel's need for substantial Jewish immigration from the United States, and though I believe that every conceivable measure should be taken to produce that immigration, I do not accept the proposition that if we do not have "so many or so many" immigrants from America within the next decade all that we have achieved in Israel may be lost. This crisis mood has been integral to the Zionist Movement from its very inception. I suppose that by and large it served as a beneficent goal, but if overdone it may also do much harm. Nothing is psychologically more frustrating than palpably unattainable goals.

I do not know how many immigrants Israel needs from America within the next decade in order to be "saved." Nor is my opinion of American Jewry so pessimistic as to be as sure as some are that there will be no numerically significant immigration of American Jews to Israel within the forthcoming decade. One thing I am sure of. I am sure that *Israel is here to stay* and that as far as one can see, the Jewish community of America will for at least the next two generations be its chief "ally" spiritually and economically and that it must also be a primary source for whatever additional manpower Israel may need for its development.

Moreover, I also know that short of violent economic or political upheavals, such as a world war, a great economic depression, or the rise of a radical revolutionary movement, sudden unexpected changes in the outlook of large masses of people cannot be expected. Now Zionist literature has heretofore never asked the Jews of America to see themselves as potential immigrants either to *Eretz Yisrael* or the State of Israel. It is unreasonable, therefore, to expect a sudden, dramatic change in a frame of mind that has been nurtured for some two generations.

It is, moreover, obvious that conditions being as they are in the United States—and as we believe they will continue to be—the Jews of America will not be moved to make their homes in the State of Israel in order to find there greater physical security and economic welfare. What then can conceivably move an American Jew to determine to cast his lot with his brethren in Israel? It can be but one thing: the passionate desire to live as a Jew a spiritually more satisfying life and the conviction that Israel offers him the opportunity to fulfill that desire. A precondition, therefore, for his even considering settlement in Israel is a profound love of the Jewish people, a deep attachment to its pattern of life and the belief that that love and attachment can find their fullest and happiest fulfillment in Israel. Such love for the Jewish people and devotion to its spiritual heritage can take root only in the hearts and souls of Jews who strive to live *wherever they may be* as full a Jewish life as circumstances will permit. It is a well-established psychological truth that a born slave cannot easily appreciate freedom. Tradition has it that the Jews of Egypt were led in revolt by the tribe of Levi that was never enslaved. Moses knew best what his own people lacked because he was raised in the palace, and Herzl could experience more profoundly the humiliation of his people because he saw what truly free nations enjoy. Thus only he who struggles to his utmost to live as a Jew outside of the State of Israel will give serious thought, and may eventually be moved, to uproot himself from his present comfortable surroundings to take up residence in the State of Israel.

Thus the concept of auto-emancipation which historically was not only the chronological forerunner but also the intellectual or spiritual fountainhead of the concept of Zionism would continue to serve its historic role. It would be the spiritual seedbed of the concept of Zionism, which without it has shown evidence of withering even as does a flower cut off from its soil.

To the extent that American Jewry has succeeded in maintaining a degree of Jewish spiritual and intellectual independence within the framework of the tremendously alluring American civilization, it has been achieved primarily through the activity of the religious forces functioning amongst us. These religious forces may have been derelict in their responsibilities to point to Israel as the place where one may best fulfill himself as a Jew. But whatever their shortcomings may have been, they have raised in America a generation that has some roots in the Jewish spiritual heritage. Within their hearts there have been implanted those Jewish emotions and within their minds those Jewish memories and ideas upon which we can hope to build in the future.

For some two thousand years, during which we were politically subjugated, we proved that we can remain spiritually and culturally independent. Through the establishment of the State of Israel we have as a people achieved political auto-emancipation. But it has not as yet resulted in the fullness of spiritual emancipation to which we aspire. The problem of Jewish spiritual emancipation is one that continues to be of concern to Jewish educators and philosophers even in Israel. Ahad Ha'Am, in one of his most brilliant essays "Slavery Within Freedom," pointed out not only that political emancipation and spiritual emancipation do not necessarily go hand in hand, but that in Western Europe the Jews acquired political at the sacrifice of spiritual emancipation. Whether or not they had to make the sacrifice is a question that no one can now answer. But one thing is certain. In the United States that sacrifice never was, and hopefully never will be, necessary.

To suggest a line of action that envisages a period of one or two generations as a response to what is recognized by all as an immediate and urgent need—immigration to Israel from the United States—is to invite the obvious criticism of the "practical" and the "realistic" amongst us. One may even be accused of seeking thus to sidestep his responsibility to the need of the hour by calling attention to our responsibility to the need of the generations. But the prophetic qualities in the leadership of Pinsker and Herzl consisted precisely in the fact that they asked their contemporaries to undertake tasks whose fulfillment required generations in contrast to tasks suggested by the well-intentioned Baron de Hirsch or by the

Utopian revolutionaries of Eastern Europe whose programs of action envisaged, to be sure, hard labor but promised immediate results.

It was because the Jews of Eastern Europe had fulfilled in their lives the challenge of spiritual auto-emancipation so gloriously, that they had the courage, the vision and the will when the hour arrived, to give a total response to the call of political auto-emancipation.

But Zionist propaganda in the United States by and large took a neutral, and at times even a negative, attitude towards the possibilities of living a spiritually satisfying Jewish life in the Diaspora. Thus with few, insignificant exceptions no effort was made by Zionists as such to keep as intact as possible the essential framework and content of Jewish life in the communal sphere and more especially in the sphere of personal and family living. Zionism in America was thus denied both of the resources that could have given it significant spiritual and intellectual body. It did not demand of its followers completely to identify themselves personally with the national act of political auto-emancipation by joining the ranks of the pioneers who laid the foundations of the State of Israel on the land and in the cities of Palestine, nor with those who in the United States were laying the foundations of Jewish spiritual auto-emancipation in this great democracy.

And now we may well have come to that moment in Jewish history when a redefinition of the two concepts of Zionism and auto-emancipation may help us to see our way more clearly in the future. The concept of Zionism should be increasingly identified with the obligation to fulfill the act of auto-emancipation in both its political and spiritual connotations by giving serious thought and making an honest effort to make one's physical as well as spiritual home in Israel. The concept of auto-emancipation should point to our responsibility to live our personal lives no matter where we live and to fashion the life of the Jewish community, no matter in what country, within the framework of Jewish thought, Jewish mores and Jewish aspirations for the whole of mankind. That means that we must, wherever we are, strive to know as fully as possible the Hebrew language and its literature from the Bible to our day; to have the Sabbath, our festivals and dietary laws as well as the Jewish attitudes towards the great moral issues of life—the family, social justice, universal peace—reflected in our personal and family lives. That means that as a community our activities must be directed primarily towards the goal of helping the individual Jew live more fully and satisfyingly as a Jew.

Only a Zionism which is built on such broad and deep foundations of spiritual auto-emancipation will be able ultimately to flourish in America. And it will be primarily from the ranks of those American Jews who will strive here to achieve spiritual emancipation as Jews that there will hopefully come in goodly number those who will respond to the call of Israel with body and soul. Thus also will we be able to be as a people what we have been these thousands of years: a people not limited to one geographic area large or small, but a world people with a world view that has a message for the whole of mankind and that can give meaning and content to a human life no matter where it is lived; a people whose spiritual roots are firmly imbedded in Zion, but whose "descendants shall be known among the nations, and their offspring in the midst of the peoples; all who see them shall acknowledge them, that they are a people whom the Lord has blessed" (Isaiah 61:9).

CHAPTER XIII

Towards a Jewish Version of American Civilization[1]

The subject before us has two distinct, though overlapping, aspects. The one is related to the question of the place within the American democratic order of any privately supported school which segregates its pupils from the rest of the children of the community for any reason whatsoever, whether it be rooted in educational theory or in religious convictions. The other aspect is concerned with the internal order of the school, once it is established. Assuming a satisfactory philosophy for the place of the Jewish religious day school in the American democratic order of society, what would distinguish a day school administered under the auspices of the Conservative Movement from that administered under the auspices of other Jewish religious movements?

Obviously, one cannot discuss this second aspect of the subject without first formulating what he believes to be the philosophy of the Conservative Movement in Judaism and then indicating how that does or should affect the administration, curriculum and methodology of all its schools. While the two aspects overlap, they are sufficiently distinctive to require separate treatment.

Since I have previously had occasion to formulate some of my opinions on the philosophy of the Conservative Movement,[2] I shall here devote my remarks primarily to a statement on the place of a religiously centered, voluntarily supported day school in politically democratic America.

While there is no doubt in my mind that much of the hesitancy regarding the day school within the Conservative Movement stemmed from the fear of assuming the tremendous financial responsibility the maintenance of a day school involves, I am equally certain that that was not the primary factor determining our action. We hesitated even to speak favorably about Jewish day schools because we had and have a profound concern for the maintenance of the primacy of the public school in American elementary and secondary education. This concern for the primacy of the public school is in turn rooted in a philosophy of the place that Judaism should occupy in the life of an American Jew. We will not be able to think constructively and enthusiastically about the Jewish day school until our concern for the primacy of the public school is adequately met, and until we formulate an acceptable philosophy of the place of Judaism in the life of the American Jew, within whose framework the day school takes its natural, understandable place. It is only thus that we can remove the presently existing intellectual blocks to our thinking on the day school. It is upon this task that we must, therefore, first concentrate our thought.

Many, I dare say the overwhelming majority amongst us, have deep sentimental and intellectual attachments to the public school. It supplied our basic secular educational needs and it introduced us to the vast and wonderful world of American civilization. We know that a long and hard battle had to be fought before the public school won its acknowledged place in American life. We know that it was and continues to be the chief meeting ground for children of all creeds and colors in American society and was and is therefore probably the greatest single democratizing force in

America. We know that while its future is as assured and certain as the future of any human institution can be, it is constantly under attack and an increasingly large number of children are being withdrawn from its influence.

The public school as the symbol of acceptance into American society still has a very strong hold upon the imagination and the sentiments of our people. They feel that any Jewish withdrawal from it is an act smacking of ingratitude for the benefits bestowed in the past and that it is fraught with danger for our position in America.

One cannot argue with sentimental attachments nor with intuitive forebodings. But neither can one formulate an intelligent attitude merely on the basis of sentiments and intuitions. Facts should also be taken into consideration and should play their indispensable role in our thinking. When thinking about the role of the public school in American democracy, the following facts should be borne in mind.

1. The public school was never intended to monopolize education in America. It was never intended that it should meet *all* the educational needs of *all* the children. Thus, from the very beginning, all instruction in religion was specifically excluded from the curriculum of the public school. Nor was attendance in the public school ever obligatory upon every child. One of the great bulwarks of American democracy was the fact that the State never claimed for itself and was never granted the right to be the sole agency in the education of the child. The State sought merely to assure that its future citizens should receive the education deemed indispensable for an intelligent participation in the civic life of a political democracy and in the economic life of a highly industrialized and mechanized society. The public school was established in order to guarantee to every child the opportunity to receive that minimum instruction. The child who could receive the necessary instruction outside the public school was permitted to do so.

Hence, there was never a time in American history when

private schools either under religious or nonreligious auspices were considered un-American, as being contrary to the best interest of America or of democracy. On the contrary, it was always recognized, and in the twentieth century it was tragically demonstrated, that a state monopoly of the institutions for the education of the young was a universal characteristic of political tyrannies and the greatest single danger to the preservation of democratic institutions.

An oversentimentalized loyalty to the public school as the exclusive educational institution for the young would lay the best possible basis for the ultimate defeat of the very purpose that that loyalty ostensibly seeks to serve, for it would be the first step towards transforming the public school from a democratizing institution into an institution for *gleichgeschaltung,* for the forceful imposition of a uniformity of thought indispensable to a dictatorship but anathema to a democracy. That the danger of totalitarianism is a constant threat to every democratic society should never be forgotten, and least of all by us of this generation. That complete state monopoly of education is among the chief weapons of totalitarianism has also been established beyond reasonable doubt. Hence, neither the federal nor the state governments ever put impediments in the way of any group of responsible citizens who sought to organize and maintain a school for their children. All that the State required was that acceptable standards be maintained for the teaching personnel, the physical plant and curricular content.

2. As a result of the foregoing, there exists in the United States today a vast network of non-tax-supported schools from the kindergarten through the university, with a school population running into the many millions.[3] No one argues that the graduates of these schools have a poorer understanding of the meaning of democracy, or are less loyal to America and its democratic institutions. We have long passed the day when we imagine that mere physical proximity teaches people to love one another or even understand one another. Personal

contacts are very helpful, but only when the proper spiritual and intellectual attitude is simultaneously inculcated. The existence of the large Catholic parochial school system as well as of the other many private religious and nonreligious schools invalidate *a priori* any attack upon the Jewish day school as a clannish, un-American institution.

3. Furthermore, the dominance of the public school in American life is assured as long as it remains *the only tax-supported* educational institution for elementary and high school education. The determinative part that taxes play in giving predominance to any institution thus supported is too obvious to need proof.

Considering the size of the American Jewish community and the fact that it does not have the army of nonsalaried teachers available to the Catholic schools, it should be quite obvious that opposition to the Jewish day school as a threat to the public school is as realistic as opposition to the State of Israel because it is or may be a military threat to the United States.

4. To the theoretic question of whether we would prefer to see the American educational system organized along the same lines as that in Canada, *i.e.,* to have tax-supported religiously oriented schools, our answer on the basis of our own experiences would at present undoubtedly be an unequivocal "No." We do not want the taxing power of the State to be used in behalf of religious education.

But it may well be argued that depriving religiously centered schools of the benefits of the taxing power of government deprives children of the poor whose parents cannot provide non-tax-supported schooling for them, of what we would consider to be the most desirable kind of education. While theoretically, this appears to be a cogent argument, experience has not corroborated the theory. The fact of the matter seems to be that in the presently existing privately supported, religiously centered Jewish day schools, a high percentage of the school population comes from homes of the lower middle class and of the poor. But even if experience would support theory completely, I would acknowledge the gravity of the problem without accepting the implied solution. I consider this to be a situation to which there is no satisfactory solution.

We are forced to choose between two evils—between government supported religious education and the probability that many children may not get the best possible religiously centered education. I consider the second the lesser of the two evils. All human experience has taught us that government support of religion corrupts religion, for it robs it of its essence, that of voluntary personal commitment, and involves it in political maneuvering for the tax dollar.[4]

As long as the public elementary and high school remain the *only* tax-supported schools, I do not see in the non-tax-supported private school, whether religious or nonreligious, any threat to the public school, nor any danger to democracy in the United States. On the contrary, I see in the complete elimination of all but tax-supported schools a very real threat to the future of democracy in America, even as I see in tax-supported religious schools a real threat to the future of religion.

The second cause for our hesitancy regarding the day school, I consider to be much more serious and deep-rooted. I refer to the lack of clarity in our own thinking on exactly what it is we want to accomplish through a Jewish day school.

Our lack of clarity regarding the role of the Jewish day school in the life of the American Jewish community stems in turn from our lack of clarity regarding the role of Judaism in our lives. Hence, the Jewish day school has been advocated by some as a center for progressive educational methods. Others saw in it the institution that would provide properly trained leaders for the American Jewish community. Still others viewed it as the most likely institution to make Jewish education more palatable. Each one of these reasons has considerable validity and is of great importance. But in themselves, they are not enough to justify intense efforts on a national level to encourage the establishment of day schools within our Movement. Nor do they furnish sufficient motivation for the maintenance of the kind of curriculum that would enable these day schools to achieve a purpose of scope and meaning equal to the great demands they must make upon the community's resources.

There have been in the past a number of day schools maintained by congregations or individuals affiliated with our Movement. But despite very ambitious beginnings, they generally proved to be little more than private schools with progressive pedagogic methods and with the Hebrew language occupying the time in the curriculum usually given to any foreign language. There were to be sure, some other "fringe benefits" of a Jewish nature, even in these highly watered versions of what a Jewish day school should be. But by and large, these schools, if judged by their specific Jewish contribution, did not, in my opinion, justify the great investment of money and effort which they required. A well-organized weekday afternoon school produced equally good results as far as the specifically Jewish element in education is concerned.

A Jewish day school must in the final analysis justify the vast effort its maintenance requires, by the quality of the specifically Jewish element it contributes to the total education of its pupils and by the role that this Jewish element should play in the structuring of their personalities. *We conceive the ultimate purpose of all Jewish education in the United States to be that of nurturing a spiritually integrated personality at whose core is the Jewish religion and whose circumference constitutes a rich and happy synthesis of its Jewish and American spiritual heritage.* We believe this goal to be not only possible of achievement but also to be the highest privilege which America—by virtue of the Constitutional principles of religious freedom and separation of Church and State—makes available to us as Jews and to every one of its citizens in relation to his own religious tradition. We believe that the Jewish day school may prove to be the most effective instrument for us as Jews to achieve that goal.

For what is the ultimate fundamental implication of the freedom of religion which the American Constitution guarantees to all residents of America and which we recognize as being basic to all other freedoms guaranteed us in our democracy? To me, that ultimate fundamental implication is this—that America not only permits but encourages its citizens to integrate their personal lives and their lives as distinguishable groups in American society around a religion, as expressed in specific beliefs and practices.

The high priority which America places upon religion as the ultimate integrating factor of the life of an individual or of a group is most vividly reflected in its treatment of religiously oriented conscientious objectors to war and in the fact that no religious community has ever been accused of lack of patriotic ardor because it does not raise the American flag above its house of worship or place it on its pulpit. Moreover, Americans take great pride in the thought that American democracy constitutes the greatest and noblest concretization thus far achieved by any society of some of the ethical and moral teachings of what we frequently refer to as the Judaeo-Christian religious tradition. That tradition is widely recognized as the ultimate source of moral sanction and spiritual authority and its maintenance as a vital force in American life is viewed as indispensable to the welfare of our democracy. Though time may have dulled the edge of much of what Washington said to his countrymen in his Farewell Address, what he said about the role of religion in human society is still by and large explicitly or implicitly acknowledged by the official organs of American society as valid: "Of all the dispositions and habits which lead to political prosperity, religion and morality are indispensable supports. . . . And let us with caution indulge the supposition that morality can be maintained without religion. Whatever may be conceded to the influence of refined education on minds of peculiar structure, reason and experience forbid us to expect that national morality can prevail in exclusion of religious principle."

American democracy grants to no other spiritual or social phenomenon, whether it be a culture, a civilization or a language, the privileges that it grants to religion. Thus it has no objection to having some of its citizens speak another language. But no language occupies a legal position in any sense on a par with English in America. America has no objection to individuals or groups preserving their own folkways or nurturing their own cultural values. But it would not tolerate the refusal, as a matter of principle, to raise the American flag above a *Kultur Verein* or a French language school or a Jewish community center. No Jewish group in America would think of celebrating Israel Independence Day without raising the American flag at the head of the march, or placing it in the position of honor at a public gathering. No Jewish teacher absenting himself on Israel Independence Day from his classroom in a public school would expect the same treatment from his superiors as he expects when he absents himself on *Yom Kippur* or *Pesah*. One need not belabor the obvious fact, which nevertheless is often not sufficiently clearly understood, that America's attitude towards Irishmen celebrating St. Patrick's Day is different from that of her attitude towards their celebrating Irish Independence Day, though, happily, it is not opposed to the latter either.

It is this unique position of religion in America which resulted in the last half-century in what Will Herberg[5] has so aptly designated as the "triple American melting pot"—the Protestant, Catholic and Jewish "pot." I believe he should have made it a quadruple melting pot. I refer to the large secularly oriented segment of American society consisting of those who find in the ideals of American democracy as expressed in the Declaration of Independence and in the Constitution an adequate spiritual core around which to integrate their personal lives.

No individual's life can be happily and harmoniously integrated around more than one center. Just as a mankind that worships essentially different gods can never achieve a real unity, thus no individual can achieve significant inner spiritual unity by "worshipping more than one god." Each life must have its own identifiable supreme center. An individual's religion, if it be religion in any true sense of the word, is that identifiable, supreme center of his being around which his whole personality is, or should be, clearly and harmoniously integrated.

Hence, where the political order and a religion were interdependent, or identical or the one subservient to the other, Jews could not remain harmoniously integrated as individuals or as a group and at the same time be fully integrated into that political order. They had either to dissociate themselves from their Jewish heritage or live in socially and most often even geographically isolated enclaves, as essentially foreign bodies within a surrounding body politic. By divorcing religion from the political order as much as is humanly possible while recognizing the primacy of religion in the life of the individual and of groups, America not only permits but invites its citizens as individuals and as groups to choose, each one for himself, and each group for itself, his and its own highest inner integrating principle.

Some ninety or more million Church and Synagogue members in the United States have taken advantage of this privilege and have at least formally indicated that the wholeness of their personal lives requires an element that does not inhere in the American tradition as such. For many of them that element represents the consciously acknowledged core around which their spiritual personalities are integrated.

This revolutionary, historic fact implies yet another very significant truth. It implies that within the framework of the American political order, there co-exist in friendly relationship and in complete mutual toleration, various recognized versions of what in its totality is called American civilization. Around every recognized ultimate integrating center, a legitimate version of American civilization is developed.

Thus, when we rightly protest the designation of American civilization as being exclusively or even essentially Christian, we are reaffirming the proposition that there is more than one legitimate version of American civilization. There are today a goodly number of such versions, the most widely accepted among them being the various Protestant versions, the Catholic, the Jewish, and the secularist version.

It is our unprecedented privilege and opportunity to live as full and equal citizens of a country in which we can preserve the inner harmony and unity of our lives as Jews, both as individuals and as a community, because our American citizenship does not require us to do anything in violation of the Jewish religion. There is nothing in the Declaration of Independence, nor in the Constitution and in the legislation enacted under it, which makes it impossible for me to observe whatever laws of the Torah are observable in the Diaspora. Moreover, the Jewish religion as the core or the integrating principle of my life as a citizen of America does not prevent me from fulfilling completely and conscientiously all of my responsibilities as a loyal citizen of America. On the contrary, it is platitudinous by now to repeat Justice Brandeis' words that "the better a Jew one is, the better American he will be."

When I say that American democracy is rooted in Judaism, I do not think primarily of the historic role played by the Bible in early American life, important as that role undoubtedly was. Nor do I mean that Americanism and Judaism are or should be identical.[6] I mean that the political order established by the Declaration of Independence and the Constitution of the United States and the laws enacted in compliance with their spirit and letter are as full an implementation of the laws of justice and the principles of righteousness enunciated in the Torah, as has as yet been achieved by any human society. But Judaism demands more of its followers than justice and righteousness. It requires them also to live lives of mercy, of love and holiness. It asks them to be ever conscious that they are always in the presence of God.

In regard to these all-important, central aspects of my life, Americanism as reflected in the Declaration of Independence, the Constitution, and all that logically flows therefrom, offers no guidance. It consciously refrains from offering such guidance. On the contrary, it encourages its citizens to seek guidance in these aspects of their lives in whatever religious traditions they choose. I chose and I want my fellow Jews to choose to seek this guidance in the Torah, none of whose injunctions Americanism compels me to violate.

Thus, as I live in America, obedient to the laws of America, speaking the language of America, participating in the political, social and economic life of America while at the same time observing the Sabbath, the Festivals, the dietary laws, and praying in the synagogue, I am living what I would designate as the Jewish version of American civilization. That Jewish version may also contain a Hebrew or Yiddish or Anglo-Jewish press, a Hebrew or Yiddish or Anglo-Jewish theater, a profound spiritual and personal concern for the welfare of the State of Israel, etc., etc. These are as legitimate a part of the totality of American civilization as is the Negro spiritual, the St. Patrick's Day parade, the football game, or the automobile.

In creating a Jewish version of American civilization, we are inevitably also creating what may be an American version of Judaism. The full implications of that fact we must continuously explore. For our present purposes, I want to stress the thought that our duty as American educators is to help develop this Jewish version of American civilization, to teach it to our children and to nurture in them the desire to fulfill themselves as human beings through it. Many of us believe that to fulfill this glorious, historically unprecedented task, we need the help of the day school. It alone can offer the climate and the situation within which such a Jewish version of American civilization can be nurtured and can in turn become the pattern for the life of the Jewish community as a whole.

In the light of the foregoing, I believe we would do well if we ceased to think of ourselves as living in two civilizations in America. The very term "two civilizations" has always somehow disturbed me. It makes me feel as if I were in essence leading a kind of schizophrenic existence between two different and competing worlds. How can I at a given moment determine in which of these two worlds I am? In what civilization am I living when I watch a Broadway version of Sholom Aleikhem, or listen to a concert of modern or classical music, or read world news in a Yiddish or Hebrew newspaper? Is a typical New York or Oshkosh Bar Mitzvah party part of American or of Jewish civilization? Within which of the two civilizations was the poet Ephraim Lisitzki, whose home was in New Orleans, living while he was writing his great epic of the American Indian *Medurot Doakhot* in Hebrew? I have no way of answering these questions. Nor am I inclined to do with my life what modern critics have done to the text of the Bible, ascribing not only whole chapters of the book, and whole sentences of the same chapter, but even different words of the same sentence to different eras and literary sources. Whatever the original source of a word or sentence or chapter may have been, it is now part of an integrated whole. Thus, whatever the original source of any particular act of mine may be, insofar as it is part of me, it should be part of an integrated whole.

Hence, I do not feel that, as a human being who is a Jew in America, I live in two civilizations. I feel rather that insofar as my life is integrated around the Torah I am living in the Jewish version of American civilization. To the extent that America offers me opportunities for self-expression which are not inimical to the Torah but which are denied a fellow Jew in another country whose life is also integrated around the Torah, to that extent my total experience is different from his. The center of the circles of our total experience may be in essence the same. The circumferences vary widely in total size and in the size of the overlapping areas. It is this conception of the place of Judaism in my life and in the life of the Jewish community that justifies for me the effort to preserve it in America, and the effort to build Jewish day schools in America.

Inexorably, the truth has been pressing in upon us that when we say of the Torah and its commandments, that "they are our life and the length of our days," we either mean it in all literalness, or else the whole Jewish enterprise in America rests on quicksand. A conception of the Jewish religion as something which is but one of a number of equally important elements constituting Judaism, and of Judaism as an ancillary or secondary civilization in America cannot, and perhaps even should not, call forth the devotion which alone can preserve a meaningful Judaism in America. One cannot be expected to make a major effort and persevere for a lifetime in behalf of a cause that plays a secondary role in his life.

Our interest in establishing day schools is indeed associated with our need for providing properly trained leaders for the American Jewish community, with our desire to preserve the American Jewish community, with our concern for effective educational procedures and with our hope to make Jewish education more palatable to the child. All these reasons are very important and each one of us can elaborate upon any one of them with ease. But their importance depends, in the final analysis, upon the faith that the Jewish religion, rooted in the Bible and in the Rabbinic tradition, is the highest and noblest principle for the integration of the life of the individual Jew and of the Jewish community, and that in this land we have the opportunity to make it the center around which to develop the Jewish version of American civilization.

Hence, in considering the advisability of encouraging the establishment of day schools within our Movement, we are not turning our faces away from Americanism and walking away into a corner of our own. On the contrary, we are rather thinking in terms of putting our hands to a great and glorious task. It is great and glorious both in its emphasis upon the Jewish religious integrating principle and upon American civilization for which it is to serve as one such integrating principle. Such an approach sets a task for Jewish education in America which can challenge the imagination and employ the energies of the most creative and idealistic in our midst.

This approach implies that we believe that the Jewish element in the child's education is of supreme importance to him as a human being. That importance will be reflected in many ways—as, for example, in the time to be devoted to it. In this respect, we may perhaps learn much from the New York High School of Performing Arts. This school, which is a division of the Metropolitan Vocational High School of New York City, was organized in 1947. It is "dedicated to combining college preparatory education with training for professional work in what was named for the first time 'the performing arts'—dance, drama, and music. . . . By eliminating the free or study periods of the academic high school and substituting a thirty-hour week for the customary twenty-five- or twenty-six-hour week, the School of Performing Arts enables its students to cover in three hours (or four periods) the minimum requirements for college, and still have another three hours to spend in the second half of the day on a full 'shop' program."[7] Unless we are ready to take our Judaism as seriously as these children take their dance, drama and music, we had better not bother about a day school at all.

Having said all this, I believe a word of caution to be in place. It is of the utmost importance that our enthusiasm for the day school should not lead into two very dangerous pitfalls. It should, in the first place, not be associated with a derogation of the real contributions that the weekday Jewish school can, does and should make to the development of the Jewish version of American civilization. Nor should we close our minds to other very important educational channels at our disposal, particularly such proven channels as the Ramah Camps and extended periods of study in Israel. We may in time discover additional, hitherto unknown educational instruments.

The day school is not a panacea and cannot be, for the simple reason that in the foreseeable future it will be impossible for us to persuade a substantial minority, let alone a majority, of those now attending weekday schools to attend day schools. If we could persuade them, we could not now take care of them. Nor do I conceive it important that we eventually have more than a substantial minority, perhaps up to twenty-five percent of the total number of Jewish children of elementary and high school age, in Jewish day schools. That would be sufficient to develop the main patterns of the Jewish version of American civilization, and it would have a most beneficent influence upon the effectiveness of the weekday school and of all other educational agencies now existing or still to be created.

Notes

CHAPTER I: THE PATTERN OF A FAITH

1. A paper (previously entitled "Judaism") presented at the 1954–55 symposium of The Institute for Religious and Social Studies of The Jewish Theological Seminary of America and included in the volume *Patterns of Faith in America Today,* edited by F. Ernest Johnson (Religion and Civilization Series; New York: published by The Institute for Religious and Social Studies of The Jewish Theological Seminary of America, and distributed by Harper and Brothers, 1957), pp. 125–153.

2. Some texts omit "prescribed in the Law."

3. "A frequent epithet applied to both Gentiles and Jews opposed to the Rabbinical teachings. It is in no way associated with teachings supposed by the Jews to emanate from the philosopher Epicurus; to Jewish ears it conveys the sense of the root *pakar,* 'be free from restraint,' and so licentious and skeptical." (The quotation from the Mishnah and the two comments upon it in this and the preceding note are from *The Mishnah,* by Herbert Danby (New York: Oxford University Press, 1933), p. 397.

4. Max Kadushin, *Organic Thinking* (New York: The Jewish Theological Seminary of America, 1938), p. 13, and *The Rabbinic Mind* (New York: The Jewish Theological Seminary of America, 1952), pp. 131–138.

5. Solomon Schechter, *Studies in Judaism, First Series* (Philadelphia: The Jewish Publication Society of America, 1911), pp. 151–152.

6. *Judaism* (Cambridge: Harvard University Press, 1927), 3 volumes.

7. Schechter, *op. cit.*, p. 153.

8. See Isaac Husik, *A History of Medieval Jewish Philosophy* (New York: The Macmillan Co., 1916), pp. 28, 84.

9. Yehezkel Kaufmann, *Toldot Ha-emunah Ha-Yisraelit* (Jerusalem: Dvir, 1956), Vol. I, Book II, p. 588.

10. For references to Rabbinic sources, see Louis Ginzberg, *Legends of the Jews* (Philadelphia: The Jewish Publication Society of America, 1913), Vol. I, p. 4; Vol. V, p. 4, note 6.

11. Ethics of the Fathers 4:22.

12. Tosefta Sotah, Chapter 4. See also Sotah 11a, Sanhedrin 100b.

13. Rashi, *ad loc.*

14. Saul Lieberman, *Hellenism in Jewish Palestine* (New York: The Jewish Theological Seminary of America, 1950), pp. 83–99.

15. Yoma 8:9; Danby, *op. cit.*, p. 172.

16. Husik, *op. cit.*, p. 28.

17. Tosefta Avodah Zarah, end. See also the article "Noahide Laws" in *The Universal Jewish Encyclopedia.*

18. See especially Maimonides' *Guide for the Perplexed,* Part III, Chapters 26–49.

19. For a fuller discussion of this question, see the chapter on "A Revealed Law." See also Maimonides, *op. cit.*, Part III, Chapter 31.

20. Jerusalem Talmud, Hagigah 1:7.

21. Bava Metzia 59b.

22. Hagigah 3b.

23. Psalms 19:8–11. The whole of Psalm 119 is a paean to the Torah.

24. Ethics of the Fathers 6:1.

25. Shabbat 31a.

26. Jerusalem Talmud, Nedarim 7:4.

27. *Ibid.*

28. See the chapter on "The Multiplication of the Mitzvot."

29. Note, for example, how mildly Samson's parents rebuke him for wanting to marry a Philistine girl (Judges 14:3).

30. Sanhedrin 21b.

31. Yevamot 47b.

32. *The Kuzari,* translated by Hartwig Hirschfeld (New York: Bernard S. Richards, Inc., 1927), p. 109.

CHAPTER II: GOD, MAN, TORAH, AND ISRAEL

1. A paper (previously entitled "Some Guiding Principles for a Conservative Approach to Judaism") presented at the 1957 Rabbinical

Assembly Convention and published in the *Proceedings* (New York: Rabbinical Assembly, 1958), pp. 69–124.

2. Thus far no such document has been produced.

3. See Eruvin 13b for the discussion of the question of whether it were better that man had not been created at all.

4. See Hans Jonas, *The Phenomenon of Life* (New York: Harper and Row, 1966), pp. 83–86 and the Index there under "Freedom."

5. The subject of evil and suffering is discussed more fully in Simon Greenberg's *The Ideals of the Jewish Prayer Book* (New York: The National Academy for Adult Jewish Studies, 1942), pp. 80–117.

6. Max Kadushin, *Organic Thinking* (New York: The Jewish Theological Seminary of America, 1938), p. 237 ff. See also Max Kadushin, *The Rabbinic Mind* (New York: The Jewish Theological Seminary of America, 1952), Index under "Normal Mysticism."

6a. For an excellent analysis of the use of "know" and "believe," see Gilbert C. Ryle, *The Concept of Mind* (New York: Barnes and Noble, Inc., 1949), pages noted in Index there.

7. "Science and Human Values," *The Nation,* Vol. 183, No. 26 (December 29, 1956), p. 555.

8. *The Prophets* (New York: The Burning Bush Press, 1962), chapters 19–28.

9. *Guide for the Perplexed,* Part II, Chapter 32.

10. See Solomon Goldman, *The Book of Human Destiny,* Vol. III, *From Slavery to Freedom* (London and New York: Abelard Schuman Ltd., 1958), pp. 585–690 for an excellent summary of the various scholarly opinions on this subject.

11. For an authoritative summary of the scholarly opinion on these subjects, see William Foxwell Albright, *From the Stone Age to Christianity* (Garden City: Doubleday, 1957), pp. 254–273.

12. Exodus 22:20–23, Leviticus 19:34, Deuteronomy 9:17–19.

13. Exodus 2:23–25 and the repeated references to the exodus in the daily prayers.

14. For a fuller discussion of this question see the chapter on "The Multiplication of the Mitzvot."

15. See Heschel, *op. cit.,* pp. 432–433.

16. *Greek in Jewish Palestine* (New York: The Jewish Theological Seminary of America, 1942); *Hellenism in Jewish Palestine* (New York: The Jewish Theological Seminary of America, 1950).

16a. See Yoma 69b on God's desire that we speak the truth as we see it, even of Him.

17. This question is discussed more fully in the chapter entitled "A Revealed Law."

18. Cp. Exodus 14:30–31 with 16:1–3; Numbers 16:28–35 with 17:6–10 ff.; and see Numbers 14:11, Deuteronomy 9:24 and Psalms 78:11–17, 23–32.

19. See also the chapter on "The Concept of K'lal Yisrael."

20. See David Philipson, *The Reform Movement in Judaism* (London: The Macmillan Co., 1907). See Index there under "Palestine" and "Zionism."

21. The American Council for Judaism maintains the original Reform position.

22. Ernst Simon, "Jewish Adult Education in Nazi Germany," Year Book I, Leo Baeck Institute of Jews from Germany (London: East and West Library, 1956), p. 88.

23. Mordecai M. Kaplan, "The Covenant Proposal and Its Implementation," *The Reconstructionist,* Vol. XXII, No. 16 (December 14, 1956—Tevet 10, 5717), p. 7.

24. *Ibid.,* p. 8.

25. *Ibid.,* p. 9.

26. *Ibid.,* p. 11.

27. *Ibid.*

28. "Ahavas Yisrael vie a Gruntzil far Undzer Derziehung," *Kultur un Derziehung,* Vol. 27, No. 3 (March 1957), p. 4.

29. *Seder Eliyahu Rabbah,* M. Friedmann edition (Vienna: Verlag Achiasaf, 1904), p. 71.

30. This is exactly what those Jews in Israel who think of themselves as Canaanites are trying to achieve.

31. See also the chapter on "The Concept of K'lal Yisrael."

32. Mordecai M. Kaplan, *Judaism as a Civilization* (New York: The Macmillan Co., 1934), p. 202.

33. See the chapter entitled "The Pattern of a Faith," p. 21. See also Solomon Schechter, "The Seminary as a Witness" in *Seminary Addresses and Other Papers* (New York: The Burning Bush Press, 1959), p. 41.

33a. There is a sense in which one born a Jew can never free himself from the obligations incumbent upon him as a Jew. Basing themselves on the verses in Scripture "Neither with you only do I make this covenant and this oath; but with him that standeth here with us this day before the Lord our God, and also with him that is not here with us this day" (Deuteronomy 29:13–14), the Rabbis maintain that every Jewish soul still to be born to the end of time was present at Sinai and accepted the obligations of the covenant. Hence no Jew can by his unilateral action cast off those obligations. Therefore a Jew may not offer non-kosher food to a Jewish apostate or encourage him to violate any other law of Judaism, for though an apostate he is still subject to the laws of the Torah. Theologically, he is still held responsible for all of his violations of Jewish religious law. Religiously and sociologically, however, he has cut himself off completely from the living Jewish community. The problem has many legal and theological aspects far too complicated to be fully treated here.

34. For a fuller elaboration of this theme see the chapter entitled "Towards a Jewish Version of American Civilization."

35. *High Holiday Prayer Book* (Hartford, Conn.: Prayer Book Press, 1939), compiled and arranged by Morris Silverman, p. 393.

CHAPTER III: A REVEALED LAW

1. This chapter originally appeared as an article in *Conservative Judaism,* Vol. XIX, No. 1 (Fall 1964), pp. 36–50.

2. New York: The Jewish Theological Seminary of America, 1959.

3. See the section on the Torah in the chapter entitled "God, Man, Torah, and Israel."

4. *Sefer Ha-yovel Li-Yehezkel Kaufmann* (Jerusalem: The Magnes Press-Hebrew University, 1960), pp. 9 ff.

5. See the chapter on "The Concept of K'lal Yisrael."

6. See note 3 above.

CHAPTER IV: JUDAISM AND THE DEMOCRATIC IDEAL

1. This chapter originally appeared as an article in *Conservative Judaism,* Vol. XX, No. 2 (Winter 1966), pp. 1–16.

2. Jerusalem Talmud, Nedarim 9:3; Bereshit Rabbah 24:7.

2a. As translated by Herbert Danby in *The Mishnah* (New York: Oxford University Press, 1933).

3. Jerusalem Talmud, Terumot 8:10; Tosefta Terumot 7:20; see Saul Lieberman, *Tosefta Ki-fshutah* (New York: The Louis Rabinowitz Research Institute in Rabbinics at The Jewish Theological Seminary of America, 1955), *ad loc.;* Mishnah Terumot 8:12; *Mishneh Torah, Hilkhot Yesoday Hatorah* 5:5.

4. Midrash Tanhuma, *ad loc.*

5. From the *Aeropagitica,* quoted by Elmer Rice in *Great Expressions of Human Rights,* edited by R. M. MacIver (New York: Harper and Brothers, 1950), p. 106.

6. Sukkah 45b; see also Hullin 92a.

7. Sanhedrin 56a–b; *Mishneh Torah, Hilkhot Melakhim* 9:1.

8. Isaiah 56:1–7, Yevamot 47a–48b.

9. Tosefta Sanhedrin 13:2.

10. *Mishneh Torah, Hilkhot Melakhim* 8:11, 9:1.

CHAPTER V: SOME OF JUDAISM'S ETERNALLY RELEVANT CONTRIBUTIONS TO CIVILIZATION

1. This chapter originally appeared as an article in *The Torch,* Vol. XIII, No. 4 (Summer 1954), pp. 7–19.

2. *Mysticism and Logic* (New York: W. W. Norton and Co., 1929), pp. 47, 56.

3. "Man Against Darkness," *The Atlantic Monthly,* Vol. 182, No. 3 (September 1948), p. 55. Copyright © 1948, by The Atlantic Monthly Company, Boston, Massachusetts 02116. Reprinted with permission.

4. *Abraham Lincoln's Speeches and Letters, 1832–1865,* selected and edited by Paul M. Angle [Everyman's Library] (New York: E. P. Dutton and Co., 1957), pp. 278–279.

5. Carl J. Friedrich, *The Philosophy of Hegel* (New York: Modern Library, 1953), p. xv.

6. *Ibid.,* pp. 321–322.

7. *The Nature and Destiny of Man* (New York: Charles Scribner's Sons, 1949), Vol. I, p. 5.

8. George Gaylord Simpson, *The Meaning of Evolution* [A Mentor Book] (New York: The New American Library of World Literature, Inc., 1951), p. 147.

9. Jacques Barzun, *Darwin, Marx, Wagner* (Boston: Little, Brown and Co., 1941), p. 100.

10. *The Complete Writings of Thucydides* (New York: Modern Library, 1934), pp. 330–337.

10a. See pp. 43–44 in the chapter "God, Man, Torah, and Israel."

11. Bereshit Rabbah 34:14; see also Tosefta Yevamot 8:4 where *mevatayl* is used instead of *mema'ayt.*

12. The following passage is based on *The Mishnah* translated by Herbert Danby (London: Oxford University Press, 1933), pp. 387–388.

13. Most, but not all, of the printed Hebrew texts include here the words "from Israel." It is obviously a later interpolation, for Abel was not an Israelite.

14. For fuller development of this theme, see the chapter on "Judaism and the Democratic Ideal."

15. Vayikra Rabbah 89:9.

16. See the essay "Moses" in *Selected Essays of Ahad Ha-'Am,* translated and edited by Leon Simon (New York: Meridian Books, and Philadelphia: The Jewish Publication Society of America, 1962).

17. Abraham J. Heschel, *The Prophets* (New York: The Burning Bush Press, 1962), p. 151 ff., pp. 221–232.
18. *Ibid.*, pp. 3–26.
19. Bava Metzia 59b.
20. Heschel, *op. cit.*, pp. 146–153.
21. See also pp. 131–134.

CHAPTER VI: THE MULTIPLICATION OF THE MITZVOT

1. This chapter was originally published in *Mordecai M. Kaplan Jubilee Volume* (New York: The Jewish Theological Seminary of America, 1953), pp. 381–397.
2. It is impossible to translate a concept such as Mitzvah without doing violence to it. It is most often translated as "commandment" or "precept," "ordinance" or "obligation." Any standard Bible dictionary will furnish ample illustrations of these and other meanings acquired by this concept. In this paper we shall as far as possible avoid using any translation of it. See also note 4.
3. Thus translated by Herbert Danby in *The Mishnah* (London: Oxford University Press, 1933), p. 408; Philip Birnbaum, *Daily Prayer Book* (New York: Hebrew Publishing Company, 1949), p. 484, translates "to purify."
4. It is among the roots occurring 500–5000 times in the Bible, (William Rainey Harper, *Hebrew Vocabularies*, New York: Charles Scribner's Sons, 1890) where it is used repeatedly as synonymous with *Torah, hukim* and *mishpatim*. The Rabbis differentiated between these four concepts rather arbitrarily. Note Rashi's commentary on Genesis 26:5. Also discussion of this verse in Yoma 28b, and of Leviticus 18:4 in Yoma 67b and Maharsha's comments on both passages. See also Midrash Tanhuma on Deuteronomy 16:18, and Berakhot 5a. Each one of these concepts followed its own interesting course of development in Jewish religious and legal thought. There are also many passages in Rabbinic literature in which the term Mitzvah is used as a synonym for *tzedakah*, "charity." Thus Rashi explains Mitzvot as used in Shabbat 156a as "charity to the poor which the Aggadah always designates as Mitzvah." See also George Foot Moore, *Judaism*, Vol. II (Cambridge: Harvard University Press, 1927), p. 171, and Saul Lieberman, *Greek in Jewish Palestine* (New York: The Jewish Theological Seminary of America, 1942), p. 212.
5. Proverbs 6:23, 10:8, 13:13, 19:16; Ecclesiastes 8:5.
6. Robert Gordis, *Koheleth, The Man and His World* (New York: The Jewish Theological Seminary of America, 1951), pp. 33, 36–37. See also note 9 below.

7. He associates it with verse 20 of the same chapter and verse 20 of chapter 20.

8. Crawford H. Toy, *A Critical and Exegetical Commentary on The Book of Proverbs,* The International Critical Commentary (Edinburgh: T. and T. Clark, 1899), *ad loc.*

9. Thus translated by the Jewish Publication Society of America edition. Moffat translates "A man of sense defers to authority." Toy, *op. cit.,* translates "A wise man heeds commands," and comments "This characterization of the wise man is especially natural to the Jew of this period (4th or 3rd century B.C.) for whom all right was embodied in his Torah, but is also of universal propriety since all right conduct is conformity to law of some sort; here the law is external, divine or human."

10. Julius H. Greenstone, *Proverbs* (Philadelphia: The Jewish Publication Society of America, 1950), *ad loc.*

11. Gordis, *op. cit., ad loc.* Thus also Arnold B. Ehrlich in his *Randglossen zur Hebräischen Bibel* (Leipzig: J. C. Hinrich's Buchhandlung, 1908). He disagrees with Siegfried *"weil er Mitzva vom Gebote Gottes versteht, was aber nicht richtig ist."*

12. George A. Barton, *Ecclesiastes,* The International Critical Commentary (New York: Charles Scribner's Sons, 1908), *ad loc.*

13. *Ibid.,* p. 152.

14. *Op. cit., ad loc.*

15. The story of Rabbi Akiba (Berakhot 61b) is but the best known of the many regarding the martyrs who died in defiance of some tyrant's commands.

16. Bava Metzia 32a and Yevamot 5b ff. *Seder Eliyahu Rabbah,* M. Friedmann edition (Vienna: Verlag Achiasaf, 1904), p. 136.

17. "The duties enjoined in the Halacha were called Mitzvot, i. e. commandments. And the essence of a Mitzva was that it was a thing which God willed to have done. It was an occasion of service, a means offered to man by which he could in a given instance please God." R. Travers Herford, *Pharisaism: Its Aims and Its Method,* Crown Theological Library (New York: G. P. Putnam's Sons, 1912), p. 103. In his Introduction to the *Mishneh Torah,* Maimonides interprets the word Mitzvah as it occurs in Exodus 24:12 as referring to the Oral Law as contrasted with the Written Law.

18. For a discussion of the relative authority of the Pentateuch, the Prophets and the Writings, see Solomon Schechter, *Some Aspects of Rabbinic Theology* (New York: Behrman House, 1936), pp. 118, 124–125, and especially Ramban's discussion of the second principle in Maimonides' *Sefer Ha-mitzvot,* edited by Isaac S. Hurewitz (Jerusalem,

5686), p. 296, and the comments *ad loc.* of the *Megillat Esther* and the *Yad Halevi.* Also *Torat Nevi'im* by Zevi Hirsch Chajes (Zolkiew, 1836). Also Ephraim A. Urbach, *"Halakhah U-nevuah"* in *Tarbitz,* Vol. 17, No. 1 (Tishri 5707).

19. Maimonides, *Mishneh Torah,* Introduction. There is, of course, a vast modern literature on the history of the Oral Law. We are not, however, concerned with this long and complicated history but only with the manner in which the Tradition sought to establish the authority of the Oral Law.

20. Ramban in his commentary on the *Sefer Ha-mitzvot* (*op. cit.,* p. 10a) points out that Maimonides seems to contradict himself in that he bases the authority of *all* Rabbinic enactments, regardless of how the Rabbis arrived at them, exclusively on this Deuteronomic verse.

21. *Sefer Ha-mitzvot,* p. 13a. For a listing of the *Halakhot le-Moshe mi-Sinai* and enactments attributed to the Patriarchs, Prophets and Kings, see Chajes, *op. cit.,* chapter 9.

22. Discussed by Ramban, *op. cit.,* p. 14a. He herein follows the opinion of Rabbi Nahman bar Yitzhak in Shabbat 23a.

23. *Ibid.,* 18a. See also Maharsha on Yoma 28b: *"Mitzvotai, Hukotai,"* etc.

24. Exodus 24:12, Leviticus 27:34, Numbers 15:39, Deuteronomy 11:13, and many other passages.

25. *Megillat Esther,* on Maimonides' *Sefer Ha-mitzvot, op. cit.,* p. 8a.

26. It is interesting to note that Ramban, at the very beginning of his commentary on the *Sefer Ha-mitzvot* (p. 6b), expresses grave doubts about the validity of this tradition "even though I know that all accept it as an obvious truth." The most thorough investigation of this subject was made by Yechiel Michal Ha-Cohen Guttman in his *Behinat Hamitzvot* (Breslau, 5688). See also the second paragraph of Professor Ginzberg's letter in note 29.

27. Introduction to the *Sefer Ha-mitzvot* and the first two sections of the book itself.

28. Maimonides, *Mishneh Torah,* Vol. I (New York: Shulsinger Brothers edition, 1947), p. 12.

29. After discussing this question with me, Professor Louis Ginzberg was kind enough to send me the following communication on this subject (translated from the Hebrew; the original text may be found in the *Kaplan Jubilee Volume,* p. 388): "My recollection was correct and as I indicated to you yesterday it was Rabbi Zevi Hirsch Chajes who noted (in his glosses on Berakhot, bottom of page 4) that the author of *Megillat Esther* was not correct in stating that the Sages of the Talmud used the term 'Mitzvah' only in connection with matters which

the Torah ordained. His grandson, my friend the late Rabbi Zevi Peretz Chajes, pointed out two additional passages in classic Rabbinic sources where Mitzvah means a proper and good custom practiced by our Sages (see his remarks in *Sefer Ha-Yovel Le-ha'Rav Yisrael Halevi Mi-Breslau,* Hebrew Section, p. 174). For further examples of this use of Mitzvah see my French article *Compte Rendu d. Melanges* (Paris, 1914), p. 22.

"In my article there (p. 21, note 1), I commented on the enumeration of 613 letters found in the Ten Commandments. It is my present opinion that the enumeration of 613 Mitzvot in the Torah is an outgrowth of the *aggadah* about the number of letters in the Ten Commandments. The original wording is: 'There are 613 letters in the Ten Commandments corresponding to the numerical value of *Torah,* to teach you that they (the Commandments) contain the entire Torah.' This idea is very old and is found not only in Rabbinic literature but also in Philo. With the passage of time, the 'letters' were expanded to 'Mitzvot' and thus it was said: 'There are 613 Mitzvot in the Torah.'"

30. Avot d'Rabbi Nathan, Solomon Schechter edition (Vienna, 1887), Version B, chapter 30 towards the end. Also Vayikra Rabbah 34:3.

31. The principle of *divray Torah mi-divray Kabbalah lo yalfinan* (Hagigah 10b, Bava Kamma 2b) does not deny authority in all matters to *divray Kabbalah, i.e.* to the Prophets and Writings, but it does deny them equality of status with the Torah. The meaning of a passage in the Torah can not be made dependent upon or determined by a passage in the Prophets or Writings. But that does not mean that a passage in these books of the Scripture can not be used as a source for the validation of a Mitzvah. See also note 18.

32. For many more illustrations see literature referred to in note 18.

33. Midrash Tanhuma, *Re'eh,* paragraph 1.

34. Chajes, *op. cit.,* chapter 8.

35. Hillel formulates Leviticus 19:18 in the negative.

36. Obadiah Bertinoro in his commentary on Avot thus explains the opening paragraph: "Since this tractate is not based on any of the Mitzvot of the Pentateuch like all of the other tractates of the Mishnah . . . and since the gentile sages also wrote books which they conceived in their own minds on . . . how man should act towards his fellow man, therefore this tractate opens with the statement that 'Moses received the Torah at Sinai' in order to tell you that the ethical and moral teachings of this tractate were not conceived by the Sages of the Mishnah out of their own hearts, but that these too were revealed at Sinai." Obviously he finds it difficult to justify the authority of this tractate in any other way, since Biblical proof-texts are rarely offered to

validate the Rabbinic maxims. Nor does he have recourse to the statement that "it is a Mitzvah to obey the words of the Sages." See also note 46.

37. The tendency to sanctify every act of every day rather than only some acts on some days is reflected in the interpretation by a later generation of a difference in practice between Shammai and Hillel (Betzah 16a). Shammai would set aside his best food for the Sabbath day while Hillel did not. The Talmud explains Hillel's action by saying "because all of Hillel's actions were for the sake of Heaven, for he used to say 'Blessed be the Lord day by day' (Psalms 68:20)." The Biblical proof-text offered has, on the face of it, little to do with the idea that "all of one's actions should be for the sake of Heaven." Rashi apparently sensed the difficulty. He says that Hillel "had faith that meat appropriate for the Sabbath would be provided" later in the week. The religious issue that was involved in the controversy was not a matter of sanctifying every act but rather of having faith that the needs of each day would be provided in due time. As the tendency to sanctify every act became more clearly pronounced, the Rabbis interpreted this tradition regarding the practice of Hillel and Shammai in the light of their own dominant ideal, namely that "all of one's acts should be for the sake of Heaven." Hence man can and should serve God every day of the week as singlemindedly as on the Sabbath. Each day should be as dedicated to the service of God as the Sabbath. Hence man has the right to enjoy the best food available to him any day of the week as on the Sabbath for he thus is enabled to bless God and to serve Him daily.

A number of Talmudic anecdotes reflect the growth and intensification of this inner drive in Judaism to view every normal human act which makes for the preservation of physical health and hence for the possibility of serving God, as potentially a Mitzvah and therefore as "Torah," as something which one should know how to perform *properly*. Thus, it is recorded that Rabbi Joshua ben Korhah asked Rabbi Judah the Prince to tell him to which of his actions he attributed his longevity. When Rabbi Judah demurred, Rabbi Joshua said, "This too is Torah and requires study" (Megillah 28a). Rabbi Akiba related that one day he followed his teacher Rabbi Joshua into the privy to observe him. And when ben Azzai in amazement asked, "How could you be so brazen?", Akiba responded, "This too is Torah and requires study" (Berakhot 62a). There was a right and wrong way of performing any normal act. An act performed the right way, with the hope of pleasing God, thereby becomes a Mitzvah. Maimonides (*Mishneh Torah, Hilkhot Deot* 3:3) refers to the statements of both Bar

Kappara and Rabbi Jose to validate his position that all acts whose purpose it is to preserve the physical health of the body may be performed as a service for God. Any act which is thus performed thereby becomes a Mitzvah. See below p. 170.

38. Makkot 3:16, note 112 of *Tiferet Yisrael* commentary *ad loc.* See also the chapter entitled "A Revealed Law."

39. *Seder Eliyahu Rabbah, op. cit.,* p. 65.

40. Kiddushin 31a, *Tosafot, "Gadol Ha-metzuveh."*

41. Sifra, *Kedoshim,* chapter 9.

42. "The mere doing of a thing that is commanded in the law is not the fulfillment of the commandment; to make it such it is necessary that in the act a man should have in mind that it is a commandment and mean to fulfill it for that reason." George Foot Moore, *Judaism,* Vol. II, *op. cit.,* p. 223; see also other passages listed in Index under *Kawannah.* Also Michael Higger, *Intention in Talmudic Law* (New York, 1927). See also Maimonides (*Mishneh Torah, Hilkhot Melakhim* 8:11) to note how this relates to the "righteous among the gentiles."

43. *Etz Yosef* in the *Ein Ya'akov* of Berakhot, section 76 towards the end (Vilna edition, 5643). See also *Shulkhan Arukh, Orah Hayyim,* paragraph 231.

44. *Mishneh Torah, Hilkhot Deot,* chapter 4.

45. *Ibid.,* 3:3.

46. What many of us would consider to be an unhealthy expression of this tendency was the practice of interpreting the poetic and ethical statements of the Prophets, the Writings and even of the Rabbis themselves literally as positive commandments. The principle that "no verse ever loses its literal or plain meaning" (Shabbat 63a) which the Rabbis applied to the Pentateuch only, later saints applied to the rest of Scripture and to later Rabbinic writings. Thus it is told of Rabbi Zundel of Salant that when he walked the streets of Jerusalem or Hebron he would count the houses because it is specifically commanded "Walk about Zion, and go round about her; Count the towers thereof" (Psalms 48:13). Rabbi Hayyim of Volozhin was seen one day, after the students had left the study hall, rolling on the floor of the hall in literal fulfillment of Jose ben Yoezer's maxim (Avot 1:4)—"Let your house be a meeting place for scholars; cover yourself with the dust of their feet. . . ." Dov Katz, *Tenuat Ha-musar,* Second Edition (Tel Aviv: Betan Ha-Sefer, 1952), Vol. I, p. 108.

CHAPTER VII: SYMBOLS AND SYMBOLISM

1. A paper presented at the Fourteenth Symposium of the Conference on Science, Philosophy and Religion and published in *Symbols*

and Society, edited by Lyman Bryson, Louis Finkelstein, Hudson Hoagland, and R. M. MacIver (New York: published by The Conference on Science, Philosophy and Religion in their Relation to the Democratic Way of Life, Inc., and distributed by Harper and Brothers, 1955), pp. 535–559. The notes will refer to papers included in that volume, except where otherwise stated.

2. John E. Burchard in his chapter on "Symbolism in Architecture—The Decline of the Monumental" suggests that "a symbol must be understandable without footnotes or scholarly exegesis by *some minimum number of people* before it can properly be called a symbol, and we might suppose that minimum number to be greater than one" (p. 403). That may be true for a phenomenon consciously employed by one individual as a symbol, in order to communicate with another individual. But one can create his own symbols for his own purposes only. Some modern poets and painters who are interested primarily in "expressing themselves," rather than in communicating with others, create symbols which are meaningful at times only to themselves. One can argue that such artists and poets are not properly fulfilling their functions, but we cannot deny that they create symbols.

3. The basic role of "association of ideas" in symbolism is comprehensively discussed in Alfred Schutz's, "Symbol, Reality, and Society," Chapter VII, and is indicated in many passages in William Y. Tindall's "The Literary Symbol," Chapter XI, especially pp. 358–361.

4. Every artistic creation, whether it be literary or architectural, may be symbolic as a whole and symbolic in its details. "The literary symbol may be the work or one of its parts" (Tindall, p. 356). Modern architecture, by eschewing the ornamental, has practically eliminated that aspect of ancient and medieval architecture which contributed most to its symbolic or "monumental" significance. But as one modern architect has phrased it—"we have actually created monuments unconsciously, *and with them symbols,* as we have built our industrial society, our dams, bridges, and factories. . . . monuments often turn out to be different than expected by their builders. . . . the Romans may have expected to be remembered by their temples and law courts, and not the baths, roads, and aqueducts by which we actually remember them" (Burchard, p. 397).

5. "Not higher sensitivity, not longer memory or even quicker association sets man so far above other animals that he can regard them as denizens of a lower world: no, it is the power of using symbols—the power of *speech*—that makes him lord of the earth." Susanne K. Langer, *Philosophy in a New Key* (New York: Penguin Books, 1948), p. 20.

6. Louis Finkelstein's "The Hebrew Text of the Bible: A Study of Its Cadence Symbols," Chapter XIII, is a most interesting discussion of the symbolic meaning imbedded in the sounds of words, and the cadences and intonations of words in sentences. His attempt to establish his feeling that Nathan rebuked David not in wrath but in kindness, by analyzing the sounds of the words used by Nathan, can perhaps be further substantiated by the fact that Nathan took a rather long time to make his point, in contrast to the abrupt, explosive manner in which Elijah rebuked Ahab. Indignation, when not tempered by mercy, is not wont to clothe itself in telling folkloristic stories. Nathan, in contrast to Elijah, is interested not merely in denouncing David but in having him recognize for himself the wickedness of his deed. He appears in this story not so much as the angry prophet, but rather as the kindly teacher, *cf.* II Samuel 11–12 and I Kings 21.

7. The classic instance of the tactile symbol is of course the case of Helen Keller. The moving account given by her of her discovery of the fact that things have names, that what she drank was identified by a certain sequence of tactile impressions, and what that meant for her consequent mental development is well known (Langer, *op. cit.*, pp. 50–51). It is for this reason I feel that the opening statement in F. S. C. Northrop's "Linguistic Symbols and Legal Norms," Chapter IV, while it seems self-evident, needs further elucidation. He states, "Undescribed experience came first. Expressed experience, and hence language, came afterwards." An "experience" which is "undescribed" is different in kind from an "experience" that is "expressed," for an "experience" which is "expressed" is one that has entered consciousness and has thereby been transformed from an "event" into an experience. But that which remains "undescribed" has never entered consciousness, for nothing which enters consciousness remains completely "undescribed" in some manner adequate for identification by the individual undergoing the experience, although the manner of identification may not be adequate for purposes of communicating the experience to others. Hence, to speak of "undescribed" and "expressed experience," as if the concept "experience" refers to the identical phenomenon in both instances, is misleading. In the one instance, consciousness is involved. In the other it is not. And whatever is touched by consciousness is at once transformed into a category different in essence from that which is not so touched.

8. Langer, *op. cit.*, p. 52.

9. Among the papers included in this volume, that by Alfred Schutz treats this subject most comprehensively. He makes an heroic effort to distinguish between "mark, indication, sign, and symbol." Whether his

effort is also but another exercise in semantics, is, of course, a matter of opinion. See also the chapters by Tindall, pp. 338–340, Theodore M. Greene, pp. 230–236, and Robert Ulich, pp. 205–207.

10. For an excellent discussion of "natural signs" see Ernest Nagel, "Symbolism and Science," in Lyman Bryson, Louis Finkelstein, R. M. MacIver, and Richard McKeon, eds., *Symbols and Values: An Initial Study,* Thirteenth Symposium (New York: published by The Conference on Science, Philosophy and Religion in their Relation to the Democratic Way of Life, Inc., and distributed by Harper and Brothers, 1954), Chapter III, p. 39.

11. "How many Americans are aware that a gigantic symbol of Freedom rests at the peak of the national Capitol, or would be aware of the meaning of the 'delicate figure' if not suitably instructed?" (Burchard, p. 391).

12. The point made in Karl W. Deutsch's "Symbols of Political Community," Chapter III, that no one symbol, no matter how meaningful, can adequately serve the needs of any community, national or international, should here be noted. The studies referred to in the paper indicated that whenever in history there existed a "successful union, or even a successful pluralistic political community," there was always present "a *multiplicity* of unifying symbols." That does not contradict the point we wish to make, namely that each one of a group's chief "unifying symbols" tends to acquire a multiplicity of meaning or referents.

By saying that the symbol is to "rouse a multiplicity of associations from the subconscious" we mean to stress the same point that Deutsch stresses, namely, "the importance of the relatedness of the effective political symbols to the *previously acquired* memories" (p. 39).

13. The Nazi movement created its own symbol, because at the time there was no national symbol, no flag, to which Nazis could attach themselves. The flag of the Weimer Republic was anathema to them, that of the old Reich was forbidden. Nor were they interested in restoring the old Reich. They chose as their symbol the swastika—a primitive symbol or ornament—which was usually thought to be a charm, a talisman or religious token, especially a sign of good luck. It grew in "meaning" as the movement it symbolized became identified with certain well-defined slogans, attitudes, deeds, and events.

14. On the characteristics desirable for the symbols of the group, see Ulich's "Symbolism and the Education of Man" (p. 216). He is, moreover, entirely right in his emphasis upon the fact that "even the finest aspirational symbols have the charisma not in and by themselves, but only to the degree to which man understands their transparent

character and uses them for directing his thought to the superior aspects of life" (p. 225).

15. There is practically unanimous agreement among the chapters that deal with the role of symbol in literature and art, that its characteristic, if not its exclusive, purpose is that of involving the feelings or the emotions of the observer. Even Greene who is most insistent upon maintaining the position that art is "neither hedonistic nor practical" and that it does not address itself "merely to the intellect or merely to the emotions, but to both in fruitful harmony," nevertheless also writes that, "It [art] exhibits a subject-matter of human concern, and it does so in such a way as to make evident the artist's *emotive* response to this concern and to evoke in the observer a corresponding *emotive* response" (p. 235).

Tindall, basing himself on Cassirer, writes, "whereas science builds it [the universe] of facts, art builds it of feelings, intuitions of quality and the other distractions of our inner life" (p. 340).

On the relations of architecture to the emotions, see particularly Burchard's chapter, pp. 384, 386, 394–395.

16. Greene would apparently deny to any work the claim to artistic merit if it does not offer what he designates as "normative enlightenment" (p. 235). He nowhere defines what he means by that. The great artists, he says, have in common "the effort to express their normative insights as precisely and eloquently as possible. . . ." But an artist's "normative insights" may do great violence to the "normative insights" of the generality of society. Does the merit of his work depend upon the quality of his "normative insights" or on the "significant form" in which those insights have been presented? Oscar Wilde in "Pen, Pencil and Poison" concludes that "There is no essential incongruity between crime and culture . . . and neither art nor science knows anything of moral approval or disapproval."

17. See Tindall, pp. 346 ff.

18. See appendix by Paul J. Tillich and Greene to Greene's paper, p. 283.

19. There is no religious symbol that has *only* religious significance, that is, one which involves the observer only in a relationship to God, without involving him in relationship with any other referent. Such a limited religious symbol is impossible because all religious symbols involve some kind of action, and all action involves associations with specific place and time, with objects and, above all, with other human beings. These associations inevitably acquire significance in their own right and may come to be valued in and by themselves, regardless of their relationship to any ultimate reality.

The question of priority in time between the primary religious significance of a symbol and its secondary sociological, psychological or esthetic significance depends of course upon one's approach to the history of religion. If one rejects completely any kind of Revelation, then one argues that the secondary significances of the Sabbath preceded its primary religious significance. But would one argue, for example, that for the Christian the secondary significances of the Cross preceded its religious significance, or that for the Jew the secondary significance of the *Mezuzah* placed on the doorpost preceded its religious significance?

20. Albert Hofstadter's very keen analysis of "The Scientific and Literary Uses of Language" takes as one of its main theses the proposition that "in science language is an external means—a means of expression which is not itself an element in the expressed content—in literature language is an internal means [if "means" is the right word here]—a mode of expression which is itself an element in the expressed content" (p. 294). What is true of language as symbol both in science and literature is true of all kinds of symbols when used for scientific or artistic purposes.

A. J. Ayer's version of Logical Positivism which would apply the test of possible empirical verification to establish the validity or "sense" of all symbols, is excellently discussed by Whitney J. Oates in his paper, "Being and Value" (pp. 462 ff.). A fuller analysis of Ayer's position and an attempted refutation of it is presented by Wilbur M. Urban in his *Language and Reality* (New York: The Macmillan Co., 1939); see Index under "Positivism" (Logical).

21. The role of "necessary coimplicates" in all our thinking and symbolizations, whether it be scientific, artistic, or religious, is elaborately presented by Urban, *op. cit.;* see Index "Coimplicates" (of Experience).

22. See Greene's discussion of Bullough's principle of "psychic distance" as indispensable to profound and mature appreciation of the arts (p. 253).

23. See preceding reference to Greene's paper.

24. Schutz, p. 143.

CHAPTER VIII: ONE PEOPLE

1. A paper presented at the 1963 Golden Jubilee Convention of the United Synagogue of America and published in the *Proceedings* (New York: United Synagogue of America, 1964), pp. 113–123.

2. *Abraham Lincoln's Speeches and Letters, 1832–1865,* selected and edited by Paul M. Angle [Everyman's Library] (New York: E. P. Dutton and Co., 1957), p. 71.

3. See the minority, dissenting opinion by Justice Haim Cohn in the *Jewish Heritage Reader,* selected, with introduction by Morris Adler, edited by Lily Edelman [A B'nai B'rith Book] (New York: Taplinger Publishing Co., 1965), p. 8.

4. Solomon Schechter, *Seminary Addresses and Other Papers* (New York: The Burning Bush Press edition, 1959), p. 87.

5. *Ibid.,* pp. 85–86.

6. *Abraham Lincoln's Speeches and Letters, op. cit.,* p. 79.

CHAPTER IX: THE CONCEPT OF K'LAL YISRAEL

1. This chapter (previously entitled "The Role of the Concept of K'lal Yisrael in Jewish Education") originally appeared as an article in *Jewish Education,* Vol. 32, No. 3 (Spring 1962–5722), pp. 137–146.

2. For the best presentation of this subject and for the role of concepts in Judaism, see Max Kadushin's *Organic Thinking* (New York: The Jewish Theological Seminary of America, 1938) and *The Rabbinic Mind* (New York: The Jewish Theological Seminary of America, 1952).

3. *Weekday Prayer Book* (New York: Rabbinical Assembly of America, 1961), p. 79.

3a. See note 33a of the chapter "God, Man, Torah, and Israel."

4. *"Ve-lazeh amar 'u-lefi she-hotzi et atzmo min ha-k'lal' ve-lo hayetah ha-yetziah min ha-k'lal be-kiyum ha-mitzvah ki im be-emunato, u-khemo she-amar 'kafar ba-ikkar' she-ha'ikkar hu heyot ha-mitzvah elohit ve-lo enushit"*—Don Isaac Abarbanel, *Zevah Pesah, ad loc.* See also *ad loc.: Haggadah Shelaymah* by M. M. Kasher (Jerusalem: Torah Shelaymah Institute, 5715) and *Abudraham* and *Mahzor Vitry.*

5. See Ben Yehudah's *Thesaurus* under: *"K'lal"*—IV.

6. See *Law and Tradition in Judaism* by Boaz Cohen (New York: The Jewish Theological Seminary of America, 1959), p. 27, note 86.

7. Samuel H. Dinsky, "A Program for Secondary Jewish Education in the United States," *Jewish Education,* Vol. 32, No. 1 (Fall 1961–5722), p. 16.

8. Max J. Routtenberg, *Temple B'nai Sholom Bulletin* (New York: Rockville Centre, January 26, 1962).

9. Saul I. Teplitz, *To Our Colleagues* (New York: Gertz Brothers, December 1961).

10. Thus S. Y. Agnon is designated as a *"d'mut K'lal Yisrael ha-ne'eretzet gam al hugim ha'lo-datiyim ba-medinah"*—"as one having

K'lal Yisrael stature because even the non-religious hold him in high esteem." In the same article we are told that an outstanding professor is opposed *"le-hishtaltut miflagtit al mosad hinukhi gavoah ha-hayav lih'-yot dati, aval K'lal Yisraeli"*—"to party domination over an institution of higher learning which is in duty bound to be religious but K'lal Yisraelite" (*"Bar-Ilan Be-se'arah," Panim el Panim,* No. 149, 26 Adar I 5722).

11. Traditional Prayer inaugurating the new month, recited on the Sabbath preceding the new moon.

12. Shevuot 39a.

13. Mordecai M. Kaplan, *A New Zionism* (New York: Theodor Herzl Foundation, 1955), p. 107.

14. Louis Marshall, *Selected Papers and Addresses,* Charles Resnikoff, ed. (Philadelphia: The Jewish Publication Society of America, 1957), p. 713.

15. For a fuller analysis of the concept of People or Peoplehood, see the section on Israel in the chapter entitled "God, Man, Torah, and Israel."

16. Solomon Schechter, *Studies in Judaism, First Series* (Philadelphia: The Jewish Publication Society of America, 1924), p. xviii. See also Moshe Davis, *The Emergence of Conservative Judaism* (New York: The Burning Bush Press, 1963), p. 118.

17. Avot 5:14.

18. Abraham Lincoln touched upon this problem in his own profound way in the closing paragraph of the address he delivered at Cooper Union, New York, February 27, 1860.

CHAPTER X: THE ROLE OF HIGHER JEWISH LEARNING— AN EVALUATION OF THE JEWISH THEOLOGICAL SEMINARY OF AMERICA

1. A paper (previously entitled "The Jewish Theological Seminary of America—An Evaluation") presented at the sixtieth annual Rabbinical Assembly Convention, one session of which was devoted to an evaluation of the program and activities of the three bodies making up the Conservative Movement—The Rabbinical Assembly, The United Synagogue of America and The Jewish Theological Seminary of America, and published in the *Proceedings* (New York: Rabbinical Assembly, 1960), pp. 114–153.

2. Cyrus Adler, *Lectures, Selected Papers, Addresses* (Philadelphia, 1933), pp. 253–254.

3. David Philipson, *The Reform Movement in Judaism* (New York: The Macmillan Co., 1907), pp. 488–492.

4. Cyrus Adler, *op. cit.*, p. 256.

5. Solomon Schechter, *Seminary Addresses and Other Papers* (New York: The Burning Bush Press edition, 1959), p. 23.

6. *Ibid.*, p. 22.

7. *Ibid.*, p. 23.

8. *Ibid.*, p. 20.

9. *Ibid.*, p. 23.

10. *Ibid.*, p. 24.

11. *Ibid.*, p. 16.

12. *Ibid.*, p. xx.

13. *Ibid.*, p. 25.

14. *Ibid.*, p. 76.

15. *Ibid.*, p. 74.

16. *Ibid.*, p. xxv.

17. *Ibid.*, p. xxii.

18. *Ibid.*, p. xx.

19. *Ibid.*, p. 2.

20. Louis Marshall, *Selected Papers and Addresses*, Charles Reznikoff, ed. (Philadelphia: The Jewish Publication Society of America, 1957), p. 884.

21. Adler, *op. cit.*, p. 262.

22. Schechter, *op. cit.*, p. xxi.

23. Adler, *op. cit.*, pp. 262–263.

24. Marshall, *op. cit.*, p. 863.

25. Schechter, *op. cit.*, pp. xxiii–xxiv.

26. *Ibid.*, p. xxv.

27. *Ibid.*, p. 76.

28. *Ibid.*, p. xxvi.

29. Since this address was delivered, Theology and Education were added as fields of special concentration.

30. Schechter, *op. cit.*, p. 76.

31. *Ibid.*, p. 25.

CHAPTER XI: BUILDING SPIRITUAL BRIDGES

1. This chapter (previously entitled "Continuing Assignment—Building Spiritual Bridges") was originally published in *Assignment in Israel*, edited by Bernard Mandelbaum (New York: published by The Seminary Israel Institute of The Jewish Theological Seminary of America, and distributed by Harper and Brothers, 1960), pp. 1–16.

2. The First Inaugural Address.

3. Sanctification of God's name through personal action.
4. Sanctification of the Jewish people through personal action.
5. This Student Center was dedicated and has been functioning in the manner herein indicated.
6. See Psalms 118:17.
7. "And let them make Me a sanctuary, that I may dwell in their midst" (Exodus 25:8).

CHAPTER XII: AUTO-EMANCIPATION AND ZIONISM

1. This chapter is based on the address delivered by the author as president of Avukah, which was published in *The Brandeis Avukah Annual of 1932,* edited by Joseph Shalom Shubow (Boston: The Stratford Company, 1932).
2. Gittin 57a.
3. Sifra, *ad loc.*
4. Paraphrase of passage in last paragraph of Abraham Lincoln's First Inaugural Address.

CHAPTER XIII: TOWARDS A JEWISH VERSION OF AMERICAN CIVILIZATION

1. A paper (previously entitled "The Philosophy of the Conservative Day School") presented at the National Conference on Day School Education, convened at The Jewish Theological Seminary of America on April 30, 1957, by the United Synagogue Commission on Jewish Education, and published in *The Synagogue School,* Vol. XVI, No. 1 (September 1957—Tishri 5718), pp. 3–13.
2. In addition to the essays included in this volume, see also Simon Greenberg's *The Conservative Movement in Judaism: An Introduction* (New York: The National Academy for Adult Jewish Studies of the United Synagogue of America, 1955) and *Israel and Zionism: A Conservative Approach* (New York: The National Academy for Adult Jewish Studies of the United Synagogue of America, 1956).
3. See *Our Private Elementary and Secondary Schools and Their Financial Support* published by the National Association of Manufacturers, 2 East 48th Street, New York City 10017. It also offers a fair bibliography on the subject.
4. The problem of the extent to which—under the Constitution—tax money may be used to serve children attending private schools in such matters as school bus service, lunches, textbooks, etc. is one that the

Supreme Court is being challenged to solve. I have faith in the judgment of the Court.

5. *Protestant-Catholic-Jew: An Essay in American Religious Sociology* (New York: Doubleday and Co., 1955).

6. See the chapter entitled "Judaism and the Democratic Ideal."

7. May Natalie Tabak, "New York's Trade School for Stage-Struck Kids," *The Reporter,* Vol. 16, No. 7 (April 4, 1957), p. 21.

Index